How to Start a Moneymaking Liquor Store

"How to Start a Moneymaking Liquor Store"

Business and Marketing Plan Instructions

1. If you purchased this Book via Amazon's Kindle or Print-on-Demand Systems, please send proof-of-purchase to Probusconsult2@Yahoo.com and we will email you the file.

2. Feel free to edit the plan and make it more relevant to your strategic goals, objectives and business vision.

3. We have provided all of the formulas needed to prepare the financial plan. Just plug in the numbers that are based on your particular situation. Excel spreadsheets for the financials are available on the microsoft.com website and www.simplebizplanning.com/forms.htm
    http://office.microsoft.com/en-us/templates/

4. Throughout the plan, we have provided prompts or suggestions as to what values to enter into blank spaces, but use your best judgment and then delete the suggested values (?).

5. The plan also includes some separate worksheets for additional assistance in expanding some of the sections, if desired.

6. Additionally, some sections offer multiple choices and the word 'select' appears as a prompt to edit the contents of the plan.

7. Your feedback, referrals and business are always very much appreciated.

Thank you

Nat Chiaffarano, MBA
Progressive Business Consulting, Inc.
Pembroke Pines, FL 33027
ProBusConsult2@yahoo.com

The Go / No-Go Decision for Liquor Store Start-Ups

Yes/No

1. Offer marketable products/services with superior benefits? _____
2. There is a growing demand for your price/value combination? _____
3. There is a market size that provides a critical mass? _____
4. You have a realistic mission and objectives? _____
5. You have a workable business model with multiple revenue streams to make money? _____
6. You have adequate current financial resources to reach estimated positive cash flow? _____
7. You have access to future funding sources? _____
8. You have researched a competitive pricing strategy? _____
9. You have positive and conservative cash flow projections? _____
10. You have a plan to manage cash flow? _____
11. You understand the trends impacting your industry? _____
12. You have calculated a reachable breakeven target? _____
13. You lined up competent outside support services? _____
14. You lined up the required facilities/ operating locations? _____
15. You have researched suppliers for new product ideas? _____
16. You have market-oriented personnel? _____
17. You have a market-oriented managerial style? _____
18. You have trained responsive customer service skills? _____
19. You have established customer friendly policies? _____
20. Your supply chain matches your customer requirements? _____
21. You developed targeted marketing strategies? _____
22. You have competitive advantages over your competition? _____
23. You have the technical expertise and confidence to succeed? _____
24. All required permits, insurances and compliances obtained? _____
25. You have defined your ideal customer profile? _____
26. You exceed the value baseline expectations offered by competitors? _____
27. You have written a business plan that serves as a work-in-progress roadmap for strategy implementation? _____
28. You understand that failure presents valuable lessons learned for future opportunities? _____
29. You believe you have the technical expertise, managerial process control skills and growth vision to succeed? _____

Key Reasons for Liquor Store Failures

1. Poor Marketing
   a. Lack of research into client requirements, preferences & tastes.
   b. Inadequate competitor and trend analysis.
   c. Poor customer service performance
   d. Inadequate research into likely competitor responses.

2. Cash Flow Problems
   a. Poor cash flow management practices
   b. Excessive interest payment charges on borrowed funds.
   c. Trying to grow too quickly.

3. Poor Business Planning
   a. Inadequate strategic business planning (roadmap).
   b. Poor financial and sales projections.
   c. Inadequate research of state laws, potential weaknesses and threats.

4. Poor Financial Planning
   a. Inadequate capital funding
   b. Unable to seize newly revealed opportunities.

5. Failure to Embrace New Cost Saving Technologies

6. Poor Choice of Location
   a. Poor Visibility and Accessibility
   b. Proximity to competitors

7. Poor Management Practices
   a. Improper inventory management
   b. Insufficient relevant business experience.
   c. Not delegating properly (burnout)
   d. Poor cost or product quality controls
   e. Inadequate keeping of financial records (Quickbooks)
   f. Indecisiveness
   g. Lack of focus on high value producing tasks.

8. Poor Human Resource Practices
   a. Not motivating employees (compensation/empowerment)
   b. Hiring the wrong people.(attitude vs skills) (job descriptions).

9. Lack of Clear Goals/Objectives
   a. Lack of a focus
   b. Poor communication of objectives
   c. Goals were unreasonable or not measurable.

The Basic Steps to Owning a Liquor Store

Due to strict federal, state and local regulations, there are many steps that you must take before you can consider owning a liquor store. These following steps will help to put you on the right track to liquor store ownership.

1.   **Determine Eligibility**

The U.S. Department of Treasury's Alcohol and Tobacco Trade Bureau requires every seller and wholesaler of wine and spirits to register, pay special taxes and keep very detailed records of inventory and sales transactions. Before making the decision to own a liquor store business, it is important to consider the increased taxes and tight controls associated with its operation. You will also have to carefully check your personal background eligibility for liquor store ownership.

2.   **Research State Laws and Regulations**

The most important step in owning a liquor store is checking out your state's regulations. A good place to start is the Alcohol and Tobacco Trade Bureau Liquor (www.ttb.gov). Control laws and liquor regulations vary from state to state, and the bureau website features a comprehensive state directory featuring contact information and links to each state's specific website. State regulations must be followed in addition to federal regulations, and can be even stricter. It is important to keep in mind that if you have been registered and approved on the federal level, that does not automatically qualify you for a state license.

3.   **Register the Business.**

Registering the business will make you a legally recognized company. This establishes the mechanism to pay taxes on the profits of your business generates, and also enables the business to obtain a Federal Employer Identification Number so that you can tax the salaries of your employees. Contact your local city clerk's office or county clerk's office for directions on where to go to register your business. You can also register directly through the Secretary of State's office in the state where you will be conducting business. Seek advice from your attorney and accountant as to the best type of business entity to set-up, based on your financial situation and strategic business plans.

4.   **Research Location and the Competition**

Research potential locations for your business. You will need to pay close attention to local zoning restrictions. Most places have restrictions that prohibit liquor from being sold near schools, churches, libraries and hospitals. Other communities may also have more liquor stores than the local population requires, making it difficult to convince the city council to issue an additional license. Conducting detailed research into local regulations is a critical step to opening a liquor store. When scouting a location for the store, consider not only the direct competition, but also the indirect competition, such as supermarkets and wine stores. Consider how many similar stores exist in a certain area vs. how densely populated the area is. Research competitor inventory stocking, pricing and marketing strategies. Also consult the local government or Chamber of Commerce to determine if a site is eligible. Local zoning laws and ordinances limit the number and location of liquor stores in most areas. A visit to the city or town's official website will provide contact information for the person responsible for determining the eligibility of your location.

5.   Buy a Location

After researching local restrictions and evaluating potential and eligibility of certain properties, select a location and purchase it. You could get away with leasing the property, but keep in mind that your liquor license will be issued to the location as much as the individual. This could cause problems if you are ever in a situation where you have to change locations. This is why purchasing the building is the preferred course of action. If you do choose to lease the premises, make certain that you have a lengthy lease that gives you an absolute option to renew the lease at the end of the term for an extended period of time.

6.   Apply for the Appropriate Licenses and Permits

After you have established your company from a legal perspective, apply for a liquor license for that company, at the address of the building you purchased/leased. The process of applying for a liquor license varies from state to state. There is typically an Alcoholic Beverage Control Board at the State level, with local approval also needed from the local City Council. Contact the City Clerk's office in the town where you wish to do business for more information on how to apply for a liquor license in your area. Once you have studied the laws for your state, you can begin the process of license application. Copies of the liquor sale applications are available for download from each state website. The controlling agency of each state is slightly different, but is generally referred to as "Department of Alcohol Beverage Control" or "Liquor Control Board".

7.   Get a lawyer familiar with Liquor License Law

Once you have determined that you will be able to comply with the federal and state regulations to own and operate a liquor store, your next call should be to a lawyer or other professional who can assist with the navigation of the various legal issues you will come across. He or she can help you determine what kind of business entity to set-up and assist you in protection against liability issues and the purchase of special liability insurance. Because liquor stores are a high-risk endeavor, insurance can be expensive.

8.   Research Insurance Coverage

Research adequate insurance coverage with several insurance brokers and your attorney. Also research the amount and type of state mandated insurance coverage.

9.   Locate Financing

Most people looking to open a small business will need to visit the bank and apply for a small business loan. Once you have determined that you qualify to own a liquor store, writing a business plan is essential. It will be presented to potential investors and bankers. It is extremely important to include information about the steps you are taking to obtain liquor licenses and permits, because investors will be very interested in the availability, eligibility and legal issues associated with selling alcoholic beverages.

10.   Choose the Right Licensed Suppliers

Once you have discovered the perfect location for your store, you will have to stock it full of items that are more likely to sell in your area. As you go through the process of opening a liquor store, contact potential authorized wholesale suppliers in the area and research the distribution system in your state. A simple Internet Google search should provide a list of contacts to start this process. Open accounts with several authorized liquor distributors in your state. Every state has authorized liquor wholesalers who warehouse and sell alcohol to businesses that hold a valid liquor license. Obtain a complete list of these companies from the Alcoholic Beverage Control Board or the equivalent office in your state.

11.   Choose the Right Inventory Based on Area Demographics

Market and demographic research will not only determine whether your business will be popular, but will also aid you in determining which products will be your best sellers. Areas with a large university population, for example, will see a higher sale of beer kegs, and Spanish demographics prefer certain rum brands.

12.   Prevent Underage Drinking

Do not risk your license by selling to underage customers. Learn how to avoid selling alcohol to minors and train your employees to follow the rules. This can be one of the most dangerous issues for a liquor store owner. Consult with your lawyer about the best ways to avoid this most serious of legal and liability problems.

13.   Set up Security Measures

Consider the safety of your store personnel and the security of your liquor store. Liquor stores are, without a doubt, one of the most targeted stores for crime. Thoroughly research how you are going to protect your investment. Restricting access during certain hours, and/or installing high-tech gadgetry and video surveillance equipment, and posting security personnel in and around your store are options you may want to consider and enforce, but constant vigilance and a plan of action are always the key to thwarting those who are most likely to attempt a hold-up or outright thievery.

14.   Role of Technology

Before you open, make sure to purchase or lease a good computerized cash register (POS System). A good one is about $3000 but you'll make it up in time with better stock inventory management, less inventory shrinkage, and better employee management.

15.   Advertise Grand Opening.

Research whether there are any local restrictions on advertising the sale of alcohol. If no restrictions prohibit it, advertise the date of your grand opening and any special promotions in local newspapers and on a local radio station. It is generally a good idea to provide the community with a reason to visit your liquor store, such as offering free mixed drink recipe booklets, and/or wine and cheese samples.

16.   Initiate Employee Training Program
Train employees how to recommend wine and food pairings, differentiate brand qualities and convey common mixed drink recipes.

Liquor Store Valuation

The following key factors will determine the value a liquor store:

1.   Location
Liquor stores located in busy shopping centers, strip malls or near major tourist attractions generate more foot traffic and sales per unit than stores in remote areas.

2.   Margin
Typically, liquor stores located in economically disadvantaged neighborhoods obtain higher profit margins. Generally, smaller liquor units are sold more frequently in low-income neighborhoods. Liquor bottles typically have about a 75 percent profit margin compared to wine's profit margin of 25 to 35 percent.

3.   Store Lease
Leases should be at least 10 years and with a maximum escalation clause of around 4 percent a year. The less economically developed the area, the less rent will be.

4.   Lottery
Liquor stores with lotteries bring in more customers and as a result experience higher sales figures. Additionally, lotteries account for about 6 percent of store profits.

5.   Warehouse
Liquor stores including inventory storage warehouses can save business owners anywhere between 5 to 8 percent through wholesale discounts. With a large storage space, businesses can buy in bulk and take advantage of vendor discounts. Also, owning a large warehouse with inventory creates more capital raising options in the future.

Resource: http://www.loopnet.com/Liquor-Store-For-Sale/

Select a Business Entity Type

Warning: It is always recommended to get advice from your tax and legal
            professionals before setting up your legal form of business.

Sole Proprietorship

Advantages:

    Inexpensive to create and operate

    Only requires securing an occupational license.

    Profit or Loss reported on personal tax return

    Owner has complete management control.

Disadvantages:

    Personal liability for business debt

    Not a separate legal entity

    Must pay self-employment tax (15.3%) on net earnings >$400.

    Much more difficult to raise capital from investors.

    No business life after owner death.

Partnerships

Advantages:

    Income or loss flows through to partners

    Inexpensive to create and operate

Disadvantages:

    Each partner is jointly and severally liable for all debts and obligations of the partnership.

    Written detailed partnership buy/sell and relationship agreements are of vital importance.

    Must pay self-employment tax (15.3%).

    Difficult to decide disputes and partner have different objectives.

C Corporation

Advantages:

    Limited Liability: Shareholders not personally responsible for contracted debts or employee actions (unless fraud/personal harm).

    No limit to number of shareholders

    Shareholders can be individuals, trusts, tax-exempt organizations, C or S Corp or partnerships.

    No restrictions on classes or types of stock issued

    Easier to raise capital via venture capital or IPO.

    Inc. after business name adds credibility

    Unlimited life span after owner's death

    Easier to transfer ownership.

    Able to attract and keep good employees with stock option plan.

Disadvantages:

    Double taxation - taxable income subject to corporate income taxes, plus after-tax earnings or profits distributed as dividends also taxed as ordinary income at shareholders income tax rate.

    No beneficial self-employment tax treatment.

    The IRS could limit the reasonableness of your salary vs dividends

    Increased cost of doing business (annual $150 fee).

Increased legal record-keeping requirements.
Personal finances must be kept completely separate.
Closing the corporation is more complicated and costly.

Limited Liability Corporation (LLCs)

Advantages: Currently, most popular legal form.
Members not responsible for debts of the LLC, if they participate as mgrs.
Can be owned by one or more persons.
Earnings can pass through directly to owners/members for tax purposes at individual tax rates.
No limitations on the number or type of owners.
Less expensive to maintain than a corporation($50/year).
LLC. after business name adds credibility
Members can establish own membership agreements.
Fewer legal issues and requires less paperwork than corporation.
Provides protection against liability for malpractice by co-owner professionals.
Can allocate certain tax benefits disproportionately among owners.
Opportunity to take greater loss deductions.
Only what you take out of the LLC is at risk in a lawsuit.

Disadvantages: Members personally liable for their own professional practice.
No beneficial employment tax treatment.
Must pay unemployment tax (15.3%) unless 'S' election made.
Not appropriate for 'Going Public' or issuing employee shares.
State may not allow for certain business types: banking, insurance.
Requires Operating Agreement to establish each owner's percent ownership, sharing of profits/losses, rights & responsibilities, and leaving procedures.

Limited Liability Partnership (LLP)

Advantages: Limited partner not responsible for debts unless the partner actively participates in management

Disadvantages: General partners are liable for debts.

Decide whether to Federally elect Subchapter 'S' Corporate Tax Status:

Advantages: Income or loss of the entity flows through to the shareholders for income tax purposes and is not double taxed.
Shareholders generally not responsible for corporate debts.
No self-employment tax due on profits (save 15.3%)

Disadvantages: Must be a domestic corporation with no more than 75 shareholders
Shareholders must be individuals. No nonresident alien shareholders. Only one class of stock can be issued.

Personal Financial Statement of: _____ (owner name)

As of _____ (mm/dd/year)

Assets	Amount in Dollars
Cash - checking accounts	$ _____
Cash - savings accounts	$ _____
Certificates of Deposit	$ _____
Securities - stocks / bonds / mutual funds	$ _____
Notes & Contracts Receivable	$ _____
Life Insurance (cash surrender value)	$ _____
Personal Property (autos, jewelry, etc.)	$ _____
Retirement Funds (eg. IRAs, 401k)	$ _____
Real Estate (market value)	$ _____
Other assets (_____specify)	$ _____
Other assets (_____specify)	$ _____
Total Assets	**$** _____

Liabilities	Amount in Dollars
Current Debt (Credit cards, Accounts)	$ _____
Notes payable (describe below)	$ _____
Taxes payable	$ _____
Real estate mortgages (describe)	$ _____
Other liabilities (specify)	$ _____
Other liabilities (specify)	$ _____
Total Liabilities	**$** _____
Net Worth	**$** _____

Signature: _____ **Date:** _____

Notes

Many financial institutions will require information about your personal financial data. This spreadsheet will help you prepare a personal financial statement. Your personal financial statement should show only your personally held assets and liabilities (debts) outside the business. Do not include any business assets or liabilities.

If you present this financial statement to a potential lender or investor, be sure to sign and date it in the space provided. The signature is your pledge that the statement is complete and accurate to the best of your knowledge.

Step 1:   Prepare a list of all assets owned whether they are paid for or not. Enter the amount you would receive by selling the asset for cash.

Step 2:   Prepare a list of liabilities (money you owe).

Step 3:   Net worth = Total Assets - Total Liabilities

How To Choose A Business Name

Fact: Only a Federal Trademark or Service Mark Registration can give you national proprietary naming rights (www.uspto.gov).

1. The name should clearly connect with your target audience and convey a desired key benefit. Ex: Global Fine Spirits
2. The name should include concrete and visual nouns that are relevant to the nature of your business. Ex: Top Shelf Liquors
3. Incorporate adjectives that improve your business image. Ex: Merry Spirits
4. Do not make up words. Ex: Spirito
5. It may describe your geographical service area. Ex; South Florida Spirits
6. It should inform the customers as to what you do. Ex: High Spirits
7. Make it short, and easy to say, spell and remember.
8. Name a concept that is expandable, so it does not latter restrict you to a field you want to grow beyond. Ex: Hard Core Liquors
9. Avoid trendy fad names. Ex: Spirits R Us
10. Choose a distinctive name that will help you to stand out from your key competitors. Ex: Organic Wines.
11. Check to make certain that you are not encroaching on another firm's trademark or identity. (www.uspto.gov)
12. Don't use negative sounding words or phrases. Ex: Just Not Liquors
13. Do not use a strictly generic term, which cannot be trademarked. Ex: Discount Liquor Supply
14. Check to see that a domain name that is similar to your business name is available before finalizing your business name. (www.register.com)
15. Consider whether you want to be near the top of alphabetical lists in directories. Ex: AAA Spirit Sales
16. Avoid using confusing acronyms, initials or abbreviations. Ex: ProofZ

Business Name Worksheet:
Choose a business name that combines an understanding of the following:

1.   Products/Services you plan to offer:
_____

2.   The niche you plan to target:
_____

3.   Your central concept or business model theme:
_____

Location Selection Criteria Worksheet

Location Address:_____

Contact: _____

Instruction: Compare the total points for this location to others.

Legend: Grade   10 = Location offers best promise on this factor.

              Weight: 5 = This factor is of most importance.

Factors	Grade x Weight = Points
	1 – 10 1 – 5
Car Traffic Count	_____
Pedestrian Traffic Count	_____
Visibility	_____
Customer Ease of Access	_____
Supplier Ease of Access	_____
Proximity to Competition/Clustering	_____
Zoning Restrictions	_____
Parking Availability	_____
Condition of Premises	_____
Proximity to Customer Generators	_____
Neighborhood Per Capita Income	_____
Population Density	_____
Neighborhood Ethnic Make-up	_____
Age Distribution	_____
Education Distribution	_____
Profession/Occupation Distribution	_____
Growth Trend of Area	_____
Local Business Climate	_____
Area Improving/Deteriorating	_____
Crime Rate	_____
Qualified Employee Availability	_____
Labor Pay Rates	_____
Supplier Proximity	_____
Rent Contract Terms	_____
Rent Increase schedule	_____
Leasing start-up incentives	_____
Rental Rate	_____
Adequacy of utilities: water, gas, electric.	_____
Electric power availability/cost	_____
Public Transportation Availability	_____
Taxation Levels/services provided	_____
Signage Regulations/Branding	_____
Window Display Area	_____
Perception of Security/Police Services	_____
Business Open Hour Restrictions	_____
Square footage/cost:	_____
Location History	_____
Total Points:	_____

Types of Liquor Licenses

On-Site Retail Liquor Licenses

On-site retail liquor licenses include Class C licenses that allow the consumption of wine, beer or hard liquor on a licensed premise and Club licenses that are the same as Class C licenses, except the clubs possessing them may only sell the alcohol to their members. In addition, hotels may apply for B Hotel and A Hotel liquor licenses that allow consumption of alcohol in guest rooms and public areas of their premise by guests only. The B Hotel liquor license allows the sale of wine, beer and hard liquor, while the A Hotel liquor license is for the sale of wine and beer only. A Tavern liquor license is for the sale and on-site consumption of wine and beer by paying customers.

On-Site Resort Liquor License

The on-site resort liquor license is the same as an A or B Hotel license, a Tavern license or a Class C license, except that it comes with the option of being either a transferable license or a non-transferable license. The Economic Development Resort license is for million dollar resorts. To qualify for this license, a resort must provide full-course meals, have a dining facility that seats upwards of 50 people (depending on the population of the community) and have sleeping facilities or public activities on the premise. The resort's gross income must come from something other than alcohol sales.

Off-Site Resort Liquor License

The Off-Site Specially Designated Distributors (SDD) Resort license is for liquor only and may be used by a resort to promote tourism or economic development and bring visitors to the resort area.

Off-Site Retail Liquor License

The SDD off-site retail liquor license is for the sale of liquor only for consumption off the premises. The Specially Designated Merchant (SDM) license is for the sale of beer and wine for consumption away from the premise. The retail SDD license requires the merchant to have at least $5,000 worth of liquor inventory or $5,000 of funds to buy that amount of liquor and at least 50 different brands of alcohol.

On-Site 24-Hour Liquor License

The 24-hour liquor license is good only for a 24-hour period. Only organizations may profit from the sale of alcoholic beverages under this license. Law enforcement officials must approve the location of the event that will hold a special 24-hour liquor license and the organization must provide proof of non-profit status if the group is not a national organization or has never had a previous liquor license in the county. The license allows a group to sell wine, beer or hard liquor.

Industry Overview

In the United States , a liquor store is a name for a type of convenience store that specializes in the sale of alcoholic beverages. In alcoholic beverage control (ABC) states, liquor stores often sell only distilled spirits or sometimes sell distilled spirits and wine but not beer. ABC-run stores may be called ABC stores or State Stores. In Connecticut, Georgia, and Massachusetts, liquor stores are also known as "package stores" because purchased liquor must be in a sealed container and/or removed from the premises in a bag or other package.

Business Overview

_____ (company name) _____ (was/is in the process of being) formed to be a full-service retail merchant of fine wines and spirits in ____ (city). It will distinguish itself from the competition and capture market share by securing a prime storefront location in a ____ (community name) residential neighborhood. It will follow the best practices of its retail category leaders, with particular emphasis on excellent customer service, convenient store hours, a broad selection of quality inventory, innovative service offerings and competitive pricing.

The liquor store will compete on the following basis:
1. Product variety, including new product selections.
2. Easy to shop store layout and design.
3. Superior level of service.
4. Merchandise value.
5. Wraparound services, including event planning and delivery.

In order to succeed, _____ (company name) will have to do the following:
1. Conduct extensive market research to demonstrate that there is a demand for a liquor store with our aforementioned differentiation strategy.
2. Make superior customer service our number one priority.
3. Stay abreast of developments in the liquor store business.
4. Precisely assess and then exceed the expectations of all customers.
5. Form long-term, trust-based relationships with customers to secure profitable repeat business and referrals.
6. Develop process efficiencies to achieve and maintain profitability.

Marketing Strategy

The foundation for this plan is a combination of primary and secondary research, upon which the marketing strategies are built. Discussions and interviews were held with a variety of individuals and other area retail small businesses to develop financial and proforma detail. We consulted census data, county business patterns, and other directories to develop the market potential and competitive situation.

Our market strategy will be based on a cost effective approach to reach this defined target market. The basic approach to promote our products and services will be through establishing relationships with key influencers in the community and then through referral activities, once a significant client base has been established.

_____ (company name) will focus on developing loyal client relationships by offering products and services based on the customer's need for time-saving convenience, selection recommendation support and value. The newest product and service offerings, staff accessibility and value-based pricing will all serve to differentiate our company from the other providers in the area. With the help of an aggressive marketing plan, _____ (company name) expects to experience steady growth. _____ (company name) also plans to attract its customers through the use of local newspaper advertisements, circulating flyers, a systematic series of direct mailings, press releases in local newspapers, a website, and online Yellow Page directories. We will also become an active member of the local Chamber of Commerce.

The Company

The business _____ (will be/was) incorporated on _____ (date) in the state of _____, as a _____ (Corporation/LLC), and intends to register for Sub-chapter 'S' status for federal tax purposes. This will effectively shield the owner(s) from personal liability and double taxation.

Location

_____ (company name) will be located in the ___ (complex name) on _____ (address) in __ (city), __ (state). The __ (purchased/leased) space is easily accessible and provides ample parking for __ (#) customers and staff. The location is attractive due to the area demographics, which reflect our middle class target customer profile.

Competitive Edge

_____ (company name) will compete well in our market by offering competitive prices on an expanded line of quality products, event planning services, knowledgeable and approachable staff, and by using the latest software to manage inventory and enable convenient online ordering. Furthermore, we will maintain an excellent reputation for trustworthiness and integrity with the community we serve.

The Management Team

_____ (company name) will be lead by _____ (owner name) and _____ (co-owner name). ____ (owner name) has a _____ degree from _____ (institution name) and a _____ background within the industry, having spent ____ (#) years with ____ (former employer name or type of business). During this tenure, ___ (he/she) helped grow the business from $_____ in yearly revenue to over $___. ____ (co-owner name) has a ___ background, and while employed by __ was able to increase operating profit by __ percent. These acquired skills, work experiences and educational backgrounds will play a big role in the success of our convenience store. Additionally, our president, _____ (name), has an extensive knowledge of the _____ area and has identified a niche market retail opportunity to make this venture highly successful, combining his ___ (#) years of work experience in a variety of businesses. _____ (owner name) will manage all aspects of the business and service development to ensure effective customer responsiveness while monitoring day-to-day operations. Qualified and trained clerks personally trained by _____ (owner name) in customer service skills will provide additional support services. Support staff will be added as seasonal or extended hours mandate.

Start-up Funding

_____ (owner name) will financially back the new business venture with an initial investment of $ _____, and will be the principal owner. Additional funding in the amount of $_____ will be sought from _____, a local commercial bank, with a SBA loan guarantee. This money will be needed to start the company. This loan will provide start-up capital, financing for a selected site lease, remodeling renovations, inventory purchases, pay for permits and licensing, staff training and certification, equipment and working capital to cover expenses during the first year of operation.

Financial Projections

We plan to open for business on ____(date). ___ (company name) is forecasted to gross in excess of $____ in sales in its first year of operation, ending ____ (month/ year). Profit margins are forecasted to be at about __ percent. Second year operations will produce a net profit of $__. This will be generated from an investment of $__ in initial capital. It is expected that payback of our total invested capital will be realized in less than __ (#) months of operation. It is further forecasted that cash flow becomes positive from operations in year __ (one?). We project that our net profits will increase from $___ to over $ __ over the next three years.

Tactical Objectives

The following tactical objectives will specify quantifiable results and involve activities that can be easily tracked. They will also be realistic, tied to specific marketing strategies and serve as a good benchmark to evaluate our marketing plan success. (Select Choices)

1. Earn and maintain a rating as one of the best stores in the ____ (city) wine and spirits retail trade business.
2. Establish and maintain ____ (30?)% minimum gross profit margins.
3. Achieve a profitable return on investment within _____ (two?) years.
4. Earn a ____ (15?)% internal rate of return for investors over the life of the lease.
5. Recruit talented and motivated staff.
6. Capture an increasing share of the commuter traffic passing through_____.
7. Offer our customers superior products, at an affordable price.
8. Create a company whose primary goal is to exceed customer expectations.
9. To develop a cash flow that is capable of paying all salaries , as well as grow the business, by the end of the _____ (first?) year.
10. To be an active networking participant and productive member of the community by _____ (date).
11. Create over _____ (30?) % of business revenues from repeat customers by _____ (date).
12. Achieve an overall customer satisfaction rate of ____ (98?) % by _____ (date).

13.   Get a business website designed, built and operational by _____ (date), which will include an online shopping cart.
14.   Achieve total sales revenues of $_____ in _____ (year).
15.   Achieve net income more than ___ percent of net sales by the ____ (#) year.
16.   Increase overall sales by _____ (20?) percent from prior year through superior service and word-of-mouth referrals.
17.   Reduce the cost of new customer acquisition by ___ % to $ ___ by _____ (date).
18.   Provide employees with continuing training, benefits and incentives to reduce the employee turnover rate to _____%.
19.   To pursue a growth rate of ____ (20?) % per year for the first ____ (#) years.
20.   Enable the owner to draw a salary of $ _____ by the end of year ____ (one?).
21.   To reach cash break-even by the end of year ____ (one?).

Mission Statement Worksheet

Definition: A declaration of your company's reason for being in business and sets the direction, purpose and tone of the company.

Objectives: To develop an enduring statement of purpose that will provide direction and amplify your vision. To empower employees to set the correct priorities and make decisions in the best interests of the company and customers.

Methodology:
1.   Identify your target markets.
2.   Explain the customer needs you are trying to satisfy.
3.   Describe any key differentiating or value-added services.
4.   Identify the unique product benefits you offer your customers.
5.   Describe the core competencies that differentiate your company.
6.   Research the mission statements of your competitors.
7.   Research the mission statements of other respected service companies.
8.   Identify your core values.
9.   Identify ways you hope to make a difference.
10.   Identify your personal goals.
11.   Describe the larger vision and meaning behind your company that will inspire employees and customers.
12.   Describe what your customers entrust you to help them to accomplish.
13.   Describe the legacy your company wants to leave behind.

Mission Statement   (select)

Our mission is to develop into the best location to buy alcoholic beverages in ____ (city), which will be measured by our growth in sales, and in opinions and ratings published in the media. _____ (company name) will strive to provide its quality alcoholic beverages and related products and services, in a comprehensive and cost competitive manner, while providing our customers the finest service available.

We will organize our location, hours, products, staffing and staff schedule to create a positive and effective environment in order to achieve our mission and to ensure future growth. Our goal is to set ourselves apart from the competition by making customer satisfaction our number one priority and to provide customer service that is responsive, informed and respectful.

Vision Statement

_____ (company name) will strive to become one of the most respected and favored liquor stores in the _____ area.

It is our desire to become a landmark business in _____ (city), ____ (state), and become known not only for the quality of our products and services, but also for our community and charity involvement.

_____ (company name) is dedicated to operating with a constant enthusiasm for learning about the liquor store business, being receptive to implementing new ideas, and maintaining a willingness to adapt to changing customer needs and wants. To be an active and vocal member of the community, and to provide continual reinvestment through participation in community activities and financial contributions.

Keys to Success

In broad terms, the success factors relate to providing what our clients want, and doing what is necessary to be better than our competitors. The following critical success factors are areas in which our organization must excel in order to operate successfully and achieve our objectives:

1. Formulate a business plan for your new liquor store, with a marketing section that primarily focuses on finding ways to attract customers to the liquor store.
2. Create a financial plan to manage income and expenses and hire an accountant.
3. Purchase liquor from liquor manufacturers to get the liquor business up and running, and get information from the Alcohol and Tobacco Tax and Trade Bureau to find out which manufacturers are operating legally and are in compliance with federal laws.
4. Check all customer identification before selling alcohol to them.
5. Do not open the liquor store until you have received all your permits.
6. Get a security video system to monitor the liquor store's activities.
7. Computerized inventory and sales records will allow the company to identify and exploit best selling products, match volumes and profitability to service levels,

anticipate demand, manage cash flows, assist with revenue growth plans, and optimize supplier/distributor relationships.

8. Acquire liquor types and brands specifically demanded by the local area.
9. Securing regular and ongoing customer feedback
10. Providing excellent customer service that will promote customer loyalty.
11. Launch a website to showcase our services and customer testimonials, provide helpful information and facilitate online order placement.
12. Local community involvement and strategic business partnerships.
13. Conduct a targeted and cost-effective marketing campaign that seeks to differentiate our one-stop, convenient services from competitor offerings.
14. Control costs and manage budgets at all times in accordance with company goals.
15. Institute management processes and controls to insure the consistent replication of operations.
16. Recruit screened employees with a passion for delivering exceptional service.
17. Institute an employee training to insure the best techniques are consistently practiced.
18. Network aggressively within the community, as word of mouth will be our most powerful advertising asset.
19. Competitive pricing in conjunction with a differentiated service business model.
20. Build our brand awareness, which will drive customers to increase their usage of our services and make referrals.
21. Business planning with the flexibility to make changes based on gaining new insightful perspectives as we proceed.
22. Build trust by circulating to our Code of Ethics and Service Guarantees.
23. Must institute management controls to prevent shrinkage or loss of inventory due to employee theft, shoplifting, damage of items while in the store, administrative errors, and spoilage of perishable goods.
24. Must contact a qualified business attorney familiar with liquor store issues to help work through all the various legal issues.
25. A good reputation is built upon a great selection and knowledgeable staff.
26. Schedule staff trainings with winery people and distributor personnel to improve their suggestive selling knowledge and skills.
27. Obtain information from the Alcohol and Tobacco Tax and Trade Bureau to find out which liquor manufacturers are operating legally and are in compliance with federal laws.
28. Watch trends in sales, review new liquor items each month, and eliminate slow-selling liquor products from inventory every six months.
29. Contact distributors to secure a space plan to optimize sales through the correct brand placement on the shelves.

Other Business Success Factors

1. A Customer Satisfaction Survey that asks for performance feedback, suggestions, referrals, and testimonials (offer incentive/drawing).

2. A formal, Customer Needs Assessment Analysis Worksheet Process that makes the customer feel like he is receiving a custom solution.

3. A form of marketing that shares relevant information in exchange for permission to advertise to, such as a seminar.

4. A niche strategy based on an in-depth knowledge of customer needs, wants, desires, problems, pains, obstacles, etc.

5. A proposition that gives the customer plenty of options in terms of payment methods, plan components, do-it-yourself assistance, etc.

6. A guarantee that says you believe in the quality of your offering.

7. A continuous monitoring of and research into competitive offerings, and market and societal trends.

8. Business Alliances with complementary providers that enable you to be viewed as a one-stop shop or complete solution.

9. Providing the context so that the customer realizes the maximum return on their purchase investment, including applications ideas & related support.

10. Putting the interests of the customer ahead of those of the business to realize the lifetime value of the relationship.

11. The building of trust by sharing expertise, providing references and testimonials, offering guarantees, building the brand image, etc.

12. Use cost-effective, relevant value-added services to differentiate offerings.

13. A business strategy based on a combination of any two of the following three principles: cost leadership, niche focus, design differentiation.

14. Treating all failures as opportunities to analyze, learn and improve.

15. Maximize usage of core competencies, production capabilities and limited inventory selection to achieve economies of scale and faster inventory turnover. Ex: From one type of car frame, GM created multiple auto lines.

16. Find additional uses or applications for your products and services to tap into niche markets not being adequately serviced by competitors.

Company Summary

__ (company name) will be a __ (city) retailer of fine wines and spirits. _____(company name) is a start-up ___ (Corporation/Limited Liability Company) consisting of __(#) principle officers with combined industry experience of _____ (#) years.

The owner of the company will be investing $ ___ of ____ (his/her) own capital into the company and will also be seeking a loan of $ __ to cover start-up costs and future growth. _____ (company name) will be located in a _____ (purchased/rented) _____ (suite/complex) in the _____ on _____ (address) in _____ (city), _____ (state). The owner, _____ , has ___ (#) years of experience in managing _____ (retail businesses?).

The trickiest part of opening our liquor store will be orchestrating the near-simultaneous arrival of the lease and the liquor license. The State Liquor Authority demands to see that a location is chosen before awarding the license; the nightmare scenario is ending up chained to a storefront with a rejected application. We will retain an attorney and put an escape hatch into the lease: In case the liquor application falls through, the landlord-tenant agreement will automatically be moot.

The company plans to use its existing contacts and customer base to generate short-term revenues. Its long-term profitability will rely on focusing on referrals, networking within community organizations and a comprehensive marketing program that includes public relations activities and a structured referral program.

Sales are expected to reach $_____ within the first year and to grow at a conservative rate of ____ (20?) percent during the next two to five years.

Facilities Renovations

The necessary renovations are itemized as follows:	Estimate
Partition of space into functional retail areas.	_____
Build storage areas.	_____
Painting and other general cosmetic repairs	_____
Install equipment.	_____
Other _____	_____
Total:	_____

Operations

_____ (company name) will open for business on _____ (date) and will maintain the following office business hours:

Monday through Thursday:	_____	(7 AM to 11 PM?)
Friday:	_____	
Saturday:	_____	
Sunday:	_____	

The company will invest in customer relationship management software (CRM) to track real-time sales data and collect customer information, including names, email addresses, key reminder dates and preferences. This information will be used with email, e-newsletter and direct mail campaigns to build personalized fulfillment programs, establish customer loyalty and drive revenue growth.

Company Ownership

_____ (company name) is a _____ (Sole-proprietorship /Corporation/Limited Liability Corporation (LLC)) and is registered to the principal owner, _____ (owner name). The company was formed in _____ (month) of ____ (year). It will be registered as a Subchapter S to avoid double taxation, with ownership allocated as follows: _____ (owner name) ____ % and _____ (owner name) ____ %.

The owner is a _____ (year) graduate of _____ (institution name), in _____ (city, ____ (state), with a _____ degree. He/she _____ has a second degree in _____ and certification as a _____. He/she also has ____ years of executive experience in the _____ (?) industry as a _____, performing the following roles: _____.

His/her major accomplishments include: _____

Ownership Breakdown:

Name	Degrees	Responsibilities	Percent Ownership

Company Licensing & Liability Protection

We will use the services of a local attorney or liquor license consultant to help us with starting our liquor store, as these individuals have more experience with the process, and typically have more insight into the people who will be in a position to approve or deny our application for a liquor license. They will also help to work through all the various legal issues that will surface, including what kind of entity to use for our business, how to best protect against liability problems, how to meet rules against selling to under age buyers, what rules apply to advertising, and so forth. We will contact an insurance agent to find out how much insurance will cost.

Resource: http://www.cieslaciesla.com/CM/LiquorLaw/Liquor-Law.asp

After we have established our company from a legal perspective, we will apply for a liquor license for that company, at the address of the building that we have _____ (purchased/leased). It is our goal to purchase the property as the liquor license will be attached to the property.

Note: The process of applying for a liquor license varies from state to state. There is typically an Alcoholic Beverage Control Board at the State level, with local approval also needed from the local City Council. Contact the City Clerk's office in the town where you wish to do business for more information on how to apply for a liquor license in your area.   Resource: http://texasliquorlicense.com/

The typical coverage for liquor stores includes property, CGL, liquor liability and crime coverage. Our business will consider the need to acquire the following types of insurances. This will require extensive comparison shopping, through several insurance brokers, listed with our state's insurance department:
1.   Workers' Compensation Insurance,
2.   Business Policy: Property & Liability Insurance
3.   Health insurance.
4.   Commercial Auto Insurance
5.   State Unemployment Insurance
6.   Business Interruption Insurance (Business Income Insurance)
7.   Disability Insurance
8.   Life Insurance
9.   Liquor Liability
10.   Crime Coverage

We will carry business liability and property insurance and any other insurance we deem necessary after receiving counsel from our lawyer and insurance agent. Health insurance and workers' compensation will be provided for our full-time employees as part of their benefit package. We feel that this is mandatory to ensure that they do not leave the company for one that does offer these benefits. Workers' Compensation covers employees in case of harm attributed to the workplace. The Property and Liability Insurance protects the building from theft, fire, natural disasters, and being sued by a third party.   Life and Disability Insurance may be required if a bank loan is obtained.

Liquor Liability Insurance covers an insured for damages that the business becomes legally obligated to pay for injury arising from the selling, serving, or furnishing of any alcoholic beverage. As most claims against bars and restaurants are the results of fights, our liquor liability policy will include coverage for assault and battery claims. The policy will also provide our business with skilled, appointed legal counsel that does not reduce coverage and covers our employees as patrons. Finally, we must make all employees aware of the fact that liquor liability insurance will not cover sales that are contrary to law and sales to minors.

Liability Insurance includes protection in the face of day-to day accidents, unforeseen results of normal business activities, and allegations of abuse or molestation, food poisoning, or exposure to infectious disease.
Property Insurance - Property Insurance should take care of the repairs less whatever deductible you have chosen.
Loss of Income Insurance will replace our income during the time the business is shut-down. Generally this coverage is written for a fixed amount of monthly income for a fixed number of months.
Product Liability Insurance covers injuries caused by products that are designed, sold or specified by the practice.

To help save on insurance cost and claims, management will do the following:

1. Stress employee safety in our employee handbook.
2. Screen employees with interview questionnaires and will institute pre-employment drug tests and comprehensive background checks.
3. Videotape our equipment and inventory for insurance purposes.
4. Create an operations manual that shares safe techniques.
5. Limit the responsibilities that we choose to accept in our contracts.
6. Consider the financial impact of assuming the exposure ourselves.
7. Establish loss prevention programs to reduce the hazards that cause losses.
8. Consider taking higher deductibles on anything but that which involves liability insurance because of third-party involvement.
9. Stop offering services that require expensive insurance coverage or require signed releases from clients using those services.
10. Improve employee training and initiate training sessions for safety.
11. Require Certificate of Insurance from all subcontractors.
12. Make staff responsible for a portion of any damages they cause.
13. Always check for valid identification to prevent underage customers from purchasing alcohol.
14. Require all store personnel to attend TIPS [Training for Intervention Procedures] Off Premise program, which addresses the sale of alcohol at grocery stores, liquor stores and package stores to prevent illegal alcohol sales to underage or intoxicated customers
15. We will investigate the setting-up of a partial self-insurance plan.
16. Convince underwriters that our past low claims are the result of our ongoing safety programs and there is reason to expect our claims will be lower than industry averages in the future.
17. At each renewal, we will develop a service agreement with our broker and get their commitment to our goals, such as a specific reduction in the number of incidents.
18. We will assemble a risk control team, with people from both sides of our business, and broker representatives will serve on the committee as well.
19. When an employee is involved in an accident, we will insist on getting to the root cause of the incident and do everything possible to prevent similar incidents from re-occurring.
20. At renewal, we will consult with our brokers to develop a cost-saving strategy and decide whether to bid out our coverage for competitive quotes or stick with our current carrier.
21. We will set-up a captive insurance program, as a risk management technique, where our business will form its own insurance company subsidiary to finance its retained losses in a formal structure.
22. Review named assets (autos and equipment), drivers and/or key employees identified on policies to make sure these assets and people are still with our company.
23. As a portion of our business changes, that is, closes, operations change, or outsourcing occurs, we will eliminate unnecessary coverage.
24. We will make sure our workforce is correctly classified by our workers'

compensation insurer and liability insurer because our premiums are based on the type of workers used.

25. We will become active in Trade Organizations or Professional Associations, because as a benefit of membership, our business may receive substantial insurance discounts.

26. We will adopt health specific changes to our work place, such as adopting a no smoking policy at our company and allow yoga or weight loss classes to be held in our break room.

27. We will consider a partial reimbursement of health club membership as a benefit.

28. We will find out what employee training will reduce rates and get our employees involved in these programs.

The required business insurance package will be provided by _____ (insurance carrier name) . The business will open with a _____ (#) million dollar liability insurance policy, with an annual premium cost of $ _____..

The business will need to acquire the following special licenses, accreditations, certifications and permits:

1. A Sales Tax License is required through the State Department of Revenue.
2. Use Tax Registration Certificate
3. A County and/or City Occupational License.
4. Business License from State Licensing Agency
5. Permits from the Fire Department and State Health Department.
6. Building Code Inspections by the County Building Department.
7. Tobacco Tax License
8. Liquor License from the Alcoholic Beverage Control Board.
9. Sign Permit

Resources:
Workers Compensation Regulations
        http://www.dol.gov/owcp/dfec/regs/compliance/wc.htm#IL
New Hire Registration and Reporting
        www.homeworksolutions.com/new-hire-reporting-information/
State Tax Obligations
        www.sba.gov/content/learn-about-your-state-and-local-tax-obligations

Note: In most states, you are legally required to obtain a business license, and a dba certificate. A business license is usually a flat tax assessment and a percentage of your gross income. A dba stands for Doing Business As, and it is the registration of your trade name if you have one. You will be required to register your trade name within 30 days of starting your business. Instead of registering a dba, you can simply form an LLC or Corporation and it will have the same effect, namely register your business name.

Note: Check with your local County Clerk and State Offices or Chamber of Commerce to make sure you follow all legal protocols for setting up and running your business.

Control and Monopoly States in the U.S.

The extent to which a state liquor monopoly extends differs from state to state. Out of the 17 states that regulate alcohol wholesaling, only 9 (Alabama, Idaho, New Hampshire, Oregon, North Carolina, Pennsylvania, Virginia, and Utah) run liquor establishments. The others either permit ABC licensed private stores to sell liquor or contract the management and operations of the store to private firms, usually for a commission.   The 17 control or monopoly states as of 2015 were:

Alabama (All liquor stores are state-run)
Idaho (Maintains a monopoly over sales above greater than 16% ABV.)
Iowa (Does not operate retail outlets; maintains a monopoly over wholesaling of beverages greater than 6% ABV.)
Maine (State-contracted to private businesses for commission)
Michigan (Does not operate retail outlets; maintains a monopoly over wholesaling of distilled spirits only.)
Mississippi (State-contracted liquor stores)
Montana (State-contracted liquor stores, modeled after the ALGC)
New Hampshire (Beer and wine sold at supermarkets & convenience stores; spirits and liqueurs are sold only in state-run liquor stores.)
North Carolina (Beer and wine can be sold in supermarkets and convenience stores; other spirits must be sold in state-run liquor stores.)
Ohio (Licenses businesses to run liquor stores for a commission. Beverages under 21% ABV may be sold in supermarkets)
Oregon (Beer and wine can be sold in supermarkets and convenience stores; other spirits must be sold in state-run liquor stores.)
Pennsylvania (In the process of opening retail outlets inside some supermarkets.[2]
Utah (all beverages over 3.2% ABV are sold in state-run stores)
Vermont (Liquor stores are state-contracted and licensed)
Virginia (Beer and wine at supermarkets, all liquor stores are run by the state)
West Virginia (Does not operate retail outlets; maintains a monopoly over wholesaling of distilled spirits only.)
Wyoming (State-contracted stores)
Additionally, Montgomery County, Maryland is a control county, and some cities in Minnesota (notably Edina) control sales.
About one-quarter of the United States population lives in control or monopoly states.

Resources:
https://en.wikipedia.org/wiki/List_of_alcohol_laws_of_the_United_States
Block Insurance   www.blockinsurance.com
Insurance Information Institute   www.iii.org/individuals/business/
National License Directory   www.business.gov
National Association of Surety Bond Producers   www.nasbp.org
Independent Insurance Agents & Brokers of America   www.iiaa.org
Legal Zoom   www.legalzoom.com

Insurance Tracking Form

Business Name: _____ Updated: _____

Insurance Company	Contact Name / Phone	Coverage Type / Number	Cost/Year

Start-up To-Do Checklist

1. Describe your business concept and model, with special emphasis on planned multiple revenue streams and services to be offered.
2. Create Business Plan and Opening Menu of Products and Services.
3. Determine our start up costs of Liquor Store business, and operating capital and capital budget needs.
4. Seek and evaluate alternative financing options, including SBA guaranteed loan, equipment leasing, social networking loan (www.prosper.com) and/or a family loan (www.virginmoney.com).
5. Do a name search.
   Check with County Clerk Office or Department of Revenue and Secretary of State to see if the proposed name of business is available.
6. Decide on a legal structure for business.
   Common legal structure options include Sole Proprietorship, Partnership, Corporation or Limited Liability Corporation (LLC).
7. Make sure you contact your State Department of Revenue, Secretary of State, and the Internal Revenue Service to secure EIN Number and file appropriate paperwork. Also consider filing for Sub-Chapter S status with the Federal government to avoid the double taxation of business profits.
8. Protect name and logo with trademarks, if plan is to go national.
9. Find a suitable location with proper zoning.
10. Research necessary permits and requirements your local government imposes on your type of business. (Refer to: www.business.gov)
11. Call for initial inspections to determine what must be done to satisfy Fire Marshall, and Building Inspector requirements.
12. Adjust our budget based on build-out requirements.
13. Negotiate lease or property purchase contract.
14. Obtain a building permit.
15. Obtain Federal Employee Identification Number (FEIN).
16. Obtain State Sales Tax ID/Exempt Certificate.
17. Open a Business Checking Account.

18. Obtain Merchant Credit Card /PayPal Account.
19. Obtain City and County Business Licenses
20. Create a prioritized list for equipment, furniture and décor items.
21. Comparison shop and arrange for appropriate insurance coverage with product liability insurance, public liability insurance, commercial property insurance and worker's compensation insurance.
22. Locate and purchase all necessary equipment and furniture prior to final inspections.
23. Get contractor quotes for required alterations.
24. Manage the alterations process.
25. Obtain information and price quotes from possible supply distributors.
26. Set a tentative opening date.
27. Install 'Coming Soon' sign in front of building and begin word-of-mouth advertising campaign.
28. Document the preparation, project and payment process flows.
29. Create your accounting, purchasing, payroll, marketing, loss prevention, employee screening and other management systems.
30. Start the employee interview process based on established job descriptions and interview criteria.
31. Contact and interview the following service providers: uniform service, security service, trash service, utilities, telephone, credit card processing, bookkeeping, cleaning services, etc.
32. Schedule final inspections for premises.
33. Correct inspection problems and schedule another inspection.
34. Set a Grand Opening date after a month of regular operations to get the bugs out of the processes.
35. Make arrangements for website design.
36. Train staff.
37. Schedule a couple of practice lessons for friends and interested prospects.
38. Be accessible for direct customer feedback.
39. Distribute comment cards and surveys to solicit more constructive feedback.
40. Remain ready and willing to change your business concept and offerings to suit the needs of your actual customer base.

2.3.1 EMPLOYER RESPONSIBILITIES CHECKLIST

1. Apply for your SS-4 Federal Employer Identification Number (EIN) from the Internal Revenue Service. An EIN can be obtained via telephone, mail or online.
2. Register with the State's Department of Labor (DOL) as a new employer. State Employer Registration for Unemployment Insurance, Withholding, and Wage Reporting should be completed and sent to the address that appears on the form. This registration is required of all employers for the purpose of determining whether the applicants are subject to state unemployment insurance taxes.
3. Obtain Workers Compensation and Disability Insurance from an insurer. The insurance company will provide the required certificates that should be displayed.

4.   Order Federal Tax Deposit Coupons – Form 8109 – if you didn't order these when you received your EIN. To order, call the IRS at 1-800-829-1040; you will need to give your EIN. You may want to order some blanks sent for immediate use until the pre-printed ones are complete. Also ask for the current Federal Withholding Tax Tables (Circular A) – this will explain how to withhold and remit payroll taxes, and file reports.

5.   Order State Withholding Tax Payment Coupons. Also ask for the current Withholding Tax Tables.

6.   Have new employees complete an I-9 Employment Eligibility Verification form. You should have all employees complete this form prior to beginning work. Do not send it to Immigration and Naturalization Service – just keep it with other employee records in your files.

7.   Have employees complete aW-4 Employees Withholding Allowance Certificate.

Company Location

The selection of our liquor location will be driven by local zoning restrictions. Most places have restrictions that prohibit liquor from being sold near schools, churches, libraries and hospitals. Other communities may also have more liquor stores than the local population requires, making it difficult to convince the city council to issue an additional license. Conducting detailed research into local regulations will be a critical step to opening a liquor store.

In selecting our location, we will have to be mindful of the following most critical reasons for a municipality to not permit a liquor store in a particular neighborhood:

Within 300 feet of a church or school – Essentially, no retail liquor store (tavern, restaurant/bar, package liquor store, etc.) can be within 300 feet of the property line of a church or school.

More than 50 percent of neighbors must agree. For purposes of granting a liquor license, the "neighbors" are considered anyone who owns property within 250 feet of the front door of the proposed retail liquor establishment. An applicant for a liquor license must get more than 50 percent agreement from the neighbors, otherwise the license cannot be granted.

The broader neighborhood also has a voice. A majority of property owners within a 350-foot radius of a proposed liquor establishment can sign a petition and ask for a hearing before the manager of the Regulated Industries Division and "protest" the granting of a license to a business. After a hearing has been held, then the manager can withhold a license on the basis that the proposed retail liquor establishment could harm the neighborhood.

Note: Some municipalities also restrict licenses based on the distance from a residential area, whether the building is free-standing and the hours of operation.

We plan to buy a high traffic location for our business. After researching local restrictions and evaluating potential properties, we plan to select a location and purchase it. We could get by with leasing the property, but the liquor license will be issued to the location as much as the individual. This could cause problems if we ever decide or need to change locations, which is why buying the building is preferred. If we choose to rent the premises, we will make certain that we have a lengthy lease that gives our business an absolute option to renew the lease at the end of the contracted term.

____ (company name) will be located in the ___ residential area in __ (city). The site is one of the densest and ____(affluent?) markets in the state. Our storefront will be prime retail space in the _____ (northeast?) corner of the ___ Avenue building, facing _____, a main artery for vehicles and city buses coming and going from the complex. The store is centered within a cluster of __(#) residential _____ (buildings?).

_____(company name) will be located in the ___ (complex name) in ___ (city), ___ (state). It is situated on a _____ (turnpike/street/avenue) just minutes from _____ (benchmark location), in the neighborhood of ____. It borders a large parking lot which is shared by all the businesses therein. Important considerations relative to practice location are competition, visibility, accessibility, signage, community growth trends, demographics, walk by traffic, and drive by traffic patterns. A visible, busy location can make the difference between a business that is stagnant and a business that thrives.

Company Facilities

_____ (company name) signed a _____ (#) year lease for _____ (#) square foot of space. The cost is very reasonable at $____/sq. foot. We also have the option of expanding into an additional _____ sq. ft. of space. A leasehold improvement allowance of $___ /sq. ft. would be given. Consolidated area maintenance fees would be $___/month initially. _____ (company name) has obtained a _____ (three) month option on this space effective _____ (date), the submission date of this business plan, and has deposited refundable first and last lease payments, plus a $ _____ security deposit with the leasing agent.

The facilities will incorporate the following room parameters into the layout:

		Percentage	Square Footage
1.	Retail Floor Area	_____	_____
2.	Supplies Storage	_____	_____
3.	Product Inventory Storage	_____	_____
4.	Staff Room	_____	_____
5.	Admin Office	_____	_____
6.	Restroom	_____	_____
Totals:		_____	_____

Design Layout

To avoid confusing customers when they enter our store, we will direct them to their desired product by hanging signs for each type of alcohol. Our store will have "Rum," "Tequila," "Wine" and "Vodka" signs to help prevent customers from searching every aisle of our store to find what they need. Our design objective will always be ease of access to compete with convenience stores and increase sales. We will place items that are usually bought in pairs together. For example, people often buy tequila and margarita mix. We will also place cranberry and orange juices near the Vodka displays.

Start-up Summary

The start-up costs for the liquor store will be financed through a combination of an owner investment of $ _____ and a short-term bank loan of $ _____. The total start-up costs for this business are approximately $ _____ and can be broken down in the following major categories:

1.	Land, Building and Improvements	$ _____
2.	Equipment and Installation Expenses	$ _____
3.	Development Expense	$ _____
4.	Office Furniture: Work Tables and Cabinets	$ _____
5.	Initial Product Inventory	$ _____
6.	Working Capital (6 months)	$ _____
	For day-to-day operations, including payroll, etc.	
7.	Renovate Retail Space	$ _____
	Includes architect, lighting update, flooring, etc.	
8.	Marketing/Advertising Expenses	$ _____
	Includes sales brochures, direct mail, opening expenses.	
8.	Utility/ (Rent?) Deposits	$ _____
9.	Licenses and Permits	$ _____
10.	Contingency Fund	$ _____
11.	Other (Includes training, legal expenses, etc.)	$ _____
Total:		$ _____

Key Cost Estimates:

1.	Two register computer based checkout system	$4,000
2.	POS software	$3,000.
3.	Shelving and display equipment	$7,000
4.	A 5 door beer cooler (used)	$2500
5.	Cooler installation and wiring.	$2500
6.	Installed compressor system	$3000
7.	Glass breakage/motion detection alarm system installed	$3000
8.	4 camera computer based instore security camera system	$2500.

Other sample costs:
Simple signage and awning ($5,000) and austere wine racks ($3,600.00).
The registers, point-of-sale software, and back-end accounting software cost $12,000.00.
The security system ($1,950). Air-conditioning and sealing the store and basement for proper wine storage ran $18,000.00. Utilities setup cost $1,100.

The company will require $_____ in initial cash reserves and additional $_____ in assets. The start-up costs are to be financed by the equity contributions of the owner in the amount of $ _____ , as well as by a _____ (#) year commercial loan in the amount of $ _____. The funds will be repaid through earnings. These start-up expenses and funding requirements are summarized in the tables below.

Inventory

Inventory Type	Supplier	Qty	Unit Cost	Total
Bags and Supplies				
Cleaning Supplies				
Office Supplies				
Computer Supplies				
Marketing Materials				
Liquor Inventory				
Wine Inventory				
Beer Inventory				
Misc. Product Inventory				
Price Tags				
In-Store Signs				
Deposit Slips				
Business Forms				
Price Books				
Business Mail Envelopes				
Misc. Supplies				
Totals:				

Note: The average liquor store inventory is usually valued between $50,000 and $75,000. Generally speaking inventory is turned over, in a good liquor store, between eight and 10 times per year. The amount of the start-up inventory will depend on the size of our town, the number of competitors, and what we can afford to purchase.

Supply Sourcing

We will start by checking with the Liquor Control Board for alcohol beverage wholesale supplier recommendations. Initially, _____ (company name) will purchase all of its equipment from _____ and supplies from _____, the _____ (second/third?) largest supplier in _____ (state), because of the discount given for bulk purchases. However, we will also maintain back-up relationships with two smaller suppliers, namely _____ and _____. These two suppliers have competitive prices on certain products.
Note: Some states like Texas have a four-tiered distribution system where the manufacturer sells to a distributor that sells to a larger retailer, which in turn sells to smaller retailers.

Equipment Leasing

Equipment Leasing will be the smarter solution allowing our business to upgrade our equipment needs at the end of the term rather than being overly invested in outdated equipment through traditional bank financing and equipment purchase. We also intend to explore the following benefits of leasing some of the required equipment:

1.	Frees Up Capital for other uses.	2.	Tax Benefits
3.	Improves Balance Sheet	4.	Easy to add-on or trade-up
5.	Improves Cash Flow	6.	Preserves Credit Lines
7.	Protects against obsolescence	8.	Application Process Simpler

List Any Leases:

Leasing Company	Equipment Description	Monthly Payment	Lease Period	Final Disposition

Resource:

Innovative Lease Services   http://www.ilslease.com/equipment-leasing/
This company was founded in 1986 and is headquartered in Carlsbad, California. It is accredited by the Better Business Bureau, a long standing member of the National Equipment Finance Association and the National Association of Equipment Leasing Brokers and is the official equipment financing partner of Biocom.

Funding Source Matrix

Funds Source	Amount	Interest Rate	Repayment Terms	Use

Distribution or Licensing Agreements   (if any)

Note: These are some of the key factors that investors will use to determine if we have a competitive advantage that is not easily copied.

Licensor	License Rights	License Term	Fee or Royalty

Trademarks, Patents and Copyrights (if any)

Our trademark will be virtually our branding for life. Our choice of a name for our business is very important. Not only will we brand our business and services forever, but what may be worthless today will become our most valuable asset in the years to come. A trademark search by our Lawyer will be a must, because to be told down the road that we must give up our name because we did not bother to conduct a trademark search would be a devastating blow to our business. It is also essential that the name that we choose suit the expanding product or service offerings that we plan to introduce.

Note: These are some of the key factors that investors will use to determine if we have a proprietary position or competitive advantage that is not easily copied.

Resources: Patents/Trademarks www.uspto.gov / Copyright   www.copyright.gov

Innovation Strategy   (optional)

_____ (company name) will create an innovation strategy that is aligned with not only our firm's core mission and values, but also with our future technology, supplier, and growth strategies. The objective of our innovation strategy will be to create a sustainable competitive advantage . Our education and training systems will be designed to equip our staff with the foundations to learn and develop the broad range of skills needed for innovation in all of its forms, and with the flexibility to upgrade skills and adapt to changing market conditions. To foster an innovative workplace, we will ensure that employment policies facilitate efficient organizational change and encourage the expression of creativity, engage in mutually beneficial strategic alliances and allocate adequate funds for research and development. Our radical innovation strategies include _____ to achieve first mover status. Our incremental innovation strategies will include modifying the following _____ (products/services/processes) to give our customers added value for their money.
Resource:
https://hbr.org/2015/04/the-5-requirements-of-a-truly-innovative-company

2.5.9   Summary of Sources and Use of Funds

Sources:

Owner's Equity Investment	$ _____
Requested Bank Loans	$ _____
Total:	$ _____

Uses:

Capital Equipment	$ _____
Beginning Inventory	$ _____
Start-up Costs	$ _____
Working Capital	$ _____
Total:	$ _____

2.5.9.1   Funding To Date   (optional)

To date, _____'s (company name) founders have invested $_____ in _____ (company name), with which we have accomplished the following:
1. _____ (Designed/Built) the company's website
2. Developed content, in the form of ____ (#) articles, for the website.
3. Hired and trained our core staff of __(#) full-time people and ____ (#) part-time people.
4. Generated brand awareness by driving ____ (#) visitors to our website in a ___(#) month period.
5. Successfully _____ (Developed/Test Marketed) ___ (#) new _____ (products/services), which compete on the basis of _____.

6.   _____ (Purchased/Developed) and installed the software needed to _____
      (manage _____ operations?)
7.   Purchased $ _____ worth of _____ (supplies)
8.   Purchased $ _____ worth of _____ equipment.

Start-up Requirements

Start-up Expenses: Estimates
        Legal   _____   15000
        Accountant   _____   300
        POS Software Package   _____   300
        State Licenses & Permits   _____   40000?
        Store Set-up   _____   25000
        Unforeseen Contingency   _____   3000
        Market Research Survey   _____   300
        Office Supplies   _____   300
        Sales Brochures   _____   300
        Direct Mailing   _____   500
        Other Marketing Materials   _____   2000
        Logo Design   500
        Advertising (2 months)   _____   2000
        Consultants   _____   5000
        Insurance   _____
        Rent (2 months security)   _____   3000
        Rent Deposit   _____   1500
        Utility Deposit   _____   1000
        DSL Installation/Activation   _____   100
        Telecommunications Installation _____   3000
        Telephone Deposit   _____   200
        Expensed Equipment   _____   1000
        Website Design/Hosting   _____   2000
        Computer System   _____   12000
        Used Office Equipment/Furniture _____   2000
        Organization Memberships   _____   300
        Cleaning Supplies   _____   200
        Staff Training   _____   5000
        Promotional Signs   _____   7000
        Security System   _____   8000
        Other   _____
Total Start-up Expenses   _____ **(A)**

Start-up Assets:
        Cash Balance Required   _____ (T)   15000
        Start-up Equipment   _____   See schedule

Start-up Inventory _____ See schedule
Other Current Assets _____
Long-term Assets _____

Total Assets _____ **(B)**

Total Requirements _____ (A+B)

Start-up Funding

Start-up Expenses to Fund _____ (A)
Start-ups Assets to Fund _____ (B)
Total Funding Required: _____ **(A+B)**

Assets

Non-cash Assets from Start-up _____
Cash Requirements from Start-up _____ (T)
Additional Cash Raised _____ (S)
Cash Balance on Starting Date _____ (T+S=U)
Total Assets: _____ **(B)**

Liabilities and Capital

Short-term Liabilities:
Current Borrowing _____
Unpaid Expenses _____
Accounts Payable _____
Interest-free Short-term Loans _____
Other Short-term Loans _____
Total Short-term Liabilities _____ **(Z)**

Long-term Liabilities:
Commercial Bank Loan _____
Other Long-term Liabilities _____
Total Long-term Liabilities _____ **(Y)**
Total Liabilities _____ **(Z+Y = C)**

Capital

Planned Investment
Owner _____
Family _____
Other _____
Additional Investment Requirement _____
Total Planned Investment _____ **(F)**
Loss at Start-up (Start-up Expenses) (-)_____ **(A)**
Total Capital (=)_____ **(F+A=D)**
Total Capital and Liabilities _____ **(C+D)**

Total Funding _____ (C+F)

Capital Equipment List

Major Equipment	Model No.	New/ Used	Lifespan	Quantity	Unit Cost	Total Cost
Refrigeration Equipment:						
Display Coolers						
Sold Door Freezer						
Walk-in Cooler						
Frozen Food Case						
Ice Merchandiser						
Security System						
Electronic Safe						
Counter Merchandiser						
Open Front Display Cases						
Total Major Equipment						
Minor Equipment						
Computer System						
Fax Machine						
Copy Machine						
Answering Machine						
TV and DVD Player						
Office Furniture						
Accounting Software						
Microsoft Office Software						
Shelving Units						
Lockers						
Hand Truck						
Mop Station						
Marquee Sign						
Assorted Signs						
Total Minor Equipment						
Other Equipment						
Telephone headsets						
Calculator						
Filing & Storage Cabinets						
Broadband Internet Connection						
Cabinetry						
Credit Card Machine						
Pricing Guns						
Total Other Equipment						
Total Capital Equipment						

Bank Loan Request

_____ (company name) is a high-end _____ (liquor store) with a reputation for integrity, quality beverage selection, superior customer service and excellence in management. In ___ (#) years annual sales have increased by ___ % to be well over _____ dollars.

_____ (company name) was formed by _____ (owner name) as a _____ (Sole Proprietorship/S-Corporation/LLC) in ____ (month), ____ (year). In ___ (year) a combination of activities involving retail and wholesale sales, consulting, and _____ brought Gross Sales of $_____ .

The Company experienced steady growth since its inception, and incorporated in ___ (month), ____ (year), (see Appendix ___ for Articles of Incorporation). In ___ (year) Gross Sales of $____ were achieved. In ____ (year), signed contracts show that Gross Sales are expected to be $_____ (see Appendix _, current Backlog).

The Company has its address in ____ (owned/leased) premises at _____ (address)

Its activities fall under the Standard Industrial Classification SIC 5921. The owners are _____ and _____ . _____ (company name) is involved in the following activities:

Activity	Sales	Percent	Growth Rate
1. _____	_____		
2. _____	_____		
3. _____	_____		
4. Retail Liquor Sales	_____		

The majority of the Gross Sales are in __ and ___ (activity). We presently have ___ (#) permanent and ___(#) temporary employees on the payroll and ___ (#) subcontracted workers, excluding subcontracting companies (see Appendix ___ for resumes).

The company's Short Term Objectives (within the next three years) are to increase activity in all Divisions, and to achieve annual profit, net after taxes, of $___ by ___ (year). Its Long term objectives are: to maintain the level of current business achieved up to ____ (year), and then to move into _____ (new activity) and increased new _____ (new activity).

To implement these objectives the company needs:

A loan of $____ at Prime plus 2%. This loan to be used for current near term expenses including _____, _____ and _____ It will be repaid in five years.
A line of credit of $____ to take advantage of discounts available, avoid associated penalties, and expand into high profit areas requiring positive cash flow.

The prospects for _____ ' (company name) continued growth are excellent, with ___ (#) _____ (contracts/sales) underway already exceeding $_____ (see Appendix __, Backlog).

For equity the company has assets of $_____ (see Appendix ___, Balance Sheet as of _____ mm/dd/year). Additionally, the company's owners are willing to offer as collateral a second mortgage on a residence with an estimated equity of $_____. The address of this residence is _____ (address).

The company's overall objective is to satisfy that market segment that demands integrity and quality _____ (beverages), and to maintain a steady growth in sales volume that will sustain the company for twenty years. ____ (owner name) has enhanced his reputation to the point where the company is regarded by many ___ (customers/professionals) as the recommended choice with their clients due to the excellence of its _____ (customer service) and management.

Market research shows that the population in _____ (city) has increased by ____ (#) between ___ (year) and ____ (year). This increase in population brought about an increase of ____ (#) new single family homes valued at over _____ dollars. This increase gives the area over ____ (#) existing homes as a potential customer market. Demographic estimates published by the State Office of Financial Management, ___ (year), indicate that an additional ____ (year) persons will need to be housed between ____ (year) and 2020. _____ (company name) intends to pursue this market vigorously. (See Appendix __ for data on anticipated changes in the population of _____ County).

Financial Objectives:

The financial objectives of _____ (company name) over the next few years are as follows:

	Year 1	Year 2	Year 3
Sales			
Net Income After Taxes			

Please review the enclosed business plan and loan proposal, and of course feel free to ask for any additional information or explanations you may want. I will call you in about one week's time to arrange an appointment so that we can discuss the loan in person.

I look forward to a mutually profitable relationship with the _____ Bank.

Very truly yours,

_____

SBA Loan Key Requirements

In order to be considered for an SBA loan, we must meet the basic requirements:
1. Must have been turned down for a loan by a bank or other lender to qualify for most SBA Business Loan Programs. 2. Required to submit a guaranty, both personal and business, to qualify for the loans. 3. Must operate for profit; be engaged in, or propose to do business in, the United States or its possessions; 4. Have reasonable owner equity to invest; 5. Use alternative financial resources first including personal assets.

All businesses must meet eligibility criteria to be considered for financing under the SBA's 7(a) Loan Program, including: size; type of business; operating in the U.S. or its possessions; use of available of funds from other sources; use of proceeds; and repayment. The repayment term of an SBA loan is between five and 25 years, depending on the lift of the assets being financed and the cash needs of the business. Working capital loans (accounts receivable and inventory) should be repaid in five to 10 years. The SBA also has short-term loan guarantee programs with shorter repayment terms.

A Business Owner Cannot Use an SBA Loan:

To purchase real estate where the participant has issued a forward commitment to the developer or where the real estate will be held primarily for investment purposes. To finance floor plan needs. To make payments to owners or to pay delinquent withholding taxes. To pay existing debt, unless it can be shown that the refinancing will benefit the small business and that the need to refinance is not indicative of poor management.

SBA Loan Programs:
Low Doc: www.sba.gov/financing/lendinvest/lowdoc.html
SBA Express www.sba,gov/financing/lendinvest/sbaexpress.html
Basic 7(a) Loan Guarantee Program
> For businesses unable to obtain loans through standard loan programs. Funds can be used for general business purposes, including working capital, leasehold improvements and debt refinancing.
> www.sba.gov/financing/sbaloan/7a.html

Certified Development Company 504 Loan Program
> Used for fixed asset financing such as purchase of real estate or machinery.
> www. Sba.gov/gopher/Local-Information/Certified-Development-Companies/

MicroLoan 7(m) Loan Program
> Provides short-term loans up to $35,000.00 for working capital or purchase of fixtures.
> www.sba.gov/financing/sbaloan/microloans.html

Other Financing Options

1. Grants:
    Health care grants, along with education grants, represent the largest percentage of grant giving in the United States. The federal government, state, county and city governments, as well as private and corporate foundations all award grants. The largest percentage of grants are awarded to non-profit organizations, health care agencies, colleges and universities, local government agencies, tribal institutions, and schools. For profit organizations are generally not eligible for grants unless they are conducting research or creating jobs.
    A. Contact your state licensing office.
    B. Foundation Grants to Individuals: www.fdncenter.org
    C. US Grants   www.grants.gov
    D. Foundation Center   www.foundationcemter.org
    E. The Grantsmanship Center   www.tgci.com
    F. Contact local Chamber of Commerce
    G. The Catalog of Federal Domestic Assistance is a major provider of business grant money.
    H. The Federal Register is a good source to keep current with the continually changing federal grants offered.
    I. FedBizOpps is a resource, as all federal agencies must use FedBizOpps to notify the public about contract opportunities worth over $25,000.

2. Friends and Family Lending   www.virginmoney.com
3. National Business Incubator Association www.nbia.org/
4. Women's Business Associations   www.nawbo.org/
5. Minority Business Development Agency   www.mbda.gov/
6. Social Networking Loans   www.prosper.com
7. Peer-to-Peer Programs   www.lendingclub.com
8. Extended Credit Terms from Suppliers   30/60/90 days.
9. Community Bank
10. Prepayments from Customers
11. Seller Financing: When purchasing an existing liquor store.
12. Business Funding Directory   www.businessfinance.com
13. FinanceNet   www.financenet.gov
14. SBA Financing   www.sbaonline.sba.gov
15. Private Investor
16. Micro-Loans   www.accionusa.org/
17. Unsecured Business Cash Advance based on future credit card transactions.
18. Kick Starter   www.kickstarter.com
19. Capital Source   www.capitalsource.com
    www.msl.com/index.cfm?event=page.sba504
    Participates in the SBA's 504 loan program. This program is for the purchase of fixed assets such as commercial real estate and machinery and equipment of a capital nature, which are defined as assets that have a minimum useful life of ten years. Proceeds cannot be used for working capital.

20. Commercial Loan Applications   www.c-loans.com/onlineapp/
21. Sharing assets and resources with other non-competing businesses.
22. Angel Investors   www.angelcapitaleducation.org
23. The Receivables Exchange   http://receivablesxchange.com/
24. Bootstrap Methods: Personal Savings/Credit Card/Second Mortgages
25. Community-based Crowd-funding   www.profounder.com
26. On Deck Capital   http://www.ondeckcapital.com/
 Created the Short Term Business Loan (up to $100,000.00) for small businesses to get quick access to capital that fits their cash flow, with convenient daily payments.
27. Royalty Lending   www.launch-capital.com/
 With royalty lending, financing is granted in return for future revenue or company performance, and payback can prove exceedingly expensive if a company flourishes.

28. Stock :Loans   Southern Lending Solutions, Atlanta. GA.
        Custom Commercial Finance, Bartlesville, OK
 A stock loan is based on the quality of stocks, Treasuries and other kinds of investments in a businessperson's personal portfolio. Possession of the company's stock is transferred to the lender's custodial bank during the loan period.
29. Lender Compatibility Searcher   www.BoeFly.com
30. Strategic Investors
 Strategic investing is more for a large company that identifies promising technologies, and for whatever reason, that company may not want to build up the research and development department in-house to produce that product, so they buy a percentage of the company with the existing technology.
31. Bartering
32. Small Business Investment Companies   www.sba.gov/INV
33. Cash-Value Life Insurance
34. Employee Stock Option Plans   www.nceo.org
35. Venture Capitalists   www.nvca.org
36. Initial Public Offering (IPO)
37. Meet investors through online sites, including LinkedIn (group discussions), Facebook (BranchOut sorts Facebook connections by profession), and CapLinked (enables search for investment-related professionals by industry and role).
38. SBA Community Advantage Approved Lenders
        www.sba.gov/content/community-advantage-approved-lenders
39. Small Business Lending Specialists
 https://www.wellsfargo.com/biz/loans_lines/compare_lines
 http://www.bankofamerica.com/small_business/business_financing/
 https://online.citibank.com/US/JRS/pands/detail.do?ID=CitiBizOverview
 https://www.chase.com/ccp/index.jsp?pg_name=ccpmapp/smallbusiness/home/page/bb_business_bBanking_programs

40. Startup America Partnership   www.s.co/about
 Based on a simple premise: young companies that grow create jobs. Once startups

apply and become a Startup America Firm, they can access and manage many types of resources through a personalized dashboard.

41.   United States Economic Development Administration   www.eda.gov/

42.   SBA Community Advantage Approved Lenders
www.sba.gov/content/community-advantage-approved-lenders

43.   Small Business Lending Specialists
https://www.wellsfargo.com/biz/loans_lines/compare_lines
http://www.bankofamerica.com/small_business/business_financing/
https://online.citibank.com/US/JRS/pands/detail.do?ID=CitiBizOverview
https://www.chase.com/ccp/index.jsp?pg_name=ccpmapp/smallbusiness/home/page/bb_business_bBanking_programs

44.   Startup America Partnership   www.s.co/about
Based on a simple premise: young companies that grow create jobs. Once startups apply and become a Startup America Firm, they can access and manage many types of resources through a personalized dashboard.

45.   United States Economic Development Administration   www.eda.gov/

46.   Small Business Loans   http://www.iabusnet.org/small-business-loans

47.   Tax Increment Financing (TIF)
A public financing method that is used for subsidizing redevelopment, infrastructure, and other community-improvement projects. TIF is a method to use future gains in taxes to subsidize current improvements, which are projected to create the conditions for said gains. The completion of a public project often results in an increase in the value of surrounding real estate, which generates additional tax revenue. Tax Increment Financing dedicates tax increments within a certain defined district to finance the debt that is issued to pay for the project. TIF is often designed to channel funding toward improvements in distressed, underdeveloped, or underutilized parts of a jurisdiction where development might otherwise not occur. TIF creates funding for public or private projects by borrowing against the future increase in these property-tax revenues.

48.   Gust   https://gust.com/entrepreneurs
Provides the global platform for the sourcing and management of early-stage investments. Gust enables skilled entrepreneurs to collaborate with the smartest investors by virtually supporting all aspects of the investment relationship, from initial pitch to successful exit.

49.   Goldman Sachs 10,000 Small Businesses   http://sites.hccs.edu/10ksb/

50.   Earnest Loans   www.meetearnest.com

51.   Biz2Credit   www.biz2credit.com

52.   Funding Circle   www.fundingcircle.com
A peer-to-peer lending service which allows savers to lend money directly to small and medium sized businesses

53.   Forward Financing
www.forwardfinancing.com/site/portfolio-item/wine-liquor-stores/

Resource: www.sba.gov/category/navigation-structure/starting-managing-business/starting-business/local-resources
http://usgovinfo.about.com/od/moneymatters/a/Finding-Business-Loans-Grants-Incentives-And-Financing.htm

Financing Options: Pros and Cons

Finance Type	Source	Pros	Cons
Internal	Retained Earnings	Maximum simplicity No equity dilution. Less big mistake potential. No monthly payments Forces innovative solutions	Under-capitalization risk. Slower growth pace.
Debt	Bank Loan	No equity give-up Establishes Relationship Limited control request Interest tax-deductible	Must pay monthly interest Limited networking value Requires personal collateral Personal Credit Score key. May require 2 yr. history. Lengthy application process May require SBA guarantee Personal guarantees.
	Credit Cards	Quick access	Tied to credit score High interest rate varies Limited funding amount. Must make monthly payments
	Family & Friends	Convenient Few contractual strings Quickly available Lower interest rate. No loan fees Can negotiate payback terms.	Usually less than $50,000. Usually one-time financing Possible family break-up. May want some control.
Equity	Angel Investors	Mentoring support Networking opportunities Patient investors No monthly payments	Difficult to locate Divergent group interests Require regular reporting Sizeable equity give-up.
	Venture Capitalists	Mentoring support Networking opportunities Only major funding source. No personal asset risk. No monthly payments. Sets stage for IPO.	Proven fast growth potential Cash-out within 3 to 5 yrs. Exercise management control Equity/profit give-up Expensive capital source. Possess veto power. Competitor defenses critical

	Private Equity Placement	Strengthens balance sheet No monthly payments Mentoring support Funded by limited partners.	Difficult to locate Equity dilution. Time consuming arrangements Want IPO/Sale or Merger.
	Strategic Industry Investors	Enhance credibility Mentoring support Resources support (Distribution/Marketing)	May decide target markets Risky dependency No selling to their competitors
Grants	SBA/ Chamber/ Foundations/ Private Companies	Free Money Money attracts investors.	High competition for funds Strictly defined use of funds Usually to develop technology Or for 'public good' causes. Long application process
Other	Strategic Alliance	No change/business structure Share complementary resources No monthly payments	Less marketing control Must monitor benefits Share confidential info.
	Franchise Financing	Pre-arranged Generally attractive terms	Terms may vary Must adhere to franchisor rules
	Vendor Financing	Lower Interest Rate Minimal Fees Favorable Terms Less Underwriting	May require a restrictive purchasing/pricing agreement
	Leasing Equipment/ Vehicles	Minimal Cash Required Flexible Terms Comparison shopping Fixed Budget Expense Fast Approvals Possible Easy Add-ons Refinancing for lower payment Update/current exchanges Off-balance sheet financing Tax advantages Manufacturer support.	Possible High Interest Rate Varying finance charges Credit Score Dependent

Products and Services   (Select)

Note: Check state laws to determine what products can be sold.

	Forecasted Revenues	Percent Contribution

Products:

	Forecasted Revenues	Percent Contribution
Alternative Snacks		
Ice Bags		
Liquor		
Beer		
Wine		
Lottery/Gaming		
Tobacco Products: Cigarettes/Cigars/Other		
Packaged Beverages (Non-Alcohol)		
Gourmet Packaged Foods		
Publications/Magazines/Newspapers		
Salty Snacks		
Energy Drinks		
Bar Accessories/Supplies		
Frozen Pizzas		
Blenders		
Gaming Supplies: Playing Cards/Poker Chips		

Store Valued Products:

	Forecasted Revenues	Percent Contribution
Phone Cards		
Gift Cards		
Prepaid Debit Cards		

Services:

	Forecasted Revenues	Percent Contribution
Party/Event Planning Services		
Private Wine Tastings		
Custom Gift Baskets		
Delivery Services		
Bartender Services		
Wine Seminars		
Wine Consulting		
Totals:		

Service Descriptions

Custom Gift Baskets

Gift items will include a limited selection of kitchen wares, cocktail recipe books, wines cookbooks, picnic items, and bartender accessories. Gift baskets will also be available in the store and over the internet. Customers will be able to purchase pre-stocked baskets and custom designed baskets, where the customer makes all content selections within a certain price range.

Mobile Bartender Services

We will provide complete bartending and liquor needs, from the glasses, to the bartenders, to the shape and type of bar itself. The service will be professional, and customizable. It will be designed for the avid party host, the busy professional caterer, and event promoter. We will take care of everything, from the liquids, to the glasses, to the people.

Party Planning Services
Includes menu and wine selection, bar supplies, invitations, decorations, budgeting, event staffing, sommelier services, food/wine pairings, specialty drink recipes, etc.

Private Wine Tastings (Check State Rules)
During the Tasting guests will learn about a designated wine growing region, while sampling and evaluating a variety of wines and cheeses.

Wine Consulting
We will offer our wine consulting service to individuals and restaurants. We will consult restaurants on how-to create a new wine list, price wines, train staff, store wines, create marketing materials and programs, improve profitability, etc.

Wine Seminars
Seminar participants will learn: proper wine tasting techniques and etiquette, wine terms and common descriptive words, the basics of the winemaking process, wine varietals and their characteristics, wine and food pairings and what makes California Wines unique.

Alternative Revenue Streams
1. Classified Ads in our Newsletter
2. Vending Machine Sales
3. Product sales and rentals.
4. Website Banner Ads
4. Content Area Sponsorship Fees
5. Online Survey Report Fees
6. Subcontracting Commissions
7. Facilities Sub-leases

Production of Products and Services

We will use the following methods to locate the best suppliers for our business:

- Attend trade shows and seminars to spot upcoming trends, realize networking opportunities and compare prices.

  Natural Products Expo   www.naturalproductsexpo.com

- Subscribe to appropriate trade magazines, journals, newsletters and blogs.

  Beverage Dynamics   www.beveragedynamics.com
  Wine & Spirits Magazine   www.wineandspiritsmagazine.com
  Old Liquors Magazine   www.oldliquorsmagazine.com
  Beverage Industry   www.bevindustry.com

- Join our trade association to make valuable contacts, get listed in any online directories, and secure training and marketing materials.

National Alcohol Beverage Control Association   www.nabca.org/

American Beverage Licensees   www.ablusa.org/

The preeminent national trade association for retail beverage alcohol license holders across the United States.

Competitive Comparison

There are only ____ (#) other liquor stores in the neighborhood. _____ (company name) will differentiate itself from its local competitors by offering a broader range of alcoholic and non-alcoholic beverages, maintaining a database of customer preferences and transaction history, offering membership club benefits to qualifying customers, using a monthly newsletter to stay-in-touch with customers and offering an array of innovative service. We will also place a heavy emphasis on the development of a staff training program to meet consumer information demands, while also serving to control operational costs.

Location: We are the only convenience and fast to-go liquor store in the _____ area, with a drive-thru window. We will use occasional surveys to solicit customer feedback and stock items requested by local residents. We will also encourage customers to make special order requests.

_____ (company name) does not have to pay for under-utilized staff. Our flexible employee scheduling procedures and use of part-timers ensure that the store is never overstaffed during slow times. We will also adopt a pay-for-performance compensation plan, and use referral incentives to generate new business.

We will reinvest major dollars every year in professional and educational materials. We will participate in online webinars to bring clients the finest selection of products and services, and industry trend information.

Our prices will be competitive with other retail businesses that offer far less in the way of benefits, innovative services, and product selection.

Technology

___(company name) will employ and maintain the latest technology to enhance its office management, inventory management, payment processing, customer profiling and record keeping systems. We will also protect ourselves and society from the dangers of underage drinking with a new biometric fingerprint identification technology that can verify ID in a fraction of the time it takes to "card" customers. This will speed checkout while offering enhanced convenience and liability protection. We will also use a Cash Register POS system to manage our liquor store. Each item that gets sold will be deducted from our inventory list. Additionally, tracking items in our store will easily be managed with handheld inventory devices that integrate with Cash Register system.

Our point of sale system will include a small form factor computer, cash drawer, receipt printer and laser bar code scanner or tabletop scanner. An optional pole display will be easily added, which will inform our customers how much they are paying so they are likely to have the cash out quickly. A laser bar code scanner will aggressively scan bar codes that might be on bags or around bottles and quickly add the item to the invoice. All these devices help to reduce the time it takes to process a customer.

Resources:
Mobile POS Systems
Vend   **www.vendhq.com/**
A retail POS software, inventory management, ecommerce & customer loyalty for iPad, Mac and PC. Easily manage & grow your business in the cloud.

Shopkeep   **www.shopkeep.com**
Charges a monthly fee of $49 per register. It customizes service for retail, quick service, restaurants and bars with features including inventory monitoring, staff management and customer marketing. Administrators can monitor business stats through an online back-end, which also syncs with an iOS app for iPhone. Shopkeep's system can also be integrated with MailChimp to manage emails to a customer listserv and Quickbooks accounting software for an additional fee.

LevelUp   **www.thelevelup.com/**
 LevelUp charges a 1.95% rate for every transaction, as well as $50 per scanner, which plugs into most POS systems or the $100 LevelUp Tablet. The scanner reads a QR code displayed on a customer's smartphone or uses near field communication technology to allow the customer to pay with the likes of ApplePay or Google Wallet. LevelUp reminds customers when they have not visited the businesses after a set period of time and provides a rewards program. Customers also have the option of leaving feedback for the owner through the LevelUp app.

Revel   **http://revelsystems.com/**
An award-winning iPad Point of Sale solution for single and multi-location businesses.

Mobile Phone Credit Card Reader   https://squareup.com/
Square, Inc. is a financial services, merchant services aggregator and mobile payments company based in San Francisco, California. The company markets several software and hardware products and services, including Square Register and Square Order. Square Register allows individuals and merchants in the United States, Canada, and Japan to accept offline debit and credit cards on their iOS or Android smartphone or tablet

computer. The app supports manually entering the card details or swiping the card through the Square Reader, a small plastic device which plugs into the audio jack of a supported smartphone or tablet and reads the magnetic stripe. On the iPad version of the Square Register app, the interface resembles a traditional cash register.

Google Wallet   https://www.google.com/wallet/
A mobile payment system developed by Google that allows its users to store debit cards, credit cards, loyalty cards, and gift cards among other things, as well as redeeming sales promotions on their mobile phone. Google Wallet can be used NFC to make secure payments fast and convenient by simply tapping the phone on any PayPass-enabled terminal at checkout.

Apple Pay   http://www.apple.com/apple-pay/
A mobile payment and digital wallet service by Apple Inc. that lets users make payments using the iPhone 6, iPhone 6 Plus, Apple Watch-compatible devices (iPhone 5and later models), iPad Air 2, and iPad Mini 3. Apple Pay does not require Apple-specific contactless payment terminals and will work with Visa's PayWave, MasterCard's PayPass, and American Express's ExpressPay terminals. The service has begun initially only for use in the US, with international roll-out planned for the future.
Resource:
www.wired.com/2015/01/shadow-apple-pay-google-wallet-expands-online-reach/

WePay   https://www.wepay.com/
An online payment service provider in the United States. WePay's payment API focuses exclusively on platform businesses such as crowdfunding sites, marketplaces andsmall business software. Through this API, WePay allows these platforms to access its payments capabilities and process credit cards for the platform's users.

Chirpify
Connects a user's PayPal account with their Twitter account in order to enable payments through tweeting.

Selby Soft POS   www.selbysoft.com/index.shtml
Liquor POS   www.liquorpos.com/liquorPOS.html
POS Software Directory for Liquor Stores
                    www.softwareadvice.com/retail/liquor-store-software-comparison/

Indyme   **www.indyme.com/en/smart-response/smart-sense-touch**
A provider of real-time shopper engagement and loss prevention technologies, presented their Smart Sense Touch™ at the RILA Retail Asset Protection Conference. Smart Sense Touch ™ is a new sensor-driven technology that will not only help deter theft, but can also alert retail associates to potential sales opportunities. The Smart Sense Touch™ features a small wireless senor with an unobtrusive design, measuring 1.5" x 4" and the sensor can be implemented in most existing retail planograms or shelving units. The Touch sensors pick up vibrations by product interactions, such as handling an item, cutting a package, or otherwise tampering with an item on a shelf or peg hook. The Touch sensors then send a message to associates when a product has been touched a

certain amount of times; retailers are able to adjust the window of touches that must occur before a message is sent. The messages regarding suspicious activity (potential shoplifting) and customers in need of assistance are differentiated so the retail associate is able to tell how they need to approach the situation. This new technology enables retailers to instantly identify in-store customer activity and execute a response strategy to leverage these previously untapped sales and loss prevention opportunities.

Future Growth Plans

Wholesale Accounts

We plan to advise all of the local businesses that sell alcohol, such as bars and restaurants, that we are available to service their urgent need for product. We will devise a special price list for them, and arrange for free delivery, if the order is above a certain minimum amount. Business-to-business sales will serve as some of the most consistent and profitable sales, because we will be selling in bulk at a fairly constant rate.

Online Sales

We will research our state laws regarding online liquor sales. because online shopping will continue to become a preferred method of shopping, so offering our clients this convenience will be a key to our success.
Ecommerce Resource: www.shopify.com

Wine Tasting Parties

We will research the offering of in-home, bridal and corporate wine-tasting parties.

Craft Beers

We will seek to establish exclusive territory arrangements with a couple of microbreweries, and become experts in the making and taste profiles of these beers. We will also position our craft beer displays by the front door so that we can compete with the fast service offered by convenience and grocery stores. We will also use the opportunity to become knowledgeable about cooking with and the cross-selling of hot wing sauces, exotic cheeses and artisan breads with certain Belgian beers.
Source: http://www.ratebeer.com/forums/tips-for-opening-a-beer-store_86642.htm

Ambassador Program

A brand ambassador is a marketing jargon for celebrity endorser or spokesmodel, a person employed by an company to promote its products or services. The brand ambassador is meant to embody the corporate identity in lifestyle, appearance, demeanor, values and ethics. The key element of brand ambassadors lies in their ability to use promotional strategies that will strengthen the customer-product/service relationship and influence a large audience to buy and consume more. Predominantly, a brand ambassador is known as a positive spokesperson, an opinion leader or a community influencer, appointed as an internal or external agent to boost product/service sales and create brand awareness. Today, brand ambassador as a term has expanded beyond celebrity branding to self branding or personal brand management. Professional figures such as good-will and non-profit ambassadors, promotional models, testimonials and brand advocates have formed as an extension of the same concept, taking into account the requirements of every company. The Brand Ambassador for our liquor store will also function as a party planner and promote the placement of our favored brands at their events. They will also take photos at these events and post them on Instagram, Facebook,etc. Our brand ambassador will also sponsor parties and non-profit events throughout the community. We will not attempt to sell our products on social networking sites, but to rather make people aware that our business exists to facilitate 'good times'.

Custom Ordering

We will develop a form that enables our customers to custom order products that we do not normally stock. We will also ask about their brand preference , bottle size, expected monthly or special occasion usage profile and any friends that might be interested in this product.

Cooler Expansion

We plan to add an energy efficient, 14-door cooler to provide products ranging from energy drinks and organic juices to growlers and smoothies enriched with natural supplements.

Home Delivery Service

We will offer free delivery to local homes within a 5 mile radius. We will provide delivery at a cost for customers within a larger radius.

Daypart Analysis

We will conduct an ongoing study to determine the hours of the day when we sell the most product, to improve staff coverage during those hours, and limit store hours, to save personnel costs, during the slow times of day.

New Product Introductions

Because large retailers rarely take chances on new products or new developers, our specialty liquor store will seize the first opportunity to offer exclusive new items. We will develop a reputation for being one of the first liquor stores to test new products and brand marketing ideas.

Wedding/Party Planning Service

We will help our wedding and party customers to determines what -- and how much -- liquor should be ordered for the big day. Customers who register online will also be able to come to liquor store tasting room for tasting samples and usage of our event planning software. There will be no service charge. And if the order is over $____ (500?), delivery will be free. We will develop the capability to plan everything for their event, because it will be a great way to start a relationship with a newly formed household.

Meet the Distiller/ Brewer/ Winemaker Events

We will provide an experience-driven retail environment where customers can attend seminar events to learn more about the product from actual production experts.

CRM Software Tools

We will be installing a customer-relationship management (CRM) suite of tools that will enable us to really localize the selection and customize the message. We will be able to send customers offers that could be of interest and really tailor our message to local customer beverage preferences.

Club Membership Program

We will create a club membership program application form that allows us to collect consumer preferences, and ask if they wish to sign up for a monthly continuity program that will enable automatic shipments of desired favorite and/or new products.

Radio Ads

We will focus on radio because people are more receptive to party or cocktail solutions when they are driving around the community. These radio ads will help to keep the brand top of mind while they are out doing their shopping.

Website Design

We will make certain to provide cocktail recipes on our website, and a place (and/or a contest) where amateur mixologists can submit their own drink ideas.

Market Analysis Summary

Wine consumption is on the increase in the United States, and customers are trading up. In fact, wine overtook coffee as the most popular meal time beverage in the U.S. in 1998 (Wine Business Monthly, 6/00). Consumption trends and demographics point to robust wine sales growth for the next 15 years.

Wine demand is likely to be boosted strongly by the aging of the U.S. population. Per capita consumption of wine increases with age, with early consumers drinking only 6.6 bottles per year. Consumption peaks at 16.4 bottles annually among adults 50-59 years old. Baby boomers, more than any other previous generation, view wine as a simple, affordable luxury. Given that the strongest growth in population over the next 10 years will be among these adults, who currently consume about 40 percent of all wines, it is easy to understand the growth projections for this industry. Additionally, comprehensive industry research has shown that down turns in the economy and the stock market appear to have no impact on wine sales. In fact, wine sales rose slightly during previous stock market declines.

As one would expect, wine consumption in the _____ (city) metropolitan area exceeds national averages, primarily due to higher per capita income levels and a more international population mix. Europeans, for example, drink 5 to 10 times more wine per capita than their American counterparts. Consequently, we conservatively base our business plan projections for the local resident segment to buy an average of ____ (15?) bottles of wine per capita per year from our store.

Each of our targeted market segment consists of people who either live, work, or vacation in the ___ area. Our target market will be seeking a liquor store that will meet their desire for responsive and knowledgeable service, convenient store hours, a broad selection of new beverage choices, innovative home-oriented services, all provided from an easy to shop store.

Our liquor store will be located on the main road through town and is used daily by thousands of commuters between the two local _____ (towns/cities?). The closest liquor store in either direction is over ____ (#) miles away.

_____ (company name) has a defined target market of middle and upper-middle class consumers that will be the basis of this business. Effective marketing combined with an optimal product and service offering mix is critical to our success. The owner possesses solid information about the market and knows a great deal about the common attributes of those that are expected to be loyal clients. This information will be leveraged to better understand who we will serve, their specific needs, and how to better communicate with them. The owner strongly believes that as more and more products become commodities that require highly competitive pricing, it will be increasingly important to focus on the development of innovative services, that can be structured, managed and possibly outsourced.

Secondary Market Research

We will research demographic information for the following reasons:
1. To determine which segments of the population, such as Hispanics and the elderly, have been growing and may now be underserved.
2. To determine if there is a sufficient population base in the designated service area to realize the company's business objectives.
3. To consider what products and services to add in the future, given the changing demographic profile and needs of our service area.

We will pay special attention to the following general demographic trends:
1. Population growth has reached a plateau and market share will most likely be increased through innovation and excellent customer service.
2. Because incomes are not growing and unemployment is high, process efficiencies and sourcing advantages must be developed to keep prices competitive.
3. The rise of non-traditional households, such as single working mothers, means developing more innovative support programs, such as day care learning centers..
4. As the population shifts toward more young to middle aged adults, ages 30 to 44, and the elderly, aged 65 and older, there will be a greater need for child-rearing and geriatric support type products and services.
5. Because of the aging population and high unemployment, new ways of dealing with the resulting stress levels will need to be developed.

We will collect the demographic statistics for the following zip code(s):

_____

We will use the following sources: www.census.gov, www.zipskinny.com, www.city-data.com, www.demographicsnow.com, www.freedemographics.com, www.ffiec.gov/geocode, www.esri.com/data/esri_data/tapestry and www.claritas.com/claritas/demographics.jsp. This information will be used to decide upon which targeted programs to offer and to make business growth projections.
Resource: www.sbdcnet.org/index.php/demographics.html

1.	**Total Population**	_____
2.	**Number of Households**	_____
3.	**Population by Race:**	White ____% Black ___%
		Asian Pacific Islander ___% Other ____%
4.	**Population by Gender**	Male ____% Female ____%
5.	**Income Figures:**	Median Household Income $_____
		Household Income Under $50K ____%
		Household Income $50K-$100K ____%
		Household Income Over $100K ____%
6.	**Housing Figures**	Average Home Value - $_____
		Average Rent $_____
7.	**Homeownership:**	Homeowners % _____
		Renters % _____
8.	**Education Achievement**	High School Diploma % _____

		College Degree	% _____
		Graduate Degree	% _____
9.	**Stability/Newcomers**	Longer than 5 years	% _____

10. **Marital Status**   ___% Married   ___% Divorced   ___% Single
                            ___% Never Married   ___% Widowed   ___% Separated

11. **Occupations**   ___%Service   ___% Sales   ___% Management
                            ___% Construction   ___% Production
                            ___% Unemployed   ___% Below Poverty Level

12. **Age Distribution**   ___%Under 5 years   ___%5-9 yrs   ___%10-12 yrs
                            ___% 13-17 yrs   ___%18-years
                            ___% 20-29   ___% 30-39   ___% 40-49   ___% 50-59
                            ___% 60-69   ___% 70-79   ___% 80+ years

13. **Prior Growth Rate**   _____ % from _____ (year)

14. **Projected Population Growth Rate**   _____ %

15. **Employment Trend**   _____

Secondary Market Research Conclusions:
This area will be demographically favorable for our business for the following reasons:
_____
_____

Primary Market Research

We plan to develop a survey for primary research purposes and mail it to a list of local home magazine subscribers, purchased from the publishers by zip code. We will also post a copy of the survey on our website and encourage visitors to take the survey. We will use the following survey questions to develop an Ideal Customer Profile of our potential client base, so that we can better target our marketing communications. To improve the response rate, we will include an attention-grabbing _____ (discount coupon/ dollar?) as a thank you for taking the time to return the questionnaire.

1. What is your zip-code?   _____
2. Are you single, divorced, separated, widowed or married?   _____
3. Are you male or female?   _____
4. What is your age?   _____
5. What is your approximate household income?   _____
6. What is your educational level?   _____
7. What is your profession?   _____
8. Are you a dual income household?
9. Do you have children? If Yes, what are their ages?   _____
10. What are your favorite magazines?   _____
11. What is your favorite local newspaper?   _____
12. What is your favorite radio station?   _____
13. What are your favorite television programs?   _____
14. What organizations are you a member of?   _____
15. Does our community have an adequate number of liquor stores?   Yes / No
16. Does your family currently patronize a local liquor store?   Yes / No
17. Are you satisfied with your current liquor store?   Yes / No

18. How many times on average per month do you visit your liquor store? _____
19. What services do you typically purchase? _____
20. What products do you typically purchase? _____
21. On average, how much do you spend on liquor store purchases per month? ____
22. What is the name of your currently patronized liquor store?
23. What are their strengths as service providers?
24. What are their weaknesses or shortcomings?
25. What would it take for us to earn your liquor store business?
26. What is the best way for us to market our liquor store?
27. Do you live in _____ community?
28. Do you work or study in _____ community?
29. Do you think you will be in need of liquor store items in the near future?
30. Would you be interested in joining a Liquor Store Club that would offer special Membership benefits?
31. Describe your experience with other liquor store establishments.
32. Please rank (1 to 17) the importance of the following factors when choosing a Liquor Store:

___ Quality of Product	___ Wine Selection
___ Reputation	___ Staff Courtesy/Friendliness
___ Waiting time before service	___ Staff Professionalism
___ Convenient location	___ Value
___ Referral/References	___ Complaint Handling
___ Security Measures	___ Convenient Layout
___ Store Cleanliness	___ In-stock availability
___ Store Signage	___ Price
___ Other _____	

33. Please prioritize the importance of the following store activities:

___ Wine Tasting	___ Spirit Tasting
___ Gift Cards	___ Sales of Accessories
___ Sales of Books/Magazines/CDs	___ Apparel Sales

34. What information would you like to see in our store newsletter?
35. Which online social groups have you joined? Choose the ones you access.

___ Facebook	___ MySpace
___ Twitter	___ LinkedIn
___ Ryze	___ Ning

36. What types of liquor store services would most interest you?
37. What is your general need for a liquor store?
     Circle Months: J F M A M J J A S O N D (All)
     Circle Days: S M T W T F S (All)
     Indicate Hours: _____ or (24 hours)
38. What are your suggestions for realizing a better liquor store experience?
39. Are you on our mailing list? Yes/No   If No, can we add you? Yes / No

40.   Would you be interested in attending a free seminar on wine/food pairings?
41.   Can you supply the name and contact info of person who might be interested in our products and services?

Please note any comments or concerns about liquor stores in general.

We very much appreciate your participation in this survey. If you provide your name, address and email address, we will sign you up for our e-newsletter, inform you of our survey results, advise you of any new liquor stores opening in your community, and enter you into our monthly drawing for a free _____.

Name   Address
Email   Phone

Market Segmentation

Market segmentation is a technique that recognizes that the potential universe of users may be divided into definable sub-groups with different characteristics. Segmentation enables organizations to target messages to the needs and concerns of these subgroups. We will segment the market based on the needs and wants of select customer groups. We will develop a composite customer profile and a value proposition for each of these segments. The purpose for segmenting the market is to allow our marketing/sales program to focus on the subset of prospects that are "most likely" to purchase our liquor store products and services. If done properly this will help to insure the highest return for our marketing/sales expenditures.

The total potential market in units is shown in the following table and chart.
   There are approximately ____ (#) businesses in ____ (city) that could potentially be our customers.
   There are ____ (#) residents in ____ (city), according to the 200? U.S. Census, with ___ (5) % projected growth over the next ten years.
   Visitors were estimated using _____ Chamber of Commerce visitation report.
   From ___ - ____ (years), an average of ____ (#) people visited the ___ (city/attraction) annually.

Even though the visitor population appears to be the largest the market segment, it is possible that much of our sales could come from local residents and businesses, due to the fact that these people and companies make purchases for the visitors using their services. The local population is extremely important, because they can carry us through the low _____ (visitation/bad weather) months, and will determine whether we become an established community destination.

Target Markets:
   Drinking Age Residents of the _____ area
   People willing to pay a premium for one-stop convenience at all hours of the day.

The profile of the _____ (company name) client consists of the following geographic, demographic, psychographic and behavior factors:

Geographics
- The geographic market is the _____ (middle class) sector within the ___ (city), with a population of _____ people.
- A ___ (10?) mile geographic area is in need of our products and services, according to our survey results.
- The total target market population is estimated to be _____(#) people.

Demographics
- Married and attended college.
- Have children, but some may have already moved out.
- A combined household income > $ _____ (60,000).
- Age range of ___ (21) to ___ (59), with a median age of ____ (48).

Psychographics
- Enjoy having dinner parties and holiday celebrations.
- Read lifestyle magazines, including Home, Country Home and Victoria.
- Maintains an active lifestyle.
- Believe on the health benefits of moderate wine consumption.

Behaviors
- Are interested in experiencing new services.
- Follow entertainment trends.

Composite Ideal Customer Profile:

By assembling this composite customer profile we will know what customer needs and wants our company needs to focus on and how best to reach our target market. We will use the information gathered from our customer research surveys to assemble the following composite customer profile:

Ideal Customer Profile

Who are they?
- age
- gender
- occupation
  location: zip codes
- income level
  marital status
  ethnic group
  education level
  family life cycle
  number of household members
  household income
  homeowner or renter
  association memberships
  leisure activities
  hobbies/interests
  core beliefs
  _____
  _____
  _____
  _____
  _____
  _____
  _____
  _____
  _____
  _____
  _____
  _____
  _____
  _____
  _____
  _____
  _____

Where are they located (zip codes)?	_____
Most popular products purchased?	_____
Most popular services purchased?	_____
Lifestyle Preferences?	Trendsetter/Trend follower/Other _____
How often do they buy?	_____
What are most important purchase factors?	Price/Brand Name/Quality/Financing/Sales Convenience/Packaging/Other_____
What is their key buying motivator?	_____
How do they buy it?	Cash/Credit/Terms/Other_____
Where do they buy it from (locations)?	_____
What problem do they want to solve?	_____
What are the key frustrations/pains that these customers have when buying?	_____
What search methods do they use?	_____
What is preferred problem solution?	_____

Target Market Segment Strategy

Our target marketing strategy will involve identifying a group of customers to which to direct our liquor store products and services. Our strategy will be the result of intently listening to and understanding customer needs, representing customers' needs to those responsible for product production and service delivery, and giving them what they want. In developing our targeted customer messages we will strive to understand things like: where they work, worship, party and play, where they shop and go to school, how they spend their leisure time, what magazines they read and organizations they belong to, and where they volunteer their time. We will use research, surveys and observation to uncover this wealth of information to get our product details and brand name in front of our customers when they are most receptive to receiving our messaging.

The target market profile consists of _____ (city) residents who are educated, successful professionals, with disposable income, and who are regular consumers of alcoholic beverages. Most of the consumers in this category rely on assistance in selecting wines and spirits. Consequently, they tend to reward the most capable merchants with loyalty and word-of-mouth advertising.

Other potential segments (geographic, demographic, preferences):
1. **Bulk Volume (Private and Business):**
   Much of this business needs to be cultivated through opportunistic networking, and diligent follow-ups of in-store inquiries and leads.
2. **Direct Deliverables** (Outside immediate store neighborhood):
   Viable only as the store earns its way into a position in which it can invest in vehicle delivery operations and line up target customers that would sustain such an operation.
3. **Intra-state shipments:**
   Contingent on expansion following the successful implementation of this business plan. This business would develop through direct-mail catalog marketing, and an

Internet sales operation.

We will focus on the following well-defined target market segments and emphasize our good value, high quality, unique and varied selections, and great service.

Professional Women
This segment is comprised of women in the age range of 25 to 50. They are married, have a household income >$100,000, own at least one home, and are socially active. They are members of at least one club or organization. They have high disposable or discretionary income and are considered the family decision-makers.

Target University Students
We will target the students of local colleges and universities, because this group has a very well-known proclivity to party!

Target Professional Young People
This group is comprised of couples between the ages of 25 and 35, and are in the process of setting up their first adult household. They both work, earn in excess of $85,000 annually, and now want to invest in themselves. They seek to communicate a successful image to their friends and may have an interest in our event planning services.

Target Aging Baby Boomers
Since people age 50 and older have more discretionary money, they are more prone to take advantage of new products and services, and believe in the status-conferring and health benefits associated with red wine consumption.

Target Seniors
Seniors with mobility problems will appreciate the convenience of our drive-thru window and open floor plan. We will offer them discounts on products and service. We also plan to visit local nursing homes, assisted living facilities and independent living centers to learn how we can better accommodate the needs and wants of seniors.

Target Local Ethnic Groups
Ongoing demographic trends suggest that, in the coming decades, programs will be serving a population of people which is increasingly diverse in economic resources, racial and ethnic background, and family structure. Our plan is to reach out to consumers of various ethnic backgrounds, especially Hispanics, who comprise nearly 13 percent of the country's total population. In addition to embarking on an aggressive media campaign of advertising with ethnic newspapers and radio stations, we will set up programs to actively recruit bilingual employees and make our store more accessible via signage printed in various languages based on the store's community. We will accurately translate our marketing materials into other languages. We will enlist the support of our bilingual employees to assist in reaching the ethnic people in our surrounding area through a referral program. We will join the nearest _____ (predominate ethnic group) Chamber of Commerce and partner with _____ (Hispanic/Chinese/Other?) Advocacy Agencies. We will also develop programs that reflect cultural influences and brand preferences.

Helpful Resources:
U.S. census Bureau Statistics   www.census.gov
U.S. Dept. of Labor/Bureau of Labor Statistics   www.bls.gov/data/home.htm
National Hispanic Medical Association

Market Needs

We plan to pay more attention to the opportunities of geographic extensions through direct shipments of wine & spirits throughout our state, and within our county with our own delivery service. We plan to market over the Internet to the _____ (#) actual and potential customers on our mailing list. As a goal, our company will seek to capture of piece of the apparently substantial demand for direct shipment sales.

Local and visiting customers desire high quality, beverages that will appeal to their aesthetics. In addition, they desire a pleasant shopping experience that allows them to learn about and purchase the beverage items they want in a comfortable, friendly, hassle-free environment.

Buying Patterns

In most cases, clients make the purchase decision on the basis of the following criteria:
1.   Referrals and relationship with other customers.
2.   Personality and expected relationship with the store personnel.
3.   Internet-based information gathering.

People have the following reasons for drinking, (in their order of importance):
1.   To be sociable   2.   Enjoyment of a meal.
3.   Relax.   4.   Feel Good.
5.   Less shy/inhibited.   6.   Forget worries.

Males are the most frequent customers of liquor stores, but it is increasingly important to be female friendly.

Liquor store purchases are driven by occasion type, with purchases directed at enjoying good times at a special social occasion. Consequently, the store must project a good times image.

_____ (company name) will gear its offerings, marketing, and pricing policies to establish a loyal client base. Our value-based pricing, easy store access, preferred membership programs, home-based services and basic quality products will be welcomed in _____ (city) and contribute to our success.

Market Growth

American Demographics projects the number of U.S. households will grow by 15% to 115 million by the year 2015. These busy households will require a greater range of convenience-driven store products and services.

We believe there is a market for our products and services in ___ (city) and that the market has potential for growth. _____ County's population in the year 2000 was ____ and is expected to grow at a rate of ___ (5)% over the next ten years. ____ (city) is dedicated to remaining a travel destination "hot spot" without loosing its "small town" feel. Because of its unique appeal it is likely to attract many vacationers and settlers for years to come. Our business will grow as customers become familiar with our unrivaled product selection and home-based entertaining services.

One important factor is that married couples in the 35 to 65 age range represent a growth segment and enjoy larger incomes than other family structures. They welcome the choice to spend their disposable income on home-based activities, such as wine-tasting parties. Overall, the environment appears very positive for the ____ (company name). The forces driving market demand, mainly economic, are strong, with industry growth healthy and new residents moving into the area resulting in a greater demand for our stress-relieving products and services.

The general industry analysis shows that _____ (city) is expected to experience _____ (double digit?) population, housing and commercial business growth. This suggests that as more families continue to move into the _____ area, there will be an increasing demand for quality beverage services, and this makes it a prime location for a liquor store that is willing to think outside-of-the-box.

Service Business Analysis

The demand for liquor stores is increasing for the following reasons:
1. Alcoholic beverages are seen as an affordable luxury during recessionary times.
2. The number of drinking age Americans is increasing almost three times as fast as the rest of the population.

Liquor super stores have increased in number more than 15% to about 1,200 stores since 2008, growing three times faster than conventional liquor stores, which still dominate with 40,000 stores, according to Nielsen. The superstores, including regional chains like Binny's Beverage Depot, ABC Fine Wine & Spirits and Total Wine & More, seek to differentiate themselves with a broader selection and an emphasis on customer service.

Successful liquors stores offer convenience and have a staff that is friendly and approachable. They understand that they are the originating point for good times, and are very supportive of customers who require help with selection recommendations and party planning advice.

Business Environment:
1. **Potential Competitors:** There are ____ (#) liquor stores in the city of _____
2. **Power of Suppliers:** In some states, distributors hold the power and only give discounts to chain stores that can buy in large volumes.
3. **Power of Buyers:** High.
4. **Substitute Products:** Substitute products are prevalent.
5. **Rivalry:** Moderate with the territorial structure that the industry experiences and moderate exit barriers.

Barriers to Entry

_____ (company name) will benefit from the following combination of barriers to entry, which cumulatively present a moderate degree of entry difficulty or obstacles in the path of other convenience store businesses wanting to enter our market.

1.	Business Experience.	2.	Community Networking
3.	Referral Program	4.	People Skills
5.	Marketing Skills	6.	Supplier Relationships
7.	Operations Management	8.	Cash Flow Management
9.	Website Design	10.	Capital Investment
11.	License Availability	12.	Owner Background Check

Competitive Analysis

Competition to a large degree depends on location, as stores take a stake in a territory that engenders best in-store sales prospects. Relationships are cultivated with better customers, both individual and wholesale, who may qualify for discounts based on volume purchases. Prices in the ____ (city) marketplace are not subject to much variance, as retailers seek to protect their margins against distributor costs that are virtually the same for all. Distributors, however, reward volume, and high-volume retailers have the capability to build a competitive advantage. Special pricing on a limited number of products is something only a high-volume retailer could afford to do.

Other competitive factors include breadth and depth of available stock, product knowledge, customer service, expense management, marketing programs, employee training and productivity, management of detailed customer information in databases, in-store merchandising and overall "good times" design, extended hours of operation, incoming and outgoing delivery efficiencies, product packaging, customer loyalty programs, out-of-area competition, pricing, and branded reputation.

Competitors:
_____ (competitor name#1) is about _____ (#) (feet/blocks/miles) from our proposed

storefront. It is our primary local competitor, although not a serious threat to our main residential base of customers, who will find our location much more convenient to their needs. Another important factor is that our selection and product knowledge will appeal to the high-income local residents, while _____ (competitor name) has more of a neighborhood grocer approach with less focus on product knowledge and store design.

_____ (competitor name#2) on _____ Street is the next nearest competitor, about _____ (#) (feet/blocks/miles?) from of our location. Although it is a high-volume shop with strength in pricing power, it remains far beyond the practical boundaries for shoppers who live in our neighborhood.

There are other direct marketers and major advertisers that can deliver into our territory, But we expect our local delivery service will be faster and more responsive than these bigger players. Internet storefronts, such as Wine.com are emerging competitors and may be more of a longer term issue, since the industry is in the process of testing and adapting to changing conditions in search of an online business model that works. We intend to develop our own website and grow with website economics that make this a self-funding outlet for sales and service.

Non-local stores that are in commuter paths of our neighborhood residents are also competitors, which will make us ever aware of the importance of cultivating personal relationships with our neighborhood residents, so we can develop a long-term loyal customer base.

We will conduct good market intelligence for the following reasons:
1.   To forecast competitors' strategies.
2.   To predict competitor likely reactions to our own strategies.
3.   To consider how competitors' behavior can be influenced in our own favor.

Overall competition in the area is _____ (weak/moderate/strong).

Competitive analysis conducted by the company owners has shown that there are _____ (# or no other?) liquor stores currently offering the same combination of products and services in the _____ (city) area. However, the existing competitors offer only a limited range of traditional products. In fact, of these, _____ (# or none) of the competitors offered a range of products and services comparable with what _____ (company name) plans to offer to its customers.

The following liquor stores are considered direct competitors in _____ (city):

Competitor	Address	Market Share	Primary Focus	Secondary Prod/Svcs	Strengths	Weaknesses

Indirect Competitors include the following:

Alternative Competitive Matrix

Competitor Name: <u>Us</u>   _____   _____   _____
Location: _____   _____   _____
Location Distance (miles)   _____   _____   _____

Comparison Items:
Sales Revenue   _____
Buying Power   _____
Product Focus   _____
Membership Programs   _____
Profitability   _____
Market Share   _____
Brand Names   _____
Specialty   _____
Services   _____
Capitalization   _____
Target Markets   _____
Delivery Area   _____
Open Days   _____
Operating Hours   _____
Operating Policies   _____
Payment Options   _____
Other Financing   _____
Pricing Strategy   _____
Price Level L/M/H   _____
Discounts   _____
Yrs in Business   _____
Reputation   _____
Reliability   _____
Quality   _____
Marketing Strategy   _____
Methods of Promotion   _____
Alliances   _____
Brochure/Catalog   _____
Website   _____
Sales Revenues   _____
No. of Staff   _____
Competitive Advantage _____
Credit Cards Accepted Y/N _____
Manufacturers Used   _____
Comments   _____

We will use the following sources of information to conduct our competition analysis:

1. Competitor company websites.
2. Mystery shopper visits.
3. Annual Reports (www.annual reports.com)
4. Thomas Net (www.thomasnet.com)
5. Trade Journals
6. Trade Associations
7. Sales representative interviews
8. Research & Development may come across new patents.
9. Market research can give feedback on the customer's perspective
10. Monitoring services will track a company or industry you select for news. Resources: www.portfolionews.com www.Office.com
11. Hoover's www.hoovers.com
12. www.zapdata.com (Dun and Bradstreet) You can buy one-off lists here.
13. www.infousa.com (The largest, and they resell to many other vendors)
14. www.onesource.com (By subscription, they pull information from many sources)
15. www.capitaliq.com (Standard and Poors).
16. Obtain industry specific information from First Research (www.firstresearch.com) or IBISWorld, although both are by subscription only, although you may be able to buy just one report.
17. Get industry financial ratios and industry norms from RMA (www.rmahq.com) or by using ProfitCents.com software.
18. Company newsletters
19. Industry and Market Research Consultants
20. Local Suppliers and Distributors
21. Customer interviews regarding competitors.
22. Analyze competitors' ads for their target audience, market position, product features, benefits, prices, etc.
23. Attend speeches or presentations made by representatives of your competitors.
24. View competitor's trade show display from a potential customer's point of view.
25. Search computer databases (available at many public libraries).
26. Review competitor Yellow Book Ads.

Market Revenue Projection

For each of our chosen target markets, we will estimate our market share in number of customers, and based on consumer behavior, how often do they buy per year? What is the average dollar amount of each purchase? We will then multiply these three numbers to project sales volume for each target market.

Target Market	Number of Customers	No. of Purchases per Year	Average Dollar Amount per Purchase	Total Sales Volume

$$A \quad x \quad B \quad x \quad C \quad = \quad D$$

Using the target market number identified in this section, and the local demographics, we have made the following assessments regarding market opportunity and revenue potential in our area:

Potential Revenue Opportunity =

	_____	Local No. of Households (>60k Income)
(x)	_____	Expected ___% Market Share
(=)	_____	Number of likely local customers
(x) $	_____	Average annual fee dollar amount
(=) $	_____	Annual Revenue Opportunity.

Or

	No. of Clients Per Day	(x)	Avg. Sale	(=)	Daily Income
Services	_____		_____		_____
Product Sales	_____		_____		_____
Other	_____		_____		_____
Total:					_____
Annualized:				(x)	300
Annual Revenue Potential:					_____

Recap:

Month	Jan Feb Mar Apr May Jun Jul Aug Sep Oct Nov Dec Total
Products	

Services

Gross Sales:	
(-) Returns	
Net Sales	

Revenue Assumptions:
1.   The sources of information for our revenue projection are:

2.   If the total market demand for our product/service = 100%, our projected sales volume represents ____% of this total market.
3.   The following factors might lower our revenue projections:

Industry Analysis   (SIC 5921)

Liquor stores are establishments engaged in the retail sale of packaged alcoholic beverages, including ale, beer, wine, and liquor, for consumption off premises.

In 2001, according to the U.S. Census Bureau, there were 28,695 establishments engaged in the retail sale of packaged alcoholic beverages. The industry employed about 136,212 people with an annual payroll of $2.1 billion. By 2003, the total number of establishments grew to 33,902. Together, they shared $13.4 billion in annual sales. The total number of employees, however, remained about the same. The average beer, wine, or liquor store generated $400,000 in sales and employed about four people.

The liquor store industry is made up of mom-and pop retail outlets, independently run chains, and corporate-owned stores. While the vast majority of stores are small, family-run operations, there are a rapidly growing number are superstores primarily engaged in other kinds of businesses.

Among the industry's top companies, most remained independently run during the 1990s. Increasingly, however, they changed their retail strategy, consolidating multiple outlets into fewer but bigger warehouse-style stores, thus saving on overhead and payroll while still moving a large inventory. The effect has been hard on smaller neighborhood retail operations comprising the bulk of the industry. The mom-and-pop shops just can't compete with the superstores and the discounters.

Following national Prohibition, the 21st Amendment to the Constitution provides states with broad powers and authority to regulate the sale and distribution of alcohol within their borders. Each state created its own unique system of alcohol beverage control. There are two general classifications. "Control" states, 18 in number, are the sole wholesalers of distilled spirits, as well as the retailers in various ways in some of these States. "License" states, of which there are 32, do not participate in the sale of alcohol beverages and regulate through the issuance of licenses to industry members that do business within their states.

In addition to meeting Federal regulations, individuals and businesses must meet each state's individual laws and regulations. These state laws and regulations, which vary widely from state to state, may be more restrictive than Federal regulations and must be met in addition to Federal requirements unless the Federal law pre-empts the State law wherein they desire to do business. For example regarding pre-emption, the Government Warning label on alcohol beverages pre-empts the states from imposing a similar requirement. Some states even prohibit the offering of free liquor in tasting events and the advertising of discounts.

Industry Trends

We will determine the trends that are impacting our consumers and indicate ways in which our customers' needs are changing and any relevant social, technical or other changes that will impact our target market. Keeping up with trends and reports will help management to carve a niche for our business, stay ahead of the competition and deliver products that our customers need and want. We will define an emerging trend as a factor that has the potential to significantly impact the market and contribute to its growth or decline.

1.   The Business Journal reports that sales at liquor stores were up in 2008, as alcohol is viewed as an affordable luxury that people turn to when they're priced out of other items.
2.   Gross sales increases have been driven by growth in the drinking-age population, (increase of 11% from 2004 to 2016) increased spirit taxes, and the consumer preference for higher-priced brands.
3.   Consumers continue to favor new products, new tastes and new packages. Flavored spirits are very popular, especially in the vodka and rum categories, and growth in flavored brandies and tequilas is expected.
4.   Distilled spirits and wine continue to market share away from beer.
5.   Supermarkets have increased their focus on liquor to drive foot traffic into their stores.
6.   States want to raise more money by selling liquor licenses to grocery stores, permitting them to sell wine and lower-proof alcohol products.
7.   Typically, liquor consumers are very liquor brand name loyal.
8.   Liquor stores with lottery sales bring in more customers and as a result experience higher sales figures.
9.   In most locations, wine and specifically alcohols with a wide array of flavors are becoming the "taste du jour".
10. Wine boutiques and mega stores are growing rapidly.
11. There is a growing interest in specialty wines, handcrafted microbrews and premium spirits.
12. Products made by independent producers are fashionable and attract customers willing to spend extra money for premium products.
13. During a recession, when a lot of people are laid off, the unemployed spend more of their free time and money on beer rather than gas to get to and from work.
14. According to the Insurance Information Institute (I.I.I.), a number of factors have combined to create a more favorable market for establishments seeking liquor liability insurance, including the responsibility assumed by owners and operators of eating and drinking establishments and stricter state liquor statutes and undercover investigations.
15. Starbucks Corp. will add beer and wine to its menu of coffees, teas and snacks at one of its Seattle locations as part of a test program.
16. Overall the online market for wine generally has continued to show a great deal of strength.
17. A retail business model, where consumers purchase wines by the case, lends itself very well to online selling.
18. The recession has forced wine consumers to trade down to bottles of less expensive wines.

19.   Consumers are staying home more and this has proven to a plus for wine retailers, as shoppers spend more for home consumption than in restaurants, because there is bigger value for the consumer in purchasing product for home consumption.
20.   Convenience stores are starting to pay attention to their wine sets.
21.   Supermarkets are seeing a shift toward value buying, with boxed wines gaining greater acceptance among customers.
22.   Profit margins seem to be driving supermarkets to sell wine, but there is probably a greater belief that there is an image to be created that appeals to an upscale food consumer.
23.   There has been a growth in sales of value-priced limited reserve wines.
24.   Many stores are continuing to cross merchandise party goods, snack foods and assorted bar accessories to encourage incremental sales.
25.   Stores are giving more ad and floor space to the best selling brands within the more traditional categories.
26.   More states are opting to privatize liquor sales as a means of increasing state tax revenues. Ex: West Virginia
27.   States are also doing more extensive background checks before issuing liquor licenses to individuals.
28.   Liquor stores are facing increased competition from wine sales made in supermarkets, on the Internet and through catalogues.
29.   New state taxes on liquor may force more potential buyers to turn to the Internet to buy wine and force smaller liquor stores out of business and others to cut inventory.

Key Industry Terms

Liquor Store
A type of convenience store which specializes in the sale of alcoholic beverages in the countries where its consumption is strongly regulated. In alcoholic beverage control (ABC) states, liquor stores often sell only distilled spirits or sometimes sell distilled spirits and wine but not beer. ABC-run stores may be called **ABC stores**.

On Premise
Any establishment that serves alcohol by the glass or single bottle or can that is intended to be consumed on the establishment premises. This is usually restaurants, bars, hotels, nightclubs, private parties and even outdoor festivals.

Off Premise
Any establishments that serves alcohol by the bottle, case or single cans that are intended to be taken off the store premises to be consumed elsewhere. This is usually liquor stores, grocery stores, gas stations and convenience stores.

Package store
Package liquor is alcohol sold in the original bottle, can or other form of container. Businesses that sell package liquor include large retail grocery stores, smaller convenience stores and stores that primarily sell package liquor. Certain types of businesses cannot sell package liquor. For example, a gas station cannot sell package liquor if its primary business is selling gasoline and servicing vehicles. However, a

convenience store that primarily sells food but also sells gasoline can sell package liquor if they meet the requirements of the City code. Package liquor cannot be consumed on the premises where purchased.

PACKAGE STORE PERMIT (P)
Permit authorizes the holder to sell liquor, malt and vinous liquors on or from licensed premises at retail to consumer for off-premise consumption.

PACKAGE STORE TASTING PERMIT (PS)
Permit authorizes the holder to conduct product tasting of distilled spirits, wine, beer and malt-based or spirit-based coolers on the licensed premises of the holder's package store or wine only package store during regular business hours.

PACKAGE STORE PERMIT (WINE ONLY) (Q)
Permit authorizes the holder to sell ale, malt liquor, wine and vinous liquors on or from licensed premises at retail to consumer for off-premise consumption. The holder of a wine-only package store permit whose premise is located in a wet area allowing the legal sale of wine for off-premise consumption only may purchase, sell, or possess vinous liquor only-- no ale or malt liquor on those premises.

Industry Benchmarks
1. Gross margin should be between 24 and 28%.
2. Rent should be 7% of revenue maximum.
3. Product mix should be up to 70% liquor or up to 40% wine.
4. Labor should represent 5 to 7% of revenue.
5. Net profit should be 8 to 12% of revenue.
6. Inventory should be turned over between eight and 10 times per year.

Industry Leaders

Constellation Brands
Produces and sells over 200 brands of beer, wine, and liquor, but most of the company's revenues come from its Wine business. Constellation Wines is the largest wine company worldwide, though that translates to less than 5% of the global wine business, given the industry's fragmentation. The company is also the US distributor of many well-known beer and spirits brands including Corona, St. Pauli Girl, and Black Velvet. The company earned $4.2 billion in revenue and $99 million in net income in 2010.

Recently, Constellation's Beer business drove more than 60 percent of its high-end category growth and claimed three of the Top 10 share-gaining spots in the U.S. beer market. Its 120 Days of Summer marketing campaign drove beer business market share gains during the July Fourth holiday, which continued throughout the summer selling season and into Labor Day.
Source:
www.bevindustry.com/articles/90692-constellation-brands-announces-q2-2018-results

Constellation Wines is the firm's biggest segment and the largest wine business in the world, markets wines across all price points, from popular to premium to super-premium, with the portfolio split about evenly between high-end and low-end brands. Constellation Wines owns 24 of the 100 bestselling brands in the US and 8 of the 20 bestselling brands in the UK. This business also includes the production of cider, where Constellation is the second largest domestic producer. Constellation Wines also sells unbranded wines wholesale in the UK. Finally, the Spirits business is the firm's smallest, accounting for only 7% of annual revenues. This segment sells both premium and value brands such as Black Velvet, Chi-Chi's prepared cocktails, Barton, and Fleischmann's. Recent acquisitions, such as last year's purchase of Svedka vodka, the fastest-growing premium vodka brand in the United States, have increased the company's premium offerings in all segments. **Crown Imports** imports and markets various brands of foreign beers, most notably Corona. The company owns six of the top 25 imported beer brands in the US.

Consumption Trends

Slowing Alcohol Consumption Decreases Demand: Western Europeans and North Americans are consuming less alcohol than they have previously. In America, per capita annual consumption has been slowing for decades, from 2.76 gallons in 1980, to 2.43 gallons in 1990, and finally 2.18 gallons in 2000. From 1970-2000 consumption in Italy dropped 44%, France dropped 34%, and Spain by 15%. From 1990 to 1998 alcohol consumption declined 6% in Western Europe, 10% in North America and 12.5% in Australasia. Several demographic trends are contributing to the decrease, including, for instance, a rising level of education (alcohol consumption is negatively correlated to education). As a result, alcohol producers face stagnant markets with low growth prospects. Constellation Brands in particular stands to lose from this trend as the majority of its sales are concentrated in the United States and other developed markets.

Popularity and Growth of Wine Consumption Drives Largest Segment's Sales:
While consumption of wine in traditional wine drinking countries has been stagnant, the popularity of wine has exploded in countries where consumption has traditionally been low, such as Denmark, the Republic of Ireland, and Norway. Growth in Asia, which had been booming for decades, is now also appearing to level off. For example, wine consumption in Japan rose 350% from 1980 to 1998, but only grew .8% in 1999. For Constellation Brands, these trends hold twofold importance; first, the decline in wine consumption in many of its largest markets limits revenue growth there. Second, the changes in demand in markets the firm has not yet entered influence future expansion prospects, which may be minimal if wine consumption continues to slow.

United States Demographic Trends Influence Consumption of Alcoholic Beverages: The majority of wine drinkers in America are part of the baby boomer generation. This generation is reaching their peak wine drinking age, and have plenty of disposable income. It is believed that the baby boomer trend will continue until around 2017, and will continue to generate profits for the alcohol industry. However, this good news is tempered by some less encouraging data concerning the youngest generation of Americans. The next generation of alcohol drinkers appears to hold off on alcohol more than their parents. The number of teenagers who said they had had a drink was 78% lower in 1999 than in 1982, and the number of college freshmen who say they drink occasionally or often is at record low levels. Since the United States is the firm's largest market with over 60% of sales, these trends are key in determining future demand for its products.

Trading Up to Higher Priced of Alcohol Consumption Necessitates Adjustments of Portfolio: The global spirits market has benefited from a shift in consumer tastes from beer to higher-priced and trendier alcoholic drinks such as wine and spirits. Constellation Brands' portfolio is about equally split between premium beverages and value drinks, so the effect of this trend on the firm is mixed. On one hand, high margin wines and imported beer brands such as Corona are well-positioned to benefit from this shift in demand. In fact, Constellation is actively making investments and launching joint ventures to gain a larger position in these businesses. On the other hand, with spirits comprising only 7% of sales, the firm cannot fully benefit from the increased popularity in that segment, and value brands across all segments are threatened by the shift in the demand away from such products.

More people are becoming interested in the making and personalizing of cocktails.

Production Trends

Rising Commodity Prices Affect Production Costs: Most commodity prices have risen dramatically over the last year. This has hit the alcohol industry hard, since agricultural commodities, such as grains, are key ingredients in producing all types of alcohol. As a player in all categories of alcoholic beverages, Constellation has felt the pressure of higher production costs. At the same time, an oversupply of grapes in all of the company's primary markets (US,UK, Australia) has the potential to increase the quantity of wine on the market, leading to competitive pricing pressures. Most recently, however, the grape glut has been decreasing somewhat, alleviating the pressure on Constellation Brands.

Potential Increases in Excise Taxes and Regulation Put Pressure on Margins: Taxes and other fees account for over half of the retail cost of alcohol. However, because the average consumer is not aware of this fact, distillers usually cannot raise prices when these taxes increase. Consumers would perceive such a move as price gouging, strongly decreasing demand. Many states in the US, Constellation's largest market, have recently considered proposals to increase excise taxes, and some have passed these proposals, impacting the firm's margins.

Industry News

Delivery Apps

Relying on guidance from California, New York and Texas alcohol regulations and licensing boards, the District of Columbia determined in August of 2014 that liquor delivery websites and apps do not necessarily have to obtain a liquor license to serve DC residents.

Source: http://techyaya.com/start-up/dc-joins-ny-tx-cali-opening-path-for-liquor-delivery-startups/

Resources:

Delivery.com   https://www.delivery.com/washington/alcohol?page=1

Drizly™   https://drizly.com/

The technology company powering a superior shopping experience for beer, wine and liquor. Combining the best selection and price, content-rich and personalized shopping experiences, and the speed and convenience of on-demand delivery, Drizly delivers "The Joy of Drinking™" to legal-age drinkers across the United States. Backed by a world-class group of angel and institutional investors, the company has become a superior place to shop for beer, wine and liquor in Austin, Baltimore, Boston, Chicago, Denver, Indianapolis, Los Angeles, Minneapolis/St. Paul, New York City, Providence, Seattle, St. Louis, Washington D.C., and other cities across the United States.

Drive-up Windows

At least 23 states allow drive-up or drive-through liquor sales, according to a 2004 study cited this week in *USA Today, but con*cern about possible resulting drunken driving crashes and deaths is prompting efforts to outlaw drive-up liquor stores.

Source: http://blog.seattlepi.com/thebigblog/2012/07/11/are-drive-up-liquor-stores-legal-in-washington/#5511101=0

SBA Loans

Watchdog's analysis of data obtained from openthebooks.com reveals, for instance, that "SBA provided more than $9 million in loan guarantees to start-up and grow liquor and tobacco small businesses" in just two states—Oklahoma and Colorado—over the past 5 years.

Source: http://dailycaller.com/2015/03/23/government-hypocrisy-sba-subsidizes-liquor-tobacco-stores/

Strategy and Implementation Summary

The liquor distribution industry is primarily based off convenience sales. This, in-turn, highlights the importance of location and price in our sales strategies. The closest liquor store is a ___ (#) minute ___ (walk/ride?) from our location. To sustain this advantage, we will negotiate with the landlord so that our leasing agreement ensures no other liquor distributor can move into the same property complex.

Location is critical to attract the traffic and customer profile required to generate planned sales volumes. The business is highly territorial. We have mapped the location of every retail liquor store in _____ (city), and we have been working with executives of _____ (real estate company name) to determine the best possible location for the store. ____ (#) target areas were identified. Among the target areas investigated, _____ (area name) has been identified as our most promising business opportunity.

Our sales strategy is based on serving our niche markets better than the competition and leveraging our competitive advantages. These advantages include superior attention to understanding and satisfying customer needs and wants, creating a one-stop 'good times' solution, and value pricing.

The objectives of our marketing strategy will be to recruit new customers, retain existing customers, get good customers to spend more and return more frequently. Establishing a loyal customer base is very important because such core customers will not only generate the most lifetime sales, but also provide valuable referrals.

We will generate word-of-mouth buzz through direct-mail campaigns, exceeding customer expectations, developing a Web site, getting involved in community events with local businesses, and donating our services at charity functions, in exchange for press release coverage. Our sales strategy will seek to convert potential and first-time customers into long-term relationships and referral agents. The combination of our competitive advantages, targeted marketing campaign and networking activities, will enable _____ (company name) to continue increasing our market share.

Promotion Strategy

Promotion strategies will be focused to the target market segment. Given the importance of word-of-mouth/referrals among the area residents, we shall strive to efficiently service all our customers to gain their business regularly, which is the recipe for our long-term success. We shall focus on direct resident marketing, publicity, wine seminars, and advertising as proposed. Our promotion strategy will focus on generating referrals from existing clients and professionals, community involvement and direct mail campaigns.

Our promotional strategies will also make use of the following tools:
- **Advertising**
  - o Yearly anniversary parties to celebrate the success of each year.

- o Yellow Pages ads in the book and online.
- o Flyers promoting special promotion events.
- 0 Doorknob hangers, if not prohibited by neighborhood associations.
- O Storefront banners to promote a themed promotional event.

- **Local Marketing / Public Relations**
  - o Client raffle for gift certificates or discount coupons
  - 0 Participation in local civic groups.
  - 0 Press release coverage of our sponsoring of events at the local community center for families and residents.
  - 0 Article submissions to magazines describing a party planning checklist.
  - O Sales Brochure to convey our program specialties to prospective customers.
  - 0 Seminar presentations to local civic groups, explaining the historical origins of various alcoholic beverages.
  - 0 Giveaway of free drink recipe booklets with store contact information.
  - 0 Celebration of local ethnic holidays such as Cinco de Mayo.

- **Local Media**
  - o Direct Mail - We will send quarterly postcards and annual direct mailings to residents with a ___ (10?) mile radius of our design center. It will contain an explanation of the benefits of our mobile services.
  - o Radio Campaign - We will make "live on the air" presentations of our trial service coupons to the disk jockeys, hoping to get the promotions broadcasted to the listening audience. We will also make our expertise available for talk radio programs.
  - o Newspaper Campaign - Placing several ads in local community newspapers to launch our initial campaign. We will include a trial coupon.
  - o Website – We will collect email addresses for a monthly newsletter.
  - o Cable TV advertising on local community-based shows focused on food, drink and entertaining.

Grand Opening

Our Grand Opening celebration will be a very important promotion opportunity to create word-of-mouth advertising results. Note: There may be local restrictions on advertising the sale of alcohol. If no restrictions prohibit it, advertise the date of your grand opening in local newspapers and on local radio. It is generally a good idea to provide the community with a reason to visit your liquor store, such as offering free wine and cheese sampling.

We will do the following things to make the open house a successful event:
1. Enlist local business support to contribute a large number of door prizes.
2. Use a sign-in sheet to create an email/mailing list.
3. Sponsor a mixed drink recipe competition.

4. Schedule appearance by local celebrities.
5. Create a festive atmosphere with balloons, beverages and music.
6. Get the local radio station to broadcast live from the event and handout fun gifts.
7. Offer an application fee waiver.
8. Giveaway our logo imprinted T-shirts as a contest prize.
9. Allow potential customers to view your facility and ask questions.
10. Print promotional flyers and pay a few kids to distribute them locally.
11. Arrange for face painting, storytelling, clowns, and snacks for everyone.
12. Arrange for local politician to do the official opening ceremony so all the local newspapers came to take pictures and do a feature story.
13. Arrange that people can tour our facility on the open day in order to see our facilities, collect sales brochures and find out more about our services.
14. Allocate staff members to perform specific duties, handout business cards and sales brochures and instruct them to deal with any questions or queries.
16. Organize a drawing with everyone writing their name and phone numbers on the back of business cards and give a voucher as a prize to start a marketing list.
17. Hand out free samples of products and coupons. (if state approved)

Value Proposition

Our value proposition will summarize why a consumer should use our services. We will enable quick access to our broad line of quality products and innovative services, out of our conveniently located and clean store in the _____ (city) area. Our value proposition will convince prospects that our services will add more value and better solve their need for a convenient, one-stop liquor store. We will use this value proposition statement to target customers who will benefit most from using our services. These are college students and baby boomers looking to socialize and create 'good time' new memories. Our value proposition will be concise and appeal to the customer's strongest decision-making drivers, which are convenience, a time-efficient and guided purchase experience, product quality and selection, and quality of personal relationships.

Positioning Statement

Our positioning strategy will be the result of conducting in-depth consumer market research to find out what benefits consumers want and how our products and services can meet those needs. Due to the increase in two-income families, many service-oriented professions are leaning toward differentiating themselves on the basis of convenience. This is also what we intend to do. For instance, we plan to have extended, "people" hours on various days of the week and offer a home delivery service, and a wine and cheese catering service.

We also plan to develop specialized services that will enable us to pursue a niche focus on specific interest based programs, such as mobile bartending service. These objectives will position us at the _____ (mid-level/high-end) of the market and will allow the company to realize a healthy profit margin in relation to its low-end, discount rivals and achieve long-term growth.

Unique Selling Proposition (USP)

Our unique selling proposition will answer the question why a customer should choose to do business with our company versus any and every other option available to them in the marketplace. Our USP will be a description of a unique important benefit that our liquor store offers to customers, so that price is no longer the key to our sales.

Our USP will include the following:

Who our target audience is: _____

What we will do for them: _____

What qualities, skills, talents, traits do we possess that others do not: _____

What are the benefits we provide that no one else offers: _____

Why that is different from what others are offering: _____

Why that solution matters to our target audience: _____

Distribution Strategy

Customers can contact the _____ (company name) by telephone, fax, internet and by dropping in. Our nearest competitors' are ____ (#) miles away in either direction. The store can also stock request items for regular area residents.

Our customers will have the following access points:

1.   **Order by Phone**

     Customers can contact us 24 hours a day, 7days a week at _____.
     Our Customer Service Representatives will be available to assist customers
     Monday through Friday from ____ a.m. to ____ p.m. EST.

2.   **Order by Fax**

     Customers may fax their orders to _____ anytime.
     They must provide: Account number, Billing and shipping address, Purchase
     order number, if applicable, Name and telephone number, Product
     number/description, Unit of measure and quantity ordered and Applicable sales
     promotion source codes.

3.   **Order Online**

     Customers can order online at www._____.com.Once the account is
     activated, customers will be able to place orders, browse the catalog, check stock
     availability and pricing, check order status and view both order and transaction
     history.

4.   **In-person**

     All customers can be serviced in person at our facilities Monday through Friday
     from ____ a.m. to ____ p.m. EST.

We plan to pursue the following distribution channels: **(select)**

1.   Our own retail outlets _____
2.   Independent retail outlets _____
3.   Chain store retail outlets _____
4.   Wholesale outlets _____
5.   Independent distributors _____
6.   Independent commissioned sales reps _____
7.   In-house sales reps _____
8.   Direct mail using own catalog or flyers _____
9.   Catalog broker agreement _____
10.   In-house telemarketing _____
11.   Contracted telemarketing call center _____
12.   Cybermarketing via own website _____
13.   Online sales via amazon, eBay, etc. _____
14.   TV and Cable Direct Marketing _____
15.   TV Home Shopping Channels (QVC) _____
16.   Mobile Units _____
17.   Franchised Business Units _____
18.   Trade Shows _____
19.   Home Party Sales Plans _____
20.   Fundraisers _____
21.   Farmer's Markets _____

Competitive Advantages

A **competitive advantage** is the thing that differentiates a business from its competitors. It is what separates our business from everyone else. It answers the questions: "Why do customers buy from us versus a competitor?", and "What do we offer customers that is unique?". We will use the following competitive advantages to set us apart from our competitors. The distinctive competitive advantages which _____ (company name) brings to the marketplace are as follows: (Note: Select only those you can support)

1.   We will offer our customers better product choices and an increasing number of up-scale products.
2.   Our shelf management software reduces out-of-stock situations.
3.   We run seasonal promotions.
4.   We will offer to special order products not available in our store.
5.   Our in-store merchandising programs provide a convenient and informative shopping experience for our customers.
6.   We closely monitor consumption trends to determine which products to list and de-list.
7.   We will initiate a Supplier Scorecard Program to provide suppliers with objective and timely feedback to realize continuous improvement in supplier related activities.
8.   Easy access to customer records, purchasing history and information about all the wines helps our sales force to provide customers with the personalized information they need to shop with confidence.

9. Our business operations will be backed by a full team of managers and owners that will each devote their time and efforts into one specialized area of the business. This specialization will increase the effectiveness of each of the aspects of our business through cost-effective micro-management.

10. By having owners of the company being the principle managers of the company we will reduce employee costs and will ensure the honesty and reliability of our staff.

11. Our owners/managers we will be able to maintain a direct relationship with our customers.

12. Our involvement with the community and our presence and availability within the store on a regular basis will give our customers the opportunity to give direct feedback into our store which will create a unique and appealing consumer environment.

13. We will enable our customers to have online access to our total inventory via our website.

14. Location: _____ (company name) is located on _____, a main road that enables us to take advantage of walk-by and drive-by-traffic. The closest competitor is ____ (#) miles into the town of _____.

15. We also have adequate parking to make shopping at our store convenient for drivers.

16. High quality: Focusing on high quality spirits will draw customers from the competition, as well as create a local market that has not existed before.

17. We will train our staff to answer most customers questions, so that their time is valued.

18. Our website will enable online ordering and pre-ordering, and the issuance of reminder notices for automatic purchases.

19. We constantly are search of the latest technology to update our operations and reinforce the image in customer minds that we are among the most progressive beverage professionals in the area.

20. We will utilize a software package that provides document management services and advanced management tools, such as basic and intermediate reporting functions, cost-benefit analysis, inventory management and audit functionality, in addition to electronic records storage and retrieval.

21. We will accommodate the customers who like the idea of one-stop shopping.

22. We will offer discounts and other incentives for referrals

23. We have the technological and professional staffing capabilities to provide our customers with the highest possible level of personalized service.

24. We have an ethnically diverse and multilingual staff, which is critical for a service-oriented business.

25. We have formed alliances that enable us to provide one-stop shopping or an array of services through a single access point.

26. We developed a specialized training program for the staff so they will be proficient at administering our service programs.

27. Our superior customer service, delivered through our trained staff, sets us apart and provides our competitive advantage

28. We guarantee minimal waiting to be serviced.

29. We have the resources to research new products and make informed usage recommendations.
30. We offer a wide variety of merchandise.
31. We have an inventory management system that reduces out-of-stock situations, and assures that needed items are in stock.
32. We regularly conduct focus groups to understand changing customer expectations.
33. We utilize reliable equipment with back-up alternatives.
34. Our store features a racetrack layout that is designed to minimize customer search time.

Branding Strategy

Our branding strategy involves what we do to shape what the customer immediately thinks our business offers and stands for. The purpose of our branding strategy is to reduce customer perceived purchase risk and improve our profit margins by allowing use to charge a premium for our liquor store products and services.

We will invest $_____ every year in maintaining our personal brand name image, which will differentiate our liquor store business from other companies. The amount of money spent on creating and maintaining a brand name will not convey any specific information about our products, but it will convey, indirectly, that we are in this market for the long haul, that we have a reputation to protect, and that we will interact repeatedly with our customers. In this sense, the amount of money spent on maintaining our brand name will signal to consumers that we will provide products and services of consistent quality.

We will use the following ways to build trust and establish our personal brand:
1. Build a consistently published blog and e-newsletter with informational content.
2. Create comprehensive social media profiles.
3. Contribute articles to related online publications.
4. Earn Career Certifications

Resources:
https://www.abetterlemonadestand.com/branding-guide/

We will use the following methodologies to implement our branding strategy:
1. Develop processes, systems and quality assurance procedures to assure the consistent adherence to our quality standards and mission statement objectives.
2. Develop business processes to consistently deliver upon our value proposition.
3. Develop training programs to assure the consistent professionalism and responsiveness of our employees.
4. Develop marketing communications with consistent, reinforcing message content.
5. Incorporate testimonials into our marketing materials that support our promises.
6. Develop marketing communications with a consistent presentation style.
   (Logo design, company colors, slogan, labels, packaging, stationery, etc.)

7. Exceed our brand promises to achieve consistent customer loyalty.
8. Use surveys, focus groups and interviews to consistently monitor what our brand means to our customers.
9. Consistently match our brand values or performance benchmarks to our customer requirements.
10. Focus on the maintenance of a consistent number of key brand values that are tied to our company strengths.
11. Continuously research industry trends in our markets to stay relevant to customer needs and wants.
12. Attach a logo-imprinted product label and business card to all products, marketing communications and invoices.
13. Develop a memorable and meaningful tagline that captures the essence of our brand.
14. Prepare a one page company overview and make it a key component of our sales presentation folder.
15. Hire and train employees to put the interests of customers first.
16. Develop a professional website that is updated with fresh content on a regular basis.
17. Use our blog to circulate content that establishes our niche expertise and opens a two-way dialogue with our customers.

Brand Positioning Statement

We will use the following brand positioning statement to summarize what our brand means to our targeted market:

To _____ (target market) _____ (company name) is the brand of _____ (product/service frame of reference) that enables the customer to _____ (primary performance benefit) because ___ (company name) _____ (products/services) _____ (are made with/offer/provide) the best _____ (key attributes)

Business SWOT Analysis

Definition: SWOT Analysis is a powerful technique for understanding our Strengths and Weaknesses, and for looking at the Opportunities and Threats faced.

Strategy: We will use this SWOT Analysis to uncover exploitable opportunities and carve a sustainable niche in our market. And by understanding the weaknesses of our business, we can manage and eliminate threats that would otherwise catch us by surprise. By using the SWOT framework, we will be able to craft a strategy that distinguishes our business from our competitors, so that we can compete successfully in the market.

Strengths   (select)

What liquor store products and services are we best at providing?
What unique resources can we draw upon?
1. Our location is in the heart of an upscale neighborhood and is in close

proximity to a popular _____ with ample parking facilities.
2. The facility has been established as a liquor store for ____ years.
3. The nearest competition is ___ miles and has a minimal inventory of convenience goods.
4. Our Store has been extensively renovated, with many upgrades.
5. Our Store has the ability to change inventory with special occasion requirements.
6. Seasoned executive management professionals, sophisticated in business knowledge, experienced in the wine and spirits trade.
7. Strong networking relationships with many different organizations, including _____.
8. Excellent staff are experienced, highly trained and customer attentive.
9. Wide diversity of product/service offerings.
10. High customer loyalty.
11. The proven ability to establish excellent personalized client service.
12. Strong relationships with suppliers, that offer flexibility and respond to special customer requirements.
13. Good referral relationships.
14. Client loyalty developed through a solid reputation with repeat clients.
15. Our practice has a focused target market of _____ (college students?).
16. Sales staff with wine and spirit education credentials.
17. _____

Weaknesses

In what areas could we improve?
Where do we have fewer resources than others?
1. Lack of developmental capital to complete Phase I start-up.
2. New comer to the area.
3. Lack of marketing experience.
4. The struggle to build brand equity.
5. A limited marketing budget to develop brand awareness.
6. Finding dependable and people oriented staff.
7. We need to develop the information systems that will improve our productivity and inventory management.
8. Don't know the needs and wants of the local population.
9. The owner must deal with the retail experience learning curve.
10. Challenges caused by the seasonal nature of the business.
11. _____

Opportunities

What opportunities are there for new and/or improved services?
What trends could we take advantage of?
1. Seasonal changes in inventory.
2. Could take market share away from existing competitors.
3. Greater need for mobile home services by time starved dual income families.

4. Growing market with a significant percentage of the target market still not aware that _____ (company name) exists.
5. The ability to develop many long-term customer relationships.
6. Expanding the range of product/service packaged offerings.
7. Greater use of direct advertising to promote our services.
8. Establish referral relationships with local businesses serving the same target market segment.
9. Networking with non-profit organizations.
10. The aging population will need and expect a greater range of __ services.
11. Increased public awareness of the importance of 'green' matters.
12. Strategic alliances offering sources for referrals and joint marketing activities to extend our reach.
13. _____ (supplier name) is offering co-op advertising.
14. A competitor has overextended itself financially and is facing bankruptcy.
15. _____

Threats

What trends or competitor actions could hurt us?
What threats do our weaknesses expose us to?
1. Another liquor store could move into this area.
2. Further declines in the economic forecast.
3. Inflation affecting operations for gas, labor, and other operating costs.
4. Keeping trained efficient staff and key personnel from moving on or starting their own business venture.
5. Imitation competition from similar indirect service providers.
6. Price differentiation is a significant competition factor.
7. The government could enact legislation that could effect reimbursements.
8. We need to do a better job of assessing the strengths and weaknesses of all of our competitors.
9. Sales of custom _____ by mass discounters..
10. _____

Recap:

We will use the following strengths to capitalize on recognized opportunities:
1. _____
2. _____
We will take the following actions to turn our weaknesses into strengths and prepare to defend against known threats.
1. _____
2. _____

Marketing Strategy

Our Marketing strategy will focus on the following:
1. Developing a reputation for great selection, an appealing store environment, competitive prices, mobile services, and exceptional customer service.
2. Developing strong relationships with our suppliers to help insure best discount deals and best supplier services obtainable.
3. Keeping the staff focused, satisfied and motivated in their roles, to help keep our productivity and customer service at the highest obtainable levels.
4. Maintaining the visibility of our store through regular advertising to our target community.
5. Reaching out to potential wholesale clients, businesses and community organizations, with commissioned independent sales reps.
6. Doing activities that can stimulate additional business: wine tastings, matching wines with food, sharing interesting and educational wine knowledge, publishing a newsletter, offering customer service through a website, free local deliveries, automatic and reminder ordering services and mobile bartending and party services.
7. Extending our market penetration beyond the physical boundaries of the store location through a direct catalog sales, outside sales reps and a website.

_____ (company name) intends to actively seek out and attract new customers, whose needs go beyond the need for convenience sales. Our online website will the primary focus of this incentive program. This service will be an interactive feature that will act as a database of our broad product selection and will primarily be focused on our wines and high end products. The goals for this service will be for it to serve as a compilation of our product selection, in which a user will be able to categorize our entire inventory in several different ways and then be able to view individual product descriptions and suggestions. The service is intended to make our customers more comfortable with our product lines. It will provide a way for our customers to survey the attributes of our wines so that they may be able to make an informed purchase decision, as the novice wine drinker may be deterred from purchasing wine due to a lack of knowledge on the intricacies of a specific product. This system seeks to create consumer demand through consumer education. The staff will also be able to access this database in the store to help serve the needs of the individual consumer.

In phase one of our marketing plan, we will gain exposure to our target markets through the use of discounts and grand opening promotional tactics. We will be taking a very aggressive marketing stance in the first year of business in hopes of gaining customer loyalty. In our subsequent years, we will focus less resources on advertising as a whole. But, we do plan to budget for advertising promotions on a continual and season specific basis.

Our marketing strategy is based on establishing _____ (company name) as the one-stop resource of choice for people in need of liquor store items, party planning, and beverage knowledge. We will start our business with our known personal referral contacts and then continue our campaign to develop recognition among other groups. We will develop and maintain a database of our contacts in the field. We will work to maintain and exploit our existing relationships throughout the start-up process and then use our marketing tools to communicate with other potential referral sources.

The marketing strategy will create awareness, interest and appeal from our target market. Its ultimate purpose is to encourage repeat purchases and get customers to refer friends and professional contacts. To get referrals we will provide incentives and excellent service, and build relationships with clients by caring about what the customer needs and wants.

Our marketing strategy will revolve around two different types of media, flyers and a website. These two tools will be used to make customers aware of our broad range of product and service offerings. One focus of our marketing strategy will be to drive customers to our website for information about our service programs and mobile specialties. We will use comment cards, newsletter sign-up forms and surveys to collect customer email addresses and feed our client relationship management (CRM) software system. This system will automatically send out, on a predetermined schedule, follow-up materials, such as article reprints, seminar invitations, email messages, surveys and e-newsletters. We will offset some of our advertising costs by asking our suppliers and other local merchants to place ads in our newsletter.

Marketing Budget

Our marketing budget will be a flexible $_____ per quarter. The marketing budget can be allocated in any way that best suits the time of year.

Marketing budget per quarter:

Newspaper Ads	$_____	Radio advertisement	$_____
Web Page	$_____	Customer raffle	$_____
Direct Mail	$_____	Sales Brochure	$_____
Home Shows	$_____	Seminars	$_____
Superpages	$_____	Google Adwords	$_____
Giveaways	$_____	Vehicle Signs	$_____
Business Cards	$_____	Flyers	$_____
Labels/Stickers	$_____	Videos/DVDs	$_____
Samples	$_____	Newsletter	$_____
Yard Signs	$_____	Email Campaigns	$_____
Sales Reps Comm.	$_____	Other	$_____

Total: $_____

Our objective in setting a marketing budget has been to keep it between _____ (5?) and _____ (7?) percent of our estimated annual gross sales.

Marketing Mix

New customers will primarily come from word-of-mouth and our referral program. The overall market approach involves creating brand awareness through targeted advertising, public relations, co-marketing efforts with select alliance partners, direct mail, email campaigns (with constant contact.com), seminars and a website.

Video Marketing

We will link to our website a series of YouTube.com based video clips that talk about our range of liquor store products and services, and demonstrate our expertise with certain brands and vintages. We will create business marketing videos that are both entertaining and informational, and improve our search engine rankings. The video will include:

Client testimonials - We will let our best customers become our instant sales force. Note: People will believe what others say about us more readily than what we say about ourselves.

Product Demonstrations - Train and pre-sell our potential clients on our most popular products and services just by talking about and showing them. Often, our potential clients don't know the full range and depth of our products and services because we haven't taken the adequate time to tell them.

Include Business Website Address

Video Tour of Liquor Store

Frequently Asked Questions - We will answer questions that we often get, and anticipate objections we might get and give great reasons to convince potential clients that we are the best liquor store in the area.

Include a Call to Action - We have the experience and the know-how to supply your next family or business event. So call us, right now, and let's get started.

Seminar - Include a portion of a seminar on how restaurants can better market their beverage selection.

Comment on industry trends and product news - We will appear more in-tune and knowledgeable in our market if we can talk about what's happening in our industry and marketplace.

Resources: www.businessvideomarketing.tv
www.hotpluto.com
www.theliquorstorechannel.com/

Example: http://www.youtube.com/watch?v=dGJyu5vQRvs

Business Cards

Our business card will include our company logo, complete contact information, name and title, association logos, slogan or markets serviced, licenses and certifications. The center of our bi-fold card will contain a listing of the brands and services we offer. We will give out multiple business cards to friends, family members, and to each customer, upon the completion of the service. We will also distribute business cards in the following ways:

1.   Attached to invoices, surveys, flyers and door hangers.
2.   Included in customer product packages.
3.   We will leave a stack of business cards in a Lucite holder with the local Chamber of Commerce and any other businesses offering free counter placement.

We will use fold-over cards because they will enable us to list all of our services and complete contact instructions on the inside of the card. We will also give magnetic business cards to new clients for posting on the refrigerator door.

We will place the following referral discount message on the back of our business cards:

91

- Our business is very dependent upon referrals. If you have associates who could benefit from our quality services, please write your name at the bottom of this card and give it to them. When your friend presents this card upon their first visit, he or she will be entitled to 10% off discount. And, on your next invoice, you will also get a 10% discount as a thank you for your referral.

Resource: www.vistaprint.com

Direct Mail Package

To build name recognition and to announce the opening of our liquor store, we will offer a mail package consisting of a tri-fold brochure containing a discount coupon to welcome our new customers. We plan to make a mailing to local subscribers of Gourmet Food and Wine themed magazines. From those identified local customers, we shall ask them to complete a survey and describe their perception of the store, and any specific products or services they would like to see added. Those customers returning completed surveys would receive a premium (giveaway) gift.

New Homeowners

We will participate in local Welcome Wagon activities for new residents, and assemble a mailing list to distribute sales literature from county courthouse records and Realtor supplied information. We will use a postcard mailing to promote a special get-acquainted offer to new residents.

Resource: www.WelcomeWagon.com

Networking

Networking will be a key to success because referrals and alliances formed can help to improve our community image and keep our practice growing. We will strive to build long-term mutually beneficial relationships with our networking contacts and join the following types of organizations:

1.   We will form a LeTip Chapter to exchange business leads.
2.   We will join the local BNI.com referral exchange group.
3.   We will join the Chamber of Commerce to further corporate relationships.
4.   We will join the Rotary Club, Lions Club, Kiwanis Club, Church Groups, etc.
5.   We will do volunteer work for American Heart Assoc. and Habitat for Humanity.
6.   We will become an affiliated member of the local board of Realtors and the Women's Council of Realtors.
7.   We will join local garden and women's clubs and wine clubs.

We will use our metropolitan _____ (city) Chamber of Commerce to target prospective business contacts. We will mail letters to each prospect describing our services. We will follow-up with phone calls.

Newsletter

We will develop a one-page newsletter to be handed out to customers to take home with them as they visit the store. The monthly newsletter will be used to build our brand and update clients on special promotions. The newsletter will be produced in-house and for the cost of paper and computer time. We will include the following types of information:

1. Our involvement with charitable events.
2. New Service/Product Introductions
3. Featured employee/customer of the month.
4. New industry technologies.
5. Customer endorsements/testimonials.
6. Classified ads from local sponsors and suppliers.
7. Announcements / Upcoming tasting events.

Resources: Microsoft Publisher

We will adhere to the following newsletter writing guidelines:
1. We will provide content that is of real value to our subscribers.
2. We will provide solutions to our subscriber's problems or questions.
3. We will communicate regularly on a weekly basis.
4. We will create HTML Messages that look professional and allow us to track how many people click on our links and/or open our emails.
5. We will not pitch our business opportunity in our Ezine very often.
6. We will focus our marketing dollars on building our Ezine subscriber list.
7. We will focus on relationship building and not the conveying of a sales message.
8. We will vary our message format with videos, articles, checklists, quotes, pictures and charts.
9. We will recommend occasionally affiliate products in some of our messages to help cover our marketing costs.
10. We will include eye-catching photos, graphics and/or videos.
11. We will consistently follow the above steps to build a database of qualified prospects and customers that have given their permission to receive the newsletter.
12. We will repackage the content from some of our blogs, while papers, press releases, and articles into our newsletters to increase readership and save production time.

Resources:
www.mailchimp.com
www.constantcontact.com/email-templates/newsletter-templates
http://lmssuccess.com/10-reasons-online-business-send-regular-newsletter-customers/
www.smallbusinessmiracles.com/how/newsletters/
www.fuelingnewbusiness.com/2010/06/01/combine-email-marketing-and-social-media-
    for-ad-agency-new-business/

Vehicle Signs
We will place magnetic signs on our vehicles and include our company name, phone number, company slogan and website address, if possible.

Advertising Wearables
We will give all preferred club members an eye-catching T-shirt or sweatshirt with our company name and logo printed across the garment to wear about town. We will also

give them away as a thank you for customer referral activities. We will ask all employees to wear our logo-imprinted shirts.

Stage Events

We will stage events to become known in our community. This is essential to attracting referrals. We will schedule regular events, such as seminar talks, demonstrations, catered open house events and fundraisers. We will offer seminars through organizations to promote the health benefits of drinking in moderation. Our in-store events will occasionally double as fundraisers for charitable organizations. We will use event registration forms, our website and an event sign-in sheet to collect the names and email addresses of all attendees. This database will be used to feed our automatic customer relationship follow-up program and newsletter service.

Sales Brochures

The sales brochure will enable us to make a solid first impression when pursing business from commercial accounts and high-end residential clients. Our sales brochure will include the following contents and become a key part of our sales presentation folder and direct mail package:

- Contact Information
- Customer Testimonials
- Competitive Advantages
- Trial Coupon
- Key Brand Name Carried

- Business Description
- List of Services/Benefits
- Owner Resume/Bio
- Map of store location.
- Business Hours

Coupons

We will use coupons with limited time expirations to get prospects to try our products and service programs. We will also accept the coupons of our competitors to help establish new client relationships. We will run ads directing people to our Web site for a $___ coupon certificate. This will help to draw in new clients and collect e-mail addresses for the distribution of a monthly newsletter.   Resource: www.Valpack.com

Websites like Groupon.com, LivingSocial, Eversave, and BuyWithMe sell discount vouchers for services ranging from custom _____ to ____ consultations. Best known is Chicago-based Groupon. To consumers, discount vouchers promise substantial savings — often 50% or more. To merchants, discount vouchers offer possible opportunities for price discrimination, exposure to new customers, online marketing, and "buzz." Vouchers are more likely to be profitable for merchants with low marginal costs, who can better accommodate a large discount and for patient merchants, who place higher value on consumers' possible future return visits.
Examples:
https://ibotta.com/rebates?retailer=any-liquor-store
https://www.groupon.com/goods/alcohol
http://thekrazycouponlady.com/tips/finance/13-ways-to-save-on-booze
https://www.retailmenot.com/coupons/liquor

Cross-Promotions

We will develop and maintain partnerships with local businesses that cater to the needs of our customers, such as beauty salons, fitness clubs and senior daycare centers, and conduct cross-promotional marketing campaigns. These cross-promotions will require the exchanging of customer mailing lists and endorsements.

Premium Giveaways

We will distribute logo-imprinted promotional products at events, also known as giveaway premiums, to foster top-of-mind awareness (www.promoideas.org). These items include business cards with magnetic backs, mugs with contact phone number, drink recipe booklets and calendars that feature important celebration date reminders.

Local Publications

We will place low-cost classified ads in neighborhood publications to advertise our organic home replacement foodservice menu options. We will also submit public relations and informative articles to improve our visibility and establish our expertise and trustworthiness. These publications include the following:

1. Neighborhood Newsletters, Newspapers and Church Bulletins
2. Local Restaurant Association Newsletter
3. Local Chamber of Commerce Newsletter
4. Realtor Magazines
5. Homeowner Association Newsletters

Resource:

Hometown News	www.hometownnews.com
Pennysaver	www.pennysaverusa.com

Doorhangers

Our doorhangers will feature a calendar of 'Free Wine Seminars'. The doorhanger will include a list of all our product categories and info about our delivery options. We will also attach our business card to the doorhanger and distribute the doorhangers multiple times to the same subdivision.

Article Submissions

We will pitch articles to consumer magazines, local newspapers, business magazines and internet articles directories to help establish our specialized expertise and improve our visibility. Hyperlinks will be placed within written articles and can be clicked on to take the customer to another webpage within our website or to a totally different website. These clickable links or hyperlinks will be keywords or relevant words that have meaning to our Liquor Store. We will create keyword-rich article titles that match the most commonly searched keywords for our topic. In fact, we will create a position whose primary function is to link our liquor store with opportunities to be published in local publications.

Sample Article Titles:
How to Get Smart About the Role of Alcohol in Your Diet

Examples:

http://blog.myfitnesspal.com/the-truth-about-alcohol-5-tips-for-smarter-holiday-sips/
http://www.builtlean.com/2012/11/26/alcohol-weight-loss/

Internet article directories include:

http://ezinearticles.com/
http://www.wahm-articles.com
http://www.articlecity.com
http://www.articledashboard.com
http://www.webarticles.com
http://www.article-buzz.com
www.articletogo.com
http://article-niche.com
www.internethomebusinessarticles.com
http://www.articlenexus.com

http://www.mommyshelpercommunity.com
http://www.ladypens.com/
http://www.amazines.com
http://www.submityourarticle.com/articles
http://www.articlecube.com
http://www.free-articles-zone.com
http://www.content-articles.com
http://superpublisher.com
http://www.site-reference.com
www.articlebin.com

Free Classified Ad Placement Opportunities

The following free classified ad sites, will enable our liquor store to thoroughly describe the benefits of our using our services:

1. **Craigslist.org**
2. Ebay Classifieds
3. Classifieds.myspace.com
4. KIJIJI.com
5. //Lycos.oodle.com
6. Webclassifieds.us
7. USFreeAds.com
8. www.oodle.com
9. Backpage.com
10. stumblehere.com
11. Classifiedads.com
12. gumtree.com
13. Inetgia2nt.com
14. www.sell.com
15. Freeadvertisingforum.com
16. Classifiedsforfree.com
17. www.olx.com
18. www.isell.com
19. Base.google.com
20. www.epage.com
21. Chooseyouritem.com
22. www.adpost.com
23. Adjingo.com
24. Kugli.com

Sample Classified Ad:

Looking for Fine Wines Priced Right? We have been serving the _____ area since _____ (year). We have the largest selection of Distilled Spirits in the area, Free local delivery. Give us a call at _____, or visit us at _____ (Website) for our wine tasting schedule.

Two-Step Direct Response Classified Advertising

We will use 'two-step direct response advertising' to motivate readers to take a step or action that signals that we have their permission to begin marketing to them in step two. Our objective is to build a trusting relationship with our prospects by offering a free unbiased, educational report in exchange for permission to continue the marketing process. This method of advertising has the following benefits:

1. Shorter sales cycle.
2. Eliminates need for cold calling.

3. Establishes expert reputation. 4. Better qualifies prospects
5. Process is very trackable. 6. Able to run smaller ads.

Sample Two Step Lead Generating Classified Ad:
FREE Report Reveals "The Health Benefits of Red Wine!"
Or….. "How to Plan a Successful Cocktail Party".
Call 24 hour recorded message and leave your name and address.
Your report will be sent out immediately.
Note: The respondent has shown they have an interest in our product specialty.
We will also include a section in the report on our wine and cheese catering service and our complete contact information, along with a time limited discount coupon.

Yellow Page Ads

Research indicates that the use of the traditional Yellow Page Book is declining, but that new residents or people who don't have many personal acquaintances will look to the Yellow Pages to establish a list of potential businesses to call upon. Even a small 2" x 2" boxed ad can create awareness and attract the desired target client, above and beyond the ability of a simple listing. We will use the following design concepts:

1. We will use a headline to sell people on what is unique about our service.
2. We will include a service guarantee to improve our credibility.
3. We will include a coupon offer and a tracking code to monitor the response rate and decide whether to increase or decrease our ad size in subsequent years.
4. We will choose an ad size equal to that of our competitors, and evaluate the response rate for future insertion commitments.
5. We will include our hours of operation, motto or slogan and logo.
6. We will include our competitive advantages.
7. We will list under the same categories as our competitors.
8. We will use some bold lettering to make our ad standout.
9. We will utilize yellow books that also offer an online dimension.

Resource: www.superpages.com www.yellowpages.com
Examples: https://www.yellowpages.com/new-york-ny/liquor-stores

Ad Information:

Book Title: _____   Coverage Area: _____
Yearly Fee: $_____   Ad Size: _____ page
Renewal date: _____   Contact: _____

Radio Advertising

Radio will give us the ability to target our audience, based on radio formats, such as news-talk, classic rock and the oldies. Radio will also be a good way to get repetition into our message, as listeners tend to be loyal to stations and parts of the day.

1. We will use radio advertising to direct prospects to our Web site, advertise a limited time promotion or call for an informational flooring brochure.
2. We will try to barter our services for radio ad spots.
3. We will use a limited-time offer to entice first-time customers to use our services.
4. We will explore the use of on-air community bulletin boards to play our public announcements about community sponsored events.

5.   We will also make the radio station aware of our expertise in the alcoholic beverage field and our availability for interviews.
6.   Our choice of stations will be driven by the market research information we collect via our surveys.
7.   We will capitalize on the fact that many stations now stream their programming on the internet and reach additional local and even national audiences, and if online listeners like what they hear in our streaming radio spot, they can click over to our website.
8.   Our radio ads will use humor, sounds, compelling music or unusual voices to grab attention.
9.   Our spots will tell stories or present situations that our target audience can relate to.
10.   We will make our call to action, a website address or vanity phone number, easy to remember and tie it in with our company name or message.

Resources: Radio Advertising Bureau   www.RAB.com
                 Radio Locator   www.radio-locator.com
                  Radio Directory   www.radiodirectory.com

Ad Information:

Length of ad "spot": ___ seconds   Development costs: $____ (onetime fee)
Length of campaign: __ (#) mos.   Runs per month: Three times per day
Cost per month.: $_____   Total campaign cost: $_____.

Script Resources:

www.voices.com/documents/secure/voices.com-commercial-scripts-for-radio-and-television-ads.pdf

http://smallbusiness.chron.com/say-30second-radio-advertising-spot-10065.html

https://voicebunny.com/blog/5-tips-make-radio-ads-grab-attention-sell/

Press Releases

We will use market research surveys to determine the media outlets that our demographic customers read and then target them with press releases. We will draft a cover letter for our media kit that explains that we would like to have the newspaper print a story about the start-up of our new local business or a milestone that we have accomplished. And, because news releases may be delivered by feeds or on news services and various websites, we will create links from our news releases to content on our website. These links which will point to more information or a special offer, will drive our clients into the sales process. They will also increase search engine ranking on our site. We will follow-up each faxed package to the media outlet with a phone call to the lifestyle section editor.

1.   Announce Grand Opening Event and the availability of services.
2.   Planned Open House Event
3   Addition of new product releases or service introduction.
4.   Support for a Non-profit Cause or other local event, such as a Blood Drive.
5.   Presentation of a free seminar or workshop.
6.   Report Survey Results
7.   Publication of an article or book on industry trends.

8.   Receiving an Association Award.
9.   Additional training/certification/licensing received.
Resources: www.1888PressRelease.com   www.ecomwire.com
              www.prweb.com   www.WiredPRnews.com
              www.PR.com   www.eReleases.com
              www.24-7PressRelease.com   www.NewsWireToday.com
              www.PRnewswire.com   www.onlinePRnews.com
              www.PRLog.org

Postcards

1.   We will use a monthly, personalized, newsletter styled postcard, that includes healthy meal suggestions, to stay-in-touch with prospects and customers.
2.   Postcards will offer cheaper mailing rates, staying power and attention grabbing graphics, but require repetition, like most other advertising methods.
3.   We will develop an in-house list of potential clients for routine communications from open house events, seminar registrations, direct response ads, etc.
4.   We will use postcards to encourage users to visit our website, and take advantage of a special offer.
Resource:
www.Postcardmania.com

Flyers

1.   We will seek permission to post flyers on the bulletin boards in local businesses, community centers, party supply stores and local colleges.
2.   We will also insert flyers into our direct mailings.
3.   We will use our flyers as part of a handout package at open house events.
4.   The flyers will feature a discount coupon.
5.   The flyers will contain a listing of our product categories and foodservice specialties, along with the benefits our financial and business services.

Referral Program

We understand the importance of setting up a formal referral network through contacts with the following characteristics:
1.   We will give a premium reward based simply on people giving referral names on the registration form or customer satisfaction survey.
2.   Send an endorsed testimonial letter from a loyal patient to the referred prospect.
3.   Include a separate referral form as a direct response device.
4.   Provide a space on the response form for leaving positive comments that can be used to build a testimonial letter, that will be sent to each referral.
5.   We will clearly state our incentive rewards, and terms and conditions.
6.   We will distribute a newsletter to stay in touch with our clients and include articles about our referral program success stories.
7.   We will encourage our staff at weekly meetings to seek referrals from their personal contacts.

Customer Reward Program

As a means of building business by word-of-mouth, customers will be encouraged and rewarded as repeat customers. This will be accomplished by offering a discounted bottle of wine to those customers who sign-up for our frequent buyer card and purchase $___ of products and services within a ___ (#) month period.

Resources:

http://www.refinery29.com/best-store-loyalty-programs

https://thrivehive.com/customer-retention-and-loyalty-programs/

http://blog.fivestars.com/5-companies-loyalty-programs/

www.americanexpress.com/us/small-business/openforum/articles/10-cool-mobile-apps-
        that-increase-customer-loyalty/

https://squareup.com/loyalty

www.consumerreports.org/cro/news/2013/10/retailer-loyalty-rewards-
        programs/index.htm

Frequent Buyer Program Types:

1.	Punch Cards	Receive something for free after ? Purchases.
2.	Dollar-for-point Systems	Accrue points toward a free product.
3.	Percentage of Purchase	Accrue points toward future purchases.

Sample: Loyalty Program

_____ (company name) LOYALTY PROGRAM

ACCRUE YOUR POINTS WITH THE FOLLOWING:

 Sign-up Bonus receive 1,000 points

 Pre-book your next visit receive 1,000 points

 Refer a Friend receive 2,500 points

 Retail Purchase receive 1 point/dollar spent

 Service Purchase receive 1 point/dollar spent

REDEEMING POINT VALUE 100 POINTS = $1

Ex: For a $100 purchase, you will redeem 10,000 points

E-mail Marketing

Our liquor store will send a promotional e-mail about an in-store wine tasting to wine aficionados, as indicated in their preferred membership application, while beer lovers receive a different e-mail promoting 12-pack specials during football season. Each segment gets notified of new products, specials and offers based on past buying patterns and what they've clicked on in our previous e-newsletters or indicated on their surveys. The objective is to tap the right customer's passion and need at the right time, with a targeted subject line and targeted content. Our general e-newsletter may appeal to most customers, but targeted mailings that reach out to our various audience segments will build even deeper relationships, and drive higher sales.

Resources:

http://www.verticalresponse.com/blog/10-retail-marketing-ideas-to-boost-sales/

www.constantcontact.com/pricing/email-marketing.jsp

Google Reviews

We will use our email marketing campaign to ask people for reviews. We will ask people what they thought of our liquor store business or services and encourage them to write a Google Review if they were impressed. We will incorporate a call to action (CTA) on our email auto signature with a link to our Google My Review page.

Source:

https://superb.digital/how-to-ask-your-clients-for-google-reviews/

Resources:

https://support.google.com/business/answer/3474122?hl=en

https://support.google.com/maps/answer/6230175?co=GENIE.Platform
%3DDesktop&hl=en

www.patientgain.com/how-to-get-positive-google-reviews

Example:

We will tell our customers to:

1.   Go to https://www.google.com/maps
2.   Type in your business name, select the listing
3.   There's a "card" (sidebar) on the left-hand side. At the bottom, they can click 'Be the First to Write a Review' or 'Write a Review' if you already have one review.

Source:

https://www.reviewjump.com/blog/how-do-i-get-google-reviews/

Facebook.com

We will use Facebook to move our businesses forward and stay connected to our customers in this fast-paced world. Content will be the key to staying in touch with our customers and keeping them informed. The content will be a rich mix of information, before and after photos, interactive questions, current trends and events, industry facts, education, promotions and specials, humor and fun. We will use the following step system to get customers from Facebook.com:

1.   We will open a free Facebook account at Facebook.com.
2.   We will convert our company Profile to a Fan Page, and continue to direct people over to the new Page. We will use the Notes feature, and tag the people we   want to notify about the new Page.
3.   We will begin by adding Facebook friends. The fastest way to do this is to allow Facebook to import our email addresses and send an invite out to all our customers.
4.   We will post a video to get our customers involved with our Facebook page. We will post a video called "How to Plan a Successful Dinner Party." The video will be first uploaded to YouTube.com and then simply be linked to our Facebook page. Video will be a great way to get people active and involved with our Facebook page.

5. We will send an email to our customers base that encourages them to check out the new video and to post their feedback about it on our Facebook page. Then we will provide a link driving customers to our Facebook page.
6. We will respond quickly to feedback, engage in the dialogue and add links to our response that direct the author to a structured mini-survey.
7. We will optimize our Facebook profile with our business keyword to make it an invaluable marketing tool and become the "go-to" expert in our industry
8. On a monthly basis, we will send out a message to all Facebook fans with a special offer, as Fan pages are the best way to interact with customers and potential customers on Facebook,
9. We will use Facebook as a tool for sharing success stories and relate the ways in which we have helped our customers.
10. We will use Facebook Connect to integrate our Facebook efforts with our regular website to share our Facebook Page activity. This will also give us statistics about our website visitors, and add social interaction to our site.

Resources:
https://www.facebook.com/advertising/?connect
http://www.socialmediaexaminer.com/how-to-set-up-a-facebook-page-for-business/
http://smallbizsurvival.com/2009/11/6-big-facebook-tips-for-small-business.html

Examples:
www.facebook.com/pages/A-B-Liquor-Store/180598115410
www.facebook.com/HarrysReserve

Facebook Profiles represent individual users and are held under a person's name. Each profile should only be controlled by that person. Each user has a wall, information tab, likes, interests, photos, videos and each individual can create events.

Facebook Groups are pretty similar to Fan Pages but are usually created for a group of people with a similar interest and they are wanting to keep their discussions private. The members are not usually looking to find out more about a business - they want to discuss a certain topic.

Facebook Fan Pages are the most viral of your three options. When someone becomes a fan of your page or comments on one of your posts, photos or videos, that is spread to all of their personal friends. This can be a great way to get your information out to lots of people...and quickly! In addition, one of the most valuable features of a business page is that you can send "updates" about new products and content to fans and your home building brand becomes more visible.

Facebook Live lets people, public figures and Pages share live video with their followers and friends on Facebook.
Source:
https://live.fb.com/about/
Resources:

https://www.facebook.com/business/a/Facebook-video-ads
http://smartphones.wonderhowto.com/news/facebook-is-going-all-live-video-streaming-your-phone-0170132/

Facebook Business Page
Resources:
https://www.facebook.com/business/learn/set-up-facebook-page
https://www.pcworld.com/article/240258/how_to_make_a_facebook_page_for_your_small_business.html
https://blog.hubspot.com/blog/tabid/6307/bid/5492/how-to-create-a-facebook-business-page-in-5-simple-steps-with-video.aspx

Small Business Promotions
This group allows members to post about their products and services and is a public group designated as a Buy and Sell Facebook group.
Source: https://www.facebook.com/groups/smallbusinesspronotions/
Resource:
https://www.facebook.com/business/a/local-business-promotion-ads
https://www.facebook.com/business/learn/facebook-create-ad-local-awareness
www.socialmediaexaminer.com/how-to-use-facebook-local-awareness-ads-to-target-customers/

Facebook Ad Builder
https://waymark.com/signup/db869ac4-7202-4e3b-93c3-80acc5988df9/?partner=fitsmallbusiness

Facebook Lead Ads   www.facebook.com/business/a/lead-ads
A type of sponsored ad that appears in your audience's timeline just like other Facebook ads. However, the goal with lead ads is literally to capture the lead's info without them leaving Facebook. That is to say, these ads don't link to a website landing page, creating an additional step.

Best social media marketing practices:
1.   Assign daily responsibility for Facebook to a single person on your staff with an affinity for dialoguing .
2.   Set expectations for how often they should post new content and how quickly they should respond to comments – usually within a couple hours.
3.   Follow and like your followers when they seem to have a genuine interest in your area of health and wellness expertise.
4.   Post on the walls of not only your own Facebook site, but also on your most active, influential posters with the largest networks.
5.   Periodically post a request for your followers to "like" your page.
6.   Monitor Facebook posts to your wall and respond every two hours throughout your business day.

We will use Facebook in the following ways to market our Liquor Store:
1. Promote our blog posts on our Facebook page
2. Post a video of our service people in action.
3. Make time-sensitive offers during slow periods
4. Create a special landing page for coupons or promotional giveaways
5. Create a Welcome tab to display a video message from our owner.
              Resource: Pagemodo.
6.   Support a local charity by posting a link to their website.
7.   Thank our customers while promoting their businesses at the same time.
8.   Describe milestone accomplishments and thank customers for their role.
9.   Give thanks to corporate accounts.
10.   Ask customers to contribute stories about _____ occurrences.
11.   Use the built-in Facebook polling application to solicit feedback.
12.   Use the Facebook reviews page to feature positive comments from customers, and to respond to negative reviews.
13.   Introduce customers to our staff with resume and video profiles.
14.   Create a photo gallery of unusual _____ (requests/jobs?) to showcase our expertise.

We will also explore location-based platforms like the following:
- FourSquare
- Facebook Places
- GoWalla
- Google Latitude

As a liquor store serving a local community, we will appreciate the potential for hyper-local platforms like these. Location-based applications are increasingly attracting young, urban influencers with disposable income, which is precisely the audience we are trying to attract. People connect to geo-location apps primarily to "get informed" about local happenings.

Foursquare.com

A web and mobile application that allows registered users to post their location at a venue ("check-in") and connect with friends. Check-in requires active user selection and points are awarded at check-in. Users can choose to have their check-ins posted on their accounts on Twitter, Facebook, or both. In version 1.3 of their iPhone application, foursquare enabled push-notification of friend updates, which they call "Pings". Users can also earn badges by checking in at locations with certain tags, for check-in frequency, or for other patterns such as time of check-in.]
Resource: https://foursquare.com/business/
Ex: https://foursquare.com/v/east-gore-liquor-store/4e90dd9677c89cb921eb3b88

Instagram

Instagram.com is an online photo-sharing, video-sharing and social networking service that enables its users to take pictures and videos, apply digital filters to them, and share them on a variety of social networking services, such as
Facebook, Twitter, Tumblr and Flickr. A distinctive feature is that it confines photos to a square shape, similar to Kodak Instamatic and Polaroid images, in contrast to the

16:9 aspect ratio now typically used by mobile device cameras. Users are also able to record and share short videos lasting for up to 15 seconds.

Resources:
http://www.wordstream.com/blog/ws/2015/01/06/instagram-marketing
Examples:
https://www.instagram.com/explore/locations/29464855/
https://www.instagram.com/explore/locations/4059108/

We will open an Instagram account and post our products regularly and link them to our website. We will use Instagram in the following ways to help amplify the story of our brand, get people to engage with our content when not at our store, and get people to visit our store or site:
1.   Let our customers and fans know about specific product availability.
2.   Tie into trends, events or holidays to drive awareness.
3.   Let people know we are open and our ambiance is spectacular.
4.   Run a monthly contest and pick the winning hashtagged photograph
        to activate our customer base and increase our exposure.
5.   Encourage the posting and collection of happy onsite or offsite customer photos.

Note: Commonly found in tweets, a hashtag is a word or connected phrase (no spaces) that begins with a hash symbol (#). They're so popular that other social media platforms including Facebook, Instagram and Google+ now support them. Using a hashtag turns a word or phrase into a clickable link that displays a feed (list) of other posts with that same hashtag. For example, if you click on #_____ in a tweet, or enter #_____ in the search box, you'll see a list of tweets all about _____.

Podcasting

Our podcasts will provide both information and advertising. Our podcasts will allow us to pull in a lot of customers. Our monthly podcasts will be heard by ____ (#) eventual subscribers. Podcasts can now be downloaded for mobile devices, such as an iPod. Podcasts will give our company a new way to provide information and an additional way to advertise. Podcasting will give our business another connection point with customers. We will use this medium to communicate on important issues, what is going on with a planned event, and other things of interest to our health conscious customers. The programs will last about 10 minutes and can be downloaded for free on iTunes. The purpose is not to be a mass medium. It is directed at a niche market with an above-average educational background and very special interests. It will provide a very direct and a reasonably inexpensive way of reaching our targeted audience with relevant information about our alcoholic beverages, products and services.
Resources:
www.apple.com/itunes/download/.
www.cbc.ca/podcasting/gettingstarted.html
www.bizjournals.com/southflorida/blog/2014/11/south-florida-entrepreneurs-how-
        podcasting-helped.html

http://www.smarttimeonline.com/category/podcast/

Blogging

We will use our blog to keep customers and prospects informed about products, events and services that relate to our liquor store business, new releases, contests, and specials. Our blog will show readers that we are a good source of expert information that they can count on. With our blog, we can quickly update our customers anytime our company releases a new product, the holding of a contest or are placing items on special pricing. We will use our blog to share customer testimonials and meaningful product usage stories and recipes. We will use the blog to supply advice on creative recipes for our beverages. Our visitors will be able to subscribe to our RSS feeds and be instantly updated without any spam filters interfering. We will also use the blog to solicit product usage recommendations and future product addition suggestions. Additionally, blogs are free and allow for constant ease of updating.

Our blog will give our company the following benefits:
1.   An cost-effective marketing tool.
2.   An expanded network.
3.   A promotional platform for new _____ services.
4.   An introduction to people with similar interests.
5.   Builds credibility and expertise recognition.

We will use our blog for the following purposes:
1.   To share customer testimonials, experiences and meaningful success stories.
2.   Update our clients anytime our company releases a new service.
3.   Supply advice on _____ options.
4.   Discuss research findings.
5.   To publish helpful content.
6,   To welcome feedback in multiple formats.
7.   Link together other social networking sites, including Twitter.
8.   To improve Google rankings.
9.   Make use of automatic RSS feeds.

We will adhere to the following blog writing guidelines:
1.   We will blog at least 2 or 3 times per week to maintain interest.
2.   We will integrate our blog into the design of our website.
3.   We will use our blog to convey useful information and not our advertisements.
4.   We will make the content easy to understand.
5.   We will focus our content on the needs of our targeted audience.

Our blog will feature the following on a regular basis:
1.   Useful articles and assessment coupons.
2.   Give away of a helpful free report in exchange for email addresses
3.   Helpful information for our professional referral sources, as well as clients, and online and offline community members.
5.   Use of a few social media outposts to educate, inform, engage and drive people

back to our blog for more information and our free report.

To get visitors to our blog to take the next action step and contact our firm we will do the following:
1. Put a contact form on the upper-left hand corner of our blog, right below the header.
2. Put our complete contact information in the header itself.
3. Add a page to our blog and title it, "Become My Customer.", giving the reader somewhere to go for the next sign-up steps.
4. At the end of each blog post, we will clearly tell the reader what to do next; such as subscribe to our RSS feed, or to sign up for our newsletter mailing list.

Resources: www.blogger.com   www.blogspot.com
             www.wordpress.com   www.tumblr.com
             www.typepad.com

http://www.bloggersideas.com/tips-for-small-business-blogging-success/
http://www.blogwritersbootcamp.com/

Examples:
http://mollysspirits.com/denver-liquor-store-spirits/blog/

Signage
We will use large, colorful neon signs in the storefront window and over coolers. This will improve our visibility and promote our product selection.

Google Maps
We will first make certain that our business is listed in Google Maps. We will do a search for our business in Google Maps. If we don't see our business listed, then we will add our business to Google Maps. Even if our business is listed in Google Maps, we will create a Local Business Center account and take control of our listing, by adding more relevant information. Consumers generally go to Google Maps for two reasons: Driving Directions And to Find a Business.
Resource: http://maps.google.com/

Bing Maps   www.bingplaces.com/
This will make it easy for customers to find our business.

Apple Maps
A web mapping service developed by Apple Inc. It is the default map system of iOS, macOS, and watchOS. It provides directions and estimated times of arrival for automobile, pedestrian, and public transportation navigation.
Resources:
ttps://mapsconnect.apple.com
 http://www.stallcupgroup.com/2012/09/19/three-ways-to-make-your-pawn-business-
    more-profitable-and-sellable/

http://www.apple.com/ios/maps/
https://en.wikipedia.org/wiki/Apple_Maps

Google Places

Google Places helps people make more informed decisions about where to go, from liquor stores to wine shops. Place Pages connect people to information from the best sources across the web, displaying photos, reviews and essential facts, as well as real-time updates and offers from business owners. We will make sure that our Google Places listing is up to date to increase our online visibility. Google Places is linked to our Google Maps listing, and will help to get on the first page of Google search page results when people search for a liquor store in our area.

Resources: http://local.google.com   http://maps.google.com/

Pay-Per-Click Advertising

Google AdWords, Yahoo! Search Marketing, and Microsoft adCenter are the three largest network operators, and all three operate under a bid-based model. Cost per click (CPC) varies depending on the search engine and the level of competition for a particular keyword. Google AdWords are small text ads that appear next to the search results on Google. In addition, these ads appear on many partner web sites, including NYTimes.com (The New York Times), Business.com, Weather.com, About.com, and many more. Google's text advertisements are short, consisting of one title line and two content text lines. Image ads can be one of several different Interactive Advertising Bureau (IAB) standard sizes. Through Google AdWords, we plan to buy placements (ads) for specific search terms through this "Pay-Per-Click" advertising program. This PPC advertising campaign will allow our ad to appear when someone searches for a keyword related to our business, organization, or subject matter. More importantly, we will only pay when a potential customer clicks on our ad to visit our website. For instance, since we operate a liquor store in ____ (city), _____ (state), we will target people using search terms such as "liquor store, fine wines, vodka, in _____ (city), _____ (state)". With an effective PPC campaign our ads will only be displayed when a user searches for one of these keywords. In short, PPC advertising will be the most cost-effective and measurable form of advertising for our liquor store.

Resources:
http://adwords.google.com/support/aw/?hl=en
www.wordtracker.com

Yahoo Local Listings

We will create our own local listing on Yahoo. To create our free listing, we will use our web browser and navigate to http://local.yahoo.com. We will first register for free with Yahoo, and create a member ID and password to list our business. Once we have accessed http://local.yahoo.com, we will scroll down to the bottom and click on "Add/Edit a Business" to get onto the Yahoo Search Marketing Local Listings page. In the lower right of the screen we will see "Local Basic Listings FREE". We will click on

the Get Started button and log in again with our new Yahoo ID and password. The form for our local business listing will now be displayed. When filling it out, we will be sure to include our full web address (http://www.companyname.com). We will include a description of our liquor products and services in the description section, but avoid hype or blatant advertising, to get the listing to pass Yahoo's editorial review. We will also be sure to select the appropriate business category and sub categories.
Examples:
https://local.yahoo.com/info-10006269

HotFrog.com

HotFrog is a fast growing free online business directory listing over 6.6 million US businesses. HotFrog now has local versions in 34 countries worldwide.

Anyone can list their business in HotFrog for free, along with contact details, and products and services. Listing in HotFrog directs sales leads and enquiries to your business. Businesses are encouraged to add any latest news and information about their products and services to their listing. HotFrog is indexed by Google and other search engines, meaning that customers can find your HotFrog listing when they use Google, Yahoo! or other search engines.

Resource: http://www.hotfrog.com/AddYourBusiness.aspx

Local.com

Local.com owns and operates a leading local search site and network in the United States. Its mission is to be the leader at enabling local businesses and consumers to find each other and connect. To do so, the company uses patented and proprietary technologies to provide over 20 million consumers each month with relevant search results for local businesses, products and services on Local.com and more than 1,000 partner sites. Local.com powers more than 100,000 local websites. Tens of thousands of small business customers use Local.com products and services to reach consumers using a variety of subscription, performance and display advertising and website products.

Resource: http://corporate.local.com/mk/get/advertising-opportunities

Corporate Incentive/ Employee Rewards Program

Our Employee Rewards Program will motivate and reward the key resources of local corporations – the people who make their business a success. We will use independent sales reps to market these programs to local corporations. It will be a versatile program, allowing the corporate client to customize it to best suit the following goals:

1.   Welcome New Hires
2.   Introduce an Employee Discount Program for our alcoholic beverages.
3.   Reward increases in sales or productivity with an Employee Incentive Program
4.   Thank Retirees for their service to the company
5.   Initiate a Loyalty Rewards Program geared towards the customers of our corporate clients or their employees.

Database Marketing

Database marketing is a form of direct marketing using databases of customers or prospects to generate personalized communications in order to promote a product or service for marketing purposes. The method of communication can be any addressable medium, as in direct marketing. With database marketing tools, we will be able to implement customer nurturing, which is a tactic that attempts to communicate with each customer or prospect at the right time, using the right information to meet that customer's need to progress through the process of identifying a problem, learning options available to resolve it, selecting the right solution, and making the purchasing decision. We will use our databases to learn more about customers, select target markets for specific campaigns, through customer segmentation, compare customers' value to the company, and provide more specialized offerings for customers based on their transaction histories, demographic profile and surveyed needs and wants. This database will gives us the capability to automate regular promotional mailings, to semi-automate the telephone outreach process, and to prioritize prospects as to interests, timing, and other notable delineators. The objective is to arrange for first meetings, which are meant to be informal introductions, and valuable fact-finding and needs-assessment events.

We will use sign-in sheets, coupons, surveys and newsletter subscriptions to collect the following information from our clients:

1. Name   2. Telephone Number
3. Email Address   4. Home Address
5. Birth Date   6. Brand Preferences

We will utilize the following types of contact management software to generate leads and stay in touch with customers to produce repeat business and referrals:

1. Act   www.act.com
2. Front Range Solutions   www.frontrange.com
3. The Turning Point   www.turningpoint.com
4. Acxiom   www.acxiom.com/products_and_services/

We will utilize contact management software, such as ACT and Goldmine, to track the following:

1. Dates for follow-ups.
2. Documentation of prospect concerns, objections or comments.
3. Referral source.
4. Marketing Materials sent.
5. Log of contact dates and methods of contact.
6. Ultimate disposition.

Cause Marketing

Cause marketing or cause-related marketing refers to a type of marketing involving the cooperative efforts of a "for profit" business and a non-profit organization for mutual benefit. The possible benefits of cause marketing for business include positive public relations, improved customer relations, and additional marketing opportunities.
Cause marketing sponsorship by American businesses is rising at a dramatic rate, because

customers, employees and stakeholders prefer to be associated with a company that is considered socially responsible. Our business objective will be to generate highly cost-effective public relations and media coverage for the launch of a marketing campaign focused on _____ (type of cause), with the help of the _____ (non-profit organization name) organization.

Resources: www.causemarketingforum.com/
                  www.cancer.org/AboutUs/HowWeHelpYou/acs-cause-marketing

Marketing Associations/Groups

We will set up a marketing association comprised of complementary businesses. We will market our liquor store as a member of a group of complementary companies. Our marketing group will include a caterer, an event planner, and a party supply store. Any business that provides event services will be a likely candidate for being a member of our marketing group. The group will joint advertise, distribute joint promotional materials, exchange mailing lists, and develop a group website. The obvious benefit is that we will increase our marketing effectiveness by extending our reach.

BBB Accreditation

We will apply for BBB Accreditation to improve our perceived trustworthiness. BBB determines that a company meets BBB accreditation standards, which include a commitment to make a good faith effort to resolve any consumer complaints. BBB Accredited Businesses pay a fee for accreditation review/monitoring and for support of BBB services to the public. BBB accreditation does not mean that the business' products or services have been evaluated or endorsed by BBB, or that BBB has made a determination as to the business' product quality or competency in performing services. We will place the BBB Accreditation Logo in all of our ads.

Sponsor Events

The sponsoring of events will allow our company to engage in what is known as experiential marketing, which is the idea that the best way to deepen the emotional bond between a company and its customers is by creating a memorable and interactive experience. We will ask for the opportunity to prominently display our company signage and the set-up of a booth from which to handout sample products and sales literature. We will also seek to capitalize on networking, speech giving and workshop presenting opportunities

Patch.com

A community-specific news and information platform dedicated to providing comprehensive and trusted local coverage for individual towns and communities. Patch makes it easy to: Keep up with news and events, Look at photos and videos from around town, Learn about local businesses, Participate in discussions and Submit announcements, photos, and reviews.

MerchantCircle.com

The largest online network of local business owners, combining social networking features with customizable web listings that allow local merchants to attract new customers. A growing company dedicated to connecting neighbors and merchants online to help build real relationships between local business owners and their customers. To date, well over 1,600,000 local businesses have joined MerchantCircle to get their business more exposure on the Internet, simply and inexpensively.

Mobile iPhone Apps

We will use new distribution tools like the iPhone App Store to give us unprecedented direct access to consumers, without the need to necessarily buy actual mobile *ads* to reach people. Thanks to Apple's iPhone and the App Store, we will be able to make cool mobile apps that may generate as much goodwill and purchase intent as a banner ad. We will research Mobile Application Development, which is the process by which application software is developed for small low-power handheld devices, such as personal digital assistants, enterprise digital assistants or mobile phones. These applications are either pre-installed on phones during manufacture, or downloaded by customers from various mobile software distribution platforms. iPhone apps make good marketing tools. The bottom line is iPhones and smartphones sales are continually growing, and people are going to their phones for information. Apps will definitely be a lead generation tool because it gives potential clients easy access to our contact and business information and the ability to call for more information while they are still "hot". Our apps will contain: directory of staffers, publications on relevant issues, office location, videos, etc.

We will especially focus on the development of apps that can accomplish the following:
1. **Mobile Reservations:** Customers can use this app to access mobile reservations linked directly to your in-house calendar. They can browse open slots and book appointments easily, while on the go.
2. **Appointment Reminders:** You can send current customers reminders of regular or special appointments through your mobile app to increase your yearly revenue per customer.
3. **Style Libraries**
   Offer a style library in your app to help customers to pick out a _____ style. Using a simple photo gallery, you can collect photos of various styles, and have customers browse and select specific _____.
4. **Customer Photos**
   Your app can also have a feature that lets customers take photos and email them to you. This is great for creating a database of customer photos for testimonial purposes, advertising, or just easy reference.
5. **Special Offers**
   Push notifications allow you to drive activity on special promotions, deals, events, and offers. If you ever need to generate revenue during a down time, push notifications allow you to generate interest easily and proactively.
6. **Loyalty Programs**
   A mobile app allows you to offer a mobile loyalty program (buy ten ___, get one free, etc.). You won't need to print up cards or track anything manually – it's all done simply through users' mobile devices.

7.   Referrals

A mobile app can make referrals easy. With a single click, a user can post to a social media account on Facebook or Twitter about their experience with your business. This allows you to earn new business organically through the networks of existing customers.

8.   Product Sales

We can sell ____ products through our mobile app. Customers can browse products, submit orders, and make payments easily, helping you open up a new revenue stream.

Resources:	http://www.apple.com/iphone/apps-for-iphone/
	http://iphoneapplicationlist.com/apps/business/
Software Development:	http://www.mutualmobile.com/
	http://www.avenuesocial.com/mob-app.php#

Flash Buying

Flash Buy will be a group where every local business can play a part. Similar to FLASH MOBBING, where individuals gather secretly to stir up some comedy, this will be an effort for us to plan a visit to a locally-owned business on a particular day, pay for the goods/services, and help the chosen business reach an epic day of profits. For example, we will plan for local business group members to visit our store on a certain date. Group members will go there, any time that they wish throughout the selected day, receive a modest discount, and this will spark a rise in profits. This will be an opportunity for other businesses to become aware of and experience our liquor store, and create word-of-mouth advertising.

Yelp.com

We will use Yelp.com to help people find our local business. Visitors to Yelp write local reviews, over 85% of them rating a business 3 stars or higher In addition to reviews, visitors can use Yelp to find events, special offers, lists and to talk with other Yelpers. As business owners, we will setup a free account to post offers, photos and message our customers. We will also buy ads on Yelp, which will be clearly labeled "Sponsored Results". We will also use the Weekly Yelp, which is available in 42 city editions to bring news about the latest business openings and other happenings.
Examples:
yelp.com/search?find_desc=24+Hour+Liquor+Stores&find_loc=Washington%2C+DC
www.yelp.com/biz/casanova-liquor-store-hudson
www.yelp.com/search?find_desc=Liquor+Store&find_loc=Washington%2C+DC

Pinterest.com

This site allows its users to create and manage image collections, known as "boards," grouped by theme, and follow others with similar tastes and interests. We will use Pinterest in the following ways to help build our brand:
1. Education: We will pin the cover image of our ebook and provide a live link to

download the paper or play the video on our website.

2. Feedback: We will use Pinterest as a virtual focus group by creating a Pinterest board that allows us to test what our target market thinks.

3. Events: We will use Pinterest to create a board that introduces an upcoming event. Some ways to promote the event include pinning information about: the speakers, workshops and other educational sessions, sponsors, location and surrounding area, and special events within the event. We will also include: Blog posts related to the topic of the event, special offers for early registration, event photos and attendee comments.

4. Results: We will visually showcase before-and-after images and create pins that showcase impressive outcomes.

5. Inside Look: We will generate greater customer engagement by giving our clients an inside look at our business through a board or boards that offer a feel for our company's people, style, ideas, projects and 'green' commitments.

Examples:

https://www.pinterest.com/puntalasmarials/

https://www.pinterest.com/qualityliquor/

Google+

We will pay specific attention to Google+, which is already playing a more important role in Google's organic ranking algorithm. We will create a business page on Google+ to achieve improved local search visibility. Google+ will also be the best way to get access to Google Authorship, which will play a huge role in SEO.

Resources:

https://plus.google.com/pages/create

http://www.google.com/+/brands/

https://www.google.com/appserve/fb/forms/plusweekly/

https://plus.google.com/+GoogleBusiness/posts

http://marketingland.com/beyond-social-benefits-google-business-73460

Examples:

https://plus.google.com/118328698620078747117

Testimonial Marketing

We will either always ask for testimonials immediately after a completed project or contact our clients once a quarter for them. We will also have something prepared that we would like the client to say that is specific to a service we offer, or anything relevant to advertising claims that we have put together. For the convenience of the client we will assemble a testimonial letter that they can either modify or just sign off on. Additionally, testimonials can also be in the form of audio or video and put on our website or mailed to potential clients in the form of a DVD or Audio CD. A picture with a testimonial is also excellent. We will put testimonials directly on a magazine ad, slick sheet, brochure, or website, or assemble a complete page of testimonials for our sales presentation folder.

Examples:

http://antietamspirits.com/testimonials/

http://www.lovescotch.com/customer-testimonials.php?page=7&pagegroup=1

We will collect customer testimonials in the following ways:
1. Our website – A page dedicated to testimonials (written and/or video).
2. Social media accounts – Facebook fan pages offer a review tab, which makes it easy to receive and display customer testimonials.
3. Google+ also offers a similar feature with Google+ Local.
4. Local search directories – Ask customers to post more reviews on Yelp and Yahoo Local.
5. Customer Satisfaction Survey Forms

We will pose the following questions to our customers to help them frame their testimonials:
1. What was the obstacle that would have prevented you from buying this product?
2. "What was your main concern about buying this product?"
3. What did you find as a result of buying this product?
4. What specific feature did you like most about this product?
5. What would be three other benefits about this product?
6. Would you recommend this product? If so, why?
7. Is there anything you'd like to add?

Resource:
https://smallbiztrends.com/2016/06/use-customer-testimonials.html

Reminder Service
We will use a four-tier reminder system in the following sequence: email, postcard, letter, phone call. We will stress the importance of staying in touch in our messages and keeping their profile updated with their activities. We will also try to determine the reason for the non-response or inactivity and what can be done to reactivate the client. The reminder service will also work to the benefit of regular clients, that want to be reminded of an agreed upon special date or coming event.
Resource:
http://www.easyivr.com/reminder-service.htm

Business Logo
Our logo will graphically represent who we are and what we do, and it will serve to help brand our image. It will also convey a sense of uniqueness and professionalism. The logo will represent our company image and the message we are trying to convey. Our business logo will reflect the philosophy and objective of the liquor store business. Our logo will incorporate the following design guidelines:
1. It will relate to our industry, our name, a defining characteristic of our company or a competitive advantage we offer.
2. It will be a simple logo that can be recognized faster.
3. It will contain strong lines and letters which show up better than thin ones.
4. It will feature something unexpected or unique without being overdrawn.
5. It will work well in black and white (one-color printing).

6. It will be scalable and look pleasing in both small and large sizes.
7. It will be artistically balanced and make effective use of color, line density and shape.
8. It will be unique when compared to competitors.
9. It will use original, professionally rendered artwork.
10. It can be replicated across any media mix without losing quality.
11. It appeals to our target audience.
12. It will be easily recognizable from a distance if utilized in outdoor advertising.

Example: https://99designs.com/logo-design/contests/liquor-store-logo-10778

Resources: www.freelogoservices.com/   www.hatchwise.com
              www.logosnap.com   www.99designs.com
              www.fiverr.com   www.freelancer.com
              www.upwork.com

Logo Design Guide:
www.bestfreewebresources.com/logo-design-professional-guide
www.creativebloq.com/graphic-design/pro-guide-logo-design-21221

Fundraisers

Community outreach programs involving charitable fundraising and showing a strong interest in the local school system will serve to elevate our status in the community as a "good corporate citizen" while simultaneously increasing store traffic. We will execute a successful fundraising program for our liquor store and build goodwill in the community, by adhering to the following guidelines:

1. Keep It Local
   When looking for a worthy cause, we will make sure it is local so the whole neighborhood will support it.
2. Plan It
   We will make sure that we are organized and outline everything we want to accomplish before planning the fundraiser.
3. Contact Local Media
   We will contact the suburban newspapers to do stories on the event and send out press releases to the local TV and radio stations.
4. Contact Area Businesses
   We will contact other businesses and have them put up posters in their stores and pass out flyers to promote the event.
5. Get Recipient Support
   We will make sure the recipients of the fundraiser are really willing to participate and get out in the neighborhood to invite everyone into our store for the event, plus help pass out flyers and getting other businesses to put up the posters.
6. Give Out Bounce Backs
   We will give a "bounce-back" coupon that allows for both a discount and an additional donation in exchange for customer next purchase. (It will have an expiration date of two weeks to give a sense of urgency.)

7.   Be Ready with plenty of product and labor on hand for the event.

Fundraiser Action Plan Checklist:
1.   Choose a good local cause for your fundraiser.
2.   Calculate donations as a percentage for normal sales.
3.   Require the group to promote and support the event.
4.   Contact local media to get exposure before and after the event.
5.   Ask area businesses to put up flyers and donate printing of materials.
6.   Use a bounce-back coupon to get new customers back.
7.   Be prepared with sufficient labor and product.
Resource:
www.thefundraisingauthority.com/fundraising-basics/fundraising-event/

Online Directory Listings

The following directory listings use proprietary technology to match customers with industry professionals in their geographical area. The local search capabilities for specific niche markets offer an invaluable tool for the customer. These directories help member businesses connect with purchase-ready buyers, convert leads to sales, and maximize the value of customer relationships. Their online and offline communities provide a quick and easy low or no-cost solution for customers to find a liquor store quickly. We intend to sign-up with all no cost directories and evaluate the ones that charge a fee.

Liquor Retail Store	www.liquorretailstore.com/directory/refine/
Liquor Store Channel	www.theliquorstorechannel.com/genre/Liquor-Stores
Liquor Maps	http://liquormaps.com/?ptype=post_listing

Resource:
https://synup.com/?utm_source=fitsmallbusiness&utm_medium=fsb_domain_ref&utm_
        campaign=fitsmallbusiness

We will make certain that our listings contain the following information:

- Business Name   - Address
- Phone number   - Days and Hours of operation
- Email address   - Website URL
- Contact Person: name, phone #, email   - Facility Photos
- Company logo   - Products/ Services offered
- Short Business description   - Affiliations
- Specialties   - Facebook Business Page Link
- Twitter Business Page Link   - LinkedIn Business Page Link

Other General Directories Include:

Listings.local.yahoo.com   Switchboard Super Pages
YellowPages.com   MerchantCircle.com
Bing.com/businessportal   Local.com
Yelp.com   BrownBook.com

InfoUSA.com iBegin.com
Localeze.com Bestoftheweb.com
YellowBot.com HotFrog.com
InsiderPages.com MatchPoint.com
CitySearch.com YellowUSA.com
Profiles.google.com/me Manta.com
Jigsaw.com LinkedIn.com
Whitepages.com PowerProfiles.com
Judysbook.com Company.com
Google.com Yahoo.com
SuperPages.com TrueLocal.com
ExpressUpdate.com Citysquares.com
MojoPages.com DMOZ
BOTW Business.com

Resource:
https://blog.hubspot.com/blog/tabid/6307/bid/10322/The-Ultimate-List-50-Local-Business-Directories.aspx#sm.003v1ogz1d24drz10zn27n7f99ha5

Get Listed http://getlisted.org/enhanced-business-listings.aspx
Universal Business Listing https://www.ubl.org/index.aspx
www.UniversalBusinessListing.org

Universal Business Listing (UBL) is a local search industry service dedicated to acting as a central collection and distribution point for business information online. UBL provides business owners and their marketing representatives with a one-stop location for broad distribution of complete, accurate, and detailed listing information.

Strategic Alliances

We will focus our efforts on building strategic relationships within the community that we serve. We will form strategic alliances to accomplish the following objectives:
1.   To share marketing expenses.
2.   To realize bulk buying power on wholesale purchases.
3.   To engage in barter arrangements.
4.   To collaborate with industry experts.
5.   To set-up mutual referral relationships.

_____ (company name) will seek out opportunities to establish viable strategic alliances, such as co-marketing with gourmet food operations, wine and spirits distributors, importers, and producers. One such opportunity, is an alliance with an upscale gourmet food market. Packaging party catering and event food services with a complement of fine wines and spirits will help promote both businesses and provide an extra measure of service to our neighborhood customers. Coordinating gift baskets with wine orders in a single delivery package presents another compelling co-marketing opportunity. Information specific to pairing wines with food can be used to stimulate sales as well.

We will develop strategic alliances with the following service providers by conducting introductory 'cold calls' to their offices and making them aware of our capabilities by distributing our brochures and business cards:

1.	Party Supply Stores	2.	Senior Daycare Centers
3.	Dance Schools	4.	Gourmet Food Stores
5.	Day Spas	6.	Boutiques
7.	Health Clubs	8.	Beauty Salons
9.	Nail Salons	10.	Bridal Centers
11.	Caterers	12.	Event Planners
13.	Corporate Offices	14.	Gift Basket Makers
15.	Cooking and Wine Schools	16.	Restaurants

We will develop a program, complete with packing materials, that teaches businesses how to use our products as part of their employee rewards strategy.

We will assemble and present a sales presentation package that includes sales brochures, business cards, and a DVD presentation of basic party planning tips, and client testimonials. We will include coupons that offer a discount or other type of introductory deal. We will ask to set-up a take-one display for our sales brochures at the business registration counter.

We will promptly give the referring business any one or combination of the following agreed upon reward options:
1.   Referral fees
2.   Free services

3.   Mutual referral exchanges

We will monitor referral sources to evaluate the mutual benefits of the alliance and make certain to clearly define and document our referral incentives prior to initiating our referral exchange program.

Monitoring Marketing Results

To monitor how well _____ (company name) is doing, we will measure how well the advertising campaign is working by taking customer surveys. What we would like to know is how they heard of us and how they like and dislike about our services. In order to get responses to the surveys, we will be give discounts as thank you rewards.

Response Tracking Methods
> Coupons: ad-specific coupons that easily enable tracking
> Landing Pages: unique web landing pages for each advertisement
> 800 Numbers: unique 1-800-# per advertisement
> Email Service Provider: Instantly track email views, opens, and clicks
> Address inclusion of dept # or suite #.

Our financial statements will offer excellent data to track all phases of sales. These are available for review on a daily basis. _____ (company name) will benchmark our objectives for sales promotion and advertising in order to evaluate our return on invested marketing dollars, and determine where to concentrate our limited advertising dollars to realize the best return. We will also strive to stay within our marketing budget.

Key Marketing Metrics
We will use the following two marketing metrics to evaluate the cost-effectiveness of our marketing campaign:
1.   The cost to acquire a new customer: The average dollar amount invested to get one new client. Example: If we invest $3,000 on marketing in a single month and end the month with 10 new customers, our cost of acquisition is $300 per new customer.
2.   The lifetime value of the average active customer. The average dollar value of an average customer over the life of their business with you. To calculate this metric for a given period of time, we will take the total amount of revenue our business generated during the time period and divide it by the total number of customers we had from the beginning of the time period.
3.   We will track the following set of statistics on a weekly basis to keep informed of the progress of our practice:
>   A.   Number of total referrals.
>   B.   Percentage increase of total referrals (over baseline).
>   C.   Number of new referral sources.
>   D.   Number of new customers/month.

Key Marketing Metrics Table
We've listed some key metrics in the following table. We will need to keep a close eye on

these, to see if we meet our own forecasted expectations. If our numbers are off in too many categories, we may, after proper analysis, have to make substantial changes to our marketing efforts.

Key Marketing Metrics	2017	2018	2019
Revenue			
Leads			
Leads Converted			
Avg. Transaction per Customer			
Avg. Dollars per Customer			
Number of Referrals			
Number of PR Appearances			
Number of Testimonials			
Number of New Club Members			
Number of Returns			
Number of BBB Complaints			
Number of Completed Surveys			
Number of Blog readers			
Number of Twitter followers			
Number of Facebook Fans			

Metric Definitions

1. Leads: Individuals who step into the store to consider a purchase.
2. Leads Converted: Percent of individuals who actually make a purchase.
3. Average Transactions Per Customer: Number of purchases per customer per month. Expected to rise significantly as customers return for more and more _____ items per month
4. Average $ Per Customer: Average dollar amount of each transaction. Expected to rise along with average transactions.
5. Referrals: Includes customer and business referrals
6. PR Appearances: Online or print mentions of the business that are not paid advertising. Expected to be high upon opening, then drop off and rise again until achieving a steady level.
7. Testimonials: Will be sought from the best and most loyal customers. Our objective is ___ (#) per month) and they will be added to the website. Some will be sought as video testimonials.
8. New Loyalty Club Members: This number will rise significantly as more customers see the value in repeated visits and the benefits of club membership.
9. Number of Returns/BBB Complaints: Our goal is zero.
10. Number of Completed Surveys: We will provide incentives for customers to complete customer satisfaction surveys.

Word-of-Mouth Marketing

We plan to make use of the following techniques to promote word-of-mouth advertising:

1. Repetitive Image Advertising
2. Provide exceptional customer service.
3. Make effective use of loss leaders.
2. Schedule in-store activities, such as demonstrations or special events.
3. Make trial easy with a coupon or introductory discount.
4. Initiate web and magazine article submissions
5. Utilize a sampling program
6. Add a forward email feature to our website.
7. Share relevant and believable testimonial letters
8. Publish staff bios.
9. Make product/service upgrade announcements
10. Hold contests or sweepstakes
12. Have involvement with community events.
13. Pay suggestion box rewards
14. Distribute a monthly newsletter
15. Share easy-to-understand information (via an article or seminar).
16. Make personalized marketing communications.
17. Structure our referral program.
18. Sharing of Community Commonalities
19. Invitations to join our community of shared interests.
20. Publish Uncensored Customer Reviews
21. Enable Information Exchange Forums
22. Provide meaningful comparisons with competitors.
23. Clearly state our user benefits.
24. Make and honor ironclad guarantees
25. Provide superior post-sale support
26. Provide support in the pre-sale decision making process
27. Host Free Informational Seminars or Workshops
28. Get involved with local business organizations
29. Issue Press Release coverage of charitable involvements
30. Hold traveling company demonstrations/exhibitions/competitions

6.4.4 Customer Satisfaction Survey

We will design a customer satisfaction survey to measure the "satisfaction quotient" of our liquor store customers. By providing a detailed snapshot of our current customer base, we will be able to generate more repeat and referral business and enhance the profitability of our company.

Our Customer Satisfaction Survey will including the following basics:

1. How do our customers rate our liquor store business?

2. How do our customers rate our competition?
3. How well do our customers rate the value of our products or services?
4. What new customer needs and trends are emerging?
5. How loyal are our customers?
6. What can be done to improve customer loyalty and repeat business?
7. How strongly do our customers recommend our business?
8. What is the best way to market our business?
9. What new value-added services would best differentiate our business from that of our competitors?
10. How can we encourage more referral business?
11. How can our pricing strategy be improved?
12. Why did our best customers first come to our store and why they continue to come back.
13. Where do they live and what their basic life situation is.

Our customer satisfaction survey will help to answer these questions and more. From the need for continual new products and services to improved customer service, our satisfaction surveys will allow our business to quickly identify problematic and underperforming areas, while enhancing our overall customer satisfaction.

Examples:

www.readsurvey.com/www-liquorstoresgp-cacustomer-survey-liquor-stores-customer-feedback-survey.html

http://smallbiztrends.com/2007/06/the-small-biz-7-survey.html

https://stellaservice.com/35-sample-customer-satisfaction-survey-questions-for-retail-brands/

Resources:

https://www.survata.com/

https://www.google.com/insights/consumersurveys/use_cases

https://www.surveymonkey.com/mp/customer-satisfaction-survey-questions/

http://www.smetoolkit.org/smetoolkit/en/content/en/6708/Customer-Satisfaction-Survey-Template-

http://smallbusiness.chron.com/common-questions-customer-service-survey-1121.html

http://smallbiztrends.com/2014/11/tailoring-survey-questions-for-your-industry.html

http://www.amplituderesearch.com/customer-satisfaction-surveys.shtml

Sales Strategy

The development of our sales strategy will start by developing a better understanding of our customer needs. To accomplish this task we will pursue the following research methods:

1. Join the associations that our target customers belong to.
2. Contact the membership director and establish a relationship to understand their member's needs, challenges and concerns.
3. Identify non-competitive suppliers who sell to our customer to learn their challenges and look for partnering solutions.
4. Work directly with our customer and ask them what their needs are and if our business may offer a possible solution.

The Management of our store will focus on daily sales revenue goals, and explaining any variances. Best value products will be identified to assist customers with smart purchase selections. Deliveries will be geared to the customer's convenience. The situation will be monitored to insure that the company invests adequately in its own delivery operations.

Sales feedback will be elicited to stimulate ideas, approaches, relate success stories, instruct in new techniques, share news, and implement improvements. Major accounts will be solicited through networking, neighborhood solicitations via sales agents, and opportunistic encounters at any time by management.

____ (company name) will keep its beverage prices competitive with other liquor stores in a __(#) mile radius of our store in order to attract commuters. Customers that purchase more than $__(100) worth of product will be given __(10)% coupon on future purchases. Our focus will be on making the mobile services we offer of the highest possible quality. Only when those services are well-established, will we consider expanding our range of services offered.

We will become a one-stop shop for wine and cheese catering services, and specialized program offerings. We will also be very active in the community, building a sold reputation with professionals and community leaders.

Our clients will be primarily obtained through word-of-mouth referrals, but we will also advertise introductory offers to introduce people to our frequent buyer and preferred club membership programs. The combination of the perception of higher quality, exceptional purchase guidance, innovative service and the recognition of superior value should turn referral leads into satisfied customers.

The company's sales strategy will be based on the following elements:
Advertising in the Yellow Pages - two inch by three inch ads describing our services will be placed in the local Yellow Pages.
Placing classified advertisements in the regional editions of gourmet magazines.
Word of mouth referrals - generating sales leads in the local community through customer referrals.

Our basic sales strategy is to:
Develop a website for lead generation by _____ (date).
Provide exceptional customer service.
Accept payment by all major credit cards, cash, PayPal and check.
Survey our customers regarding products and services they would like to see added.
Sponsor charitable and other community events.
Provide tours of the store so customers can learning how to be discriminating customers and build a trust bond with our operations.
Motivate employees with a pay-for-performance component to their straight salary compensation package, based on profits and customer satisfaction rates.
Build long-term customer relationships by putting the interests of customers first.
Establish mutually beneficial relationship with local businesses serving the entertainment and socializing needs of local residents.

Customer Retention Strategy

We will use the following post-purchase techniques to improve customer retention, foster referrals and improve the profitability of our business:

1. Keep the store sparkling clean and well-organized.
2. Use only well-trained sales associates.
3. Actively solicit customer feedback and promptly act upon their inputs.
4. Tell customers how much you appreciate their business.
5. Call regular customers by their first names.
6. Send thank you notes.
7. Offer free new product samples.
8. Change displays and sales presentations on a regular basis.
9. Practice good phone etiquette
10. Respond to complaints promptly.
11. Reward referrals.
12. Publish a monthly opt-in direct response newsletter with customized content, dependent on recipient stated information preferences .
13. Develop and publish a list of frequently asked questions.
14. Issue Preferred Customer Membership Cards.
15. Hold informational seminars and workshops.
16. Provide an emergency hotline number.
17. Publish code of ethics and our service guarantees.
18. Help customers to make accurate competitor comparisons.

19. Build a stay-in-touch (drip marketing) communications calendar.
20. Keep marketing communications focused on our competitive advantages.
21. Offer repeat user discounts and incentives.
22. Be supportive and encouraging, and not judgmental.
23. Measure customer retention and look at recurring revenue and customer surveys.
24. Build a community of shared interests by offering a website forum or discussion group for professionals and patients to allow sharing of knowledge.
25. Offer benefits above and beyond those of our competitors.
26. Issue reminder emails and holiday gift cards.

Sales Forecast

Our sales projections are based on the following:
1. Actual sales volumes of local competitors
2. Interviews with liquor store owners and managers
3. Observations of store sales and traffic at competitor establishments.
4. Government and industry trade statistics
5. Local population demographics and projections.

Regarding wine revenue potential, we are forecasting average sales of ____ (15?) bottles per capita per year for residents of _____, and an average retail price of $____ (15) per 750 ml bottle. Trade statistics show that, on a national basis, 10% of the population is responsible for 90% of alcoholic beverage consumption. The average _____ (community name) customer, representing ____ (10)% of the _____ (community name) population, therefore, would be expected to purchase ____ (three) bottles of wine per week from our store. With _____ (community name) growing from a base of ____ (#) to _____ (#) residents, we see wine revenue potential from these residents in a range of $_____ to $_____ over the course of the next _____ (#) years.

The balance of our forecasted wine sales, representing some ____ (20)% of total wine sales, will come from sources external to _____ (community name), including catering services, corporate accounts, deliveries to consumers outside _____ (community name), and visitors to the _____ complex of residences, stores, and recreational sites in the city of _____ .

Sales revenue of spirits are projected to be ____ (20)% of wine sales, based on interviews with _____ (city) store owners with a similar array of product mix we have planned. About ____ (40)% of annual sales are expected to occur in the November-December holiday period. This is in-line with the retail liquor store norm and confirmed by owner interviews and trade statistics.
Wine consumption has been growing in terms of sales volume some ____ (8-10)% annually for the last decade. This trend is expected to continue and perhaps increase to up to ____ (14)% in the next 15 years. Spirits sales will tend to remain flat during the same

time, with the exception of tequila, vodka, and rum. Our forecast assumes a ____ (7)% annual growth in total wine and spirits sales per capita.

Our sales forecast is an estimated projection of expected sales over the next three years, based on our chosen marketing strategy, government reimbursement rates and assumed competitive environment. In order to maintain competitive gas prices, the cost of gas to the consumer will never exceed 15% of wholesale cost. _____ (company name) will focus on increasing food sales in order to meet total sales forecast goals.

Sales are expected to be below average during the first year, until a regular customer base has been established. It has been estimated that it takes the average convenience store a minimum of two years to establish a significant customer base. After the customer base is built, sales will grow at an accelerated rate from word-of-mouth referrals and continued networking efforts. We expect sales to steadily increase as our marketing campaign, employee training programs and contact management system are executed. By using advertising, especially discounted introductory coupons, as a catalyst for this prolonged process, ____(company name) plans to attract more customers sooner. Throughout the first year, it is forecasted that sales will incrementally grow until profitability is reached toward the end of year ___(one?). Year two reflects a conservative growth rate of ____ (20?) percent. Year three reflects a growth rate of _____ (25?) percent. We expect to be open for business on ____ (date), and start with an initial enrollment of ____ (#) patients. With our unique product and service offerings, along with our thorough and aggressive marketing strategies, we believe that sales forecasts are actually on the conservative side.

Table: Sales Forecast

Sales	Annual Sales		
	2017	2018	2019
Wine			
Spirits			
Beer			
Non-alcohol Beverages			
Related Grocery/Produce			
Party Supplies			
Gift Merchandise			
Gift Baskets			
Catering Services			
Bartending Services			
Consulting/Seminars			
Misc.			
Total Unit Sales			
Direct Cost of Sales:			
Wine			
Spirits			
Beer			
Non-alcohol Beverages			
Related Grocery/Produce			

```
Party Supplies          _____
Gift Merchandise        _____
Gift Baskets            _____
Catering Services       _____
Bartending Services     _____
Consulting/Seminars     _____
Misc.                   _____
```
Subtotal Direct Cost of Sales   _____

Merchandising Strategy

Merchandising is that part of our marketing strategy that is involved with promoting the sales of our merchandise, as by consideration of the most effective means of selecting, pricing, displaying, and advertising items for sale in our retail store business. Through proper product placement, space allocation, and in-store promotion, sales space will be geared towards high profit margin products. Excellence in merchandising will mean that every customer easily finds what he or she wants, at a price he or she can afford, when he or she wants it.

We will use in-store merchandising to maximize sales by making products stand out from competing products or simply stand out from the clutter of messages in the store environment. We will make certain that our products are displayed properly and in sufficient quantity, in their allotted space, with the appropriate merchandising materials, and without other products encroaching on their shelf space. In-store merchandising will be our last chance to present shoppers with information about a product's features, benefits, price, and positioning.

We will create merchandising displays that will attract clients by:
Choosing market appropriate merchandise.
Strategically positioning, designing and mapping displays.
Inventory tracking and control.
Working with vendors to promote their products in-house.
Training our staff to cross-sell and up-sell products.
Setting the retail stage to encourage impulse sales
Planning our displays to convey a branded message.
Using lighting as a key accent factor.
Organizing the retail products into themed groupings.
Developing the visual layout and design of the retail area
Selecting attractive and informative signage.
Using the right mix of packaging, displays, POP media, and couponing.

We will create an environment that is comfortable, encourages sales, and attracts clients. We will regularly grow and change our displays, so customers can see that we have new products and services to offer them. We will rotate our products and educate our entire staff on each product.

Recent data from the Point-of-Purchase Advertising Institute suggest that 70 percent of supermarket shoppers and 74 percent of mass-merchant shoppers make their purchase decision inside the store, and 53 percent of these are impulse purchases. We will optimize our business revenue by tracking our merchandising strategies, and building upon the ones that produce the best results for our business.

Incorporating unique merchandising ideas into our retail business will be one of the best ways to encourage our customers to spend more time, and more money, in our store. Our retail store will use its merchandising displays to demonstrate the performance of our products and services, establish trust with our customers and encourage impulse purchases.

We will decorate the interior of our _____ store attractively. Our multi-sensory stimulating shop will undoubtedly impress our customers. We will be creative in the design of our window displays to tempt onlookers to step into our ___ store. We will keep things "touchable", and arrange cozy and plush furniture to create a warm, welcoming feeling.

To be successful, our retail area must be impressive and compelling. It must have sufficient space, excellent inventory and beautiful display furnishings.

We will develop a merchandising strategy around the following design principles:
1. We will strive to feature merchandise that is not found in competitor stores.
2. Use proper and informative signage to help sell merchandise.
3. We plan to group similar types of merchandise together for maximum visual appeal.
4. Product presentation will be designed to lead the customers through the entire display area.
5. We will designate a specific in-store location for new product introductions.
6. We will reduce the clutter to increase customer convenience.
7. We will merchandise to the four corners of the store by featuring destination categories.
8. We will set up of special displays to coincide with a specific seasonal event, also known as occasion management.
9. Adjustable shelving will give us the ability to vary the depth of each individual shelf and adjust it to allow more light to fall toward the bottom.
10. We will treat accessories as impulse items and position them near checkout counters.
11. We will display big brands with small brands, from a variety of producers and importers to capture consumer interest and help expose people to the smaller wines.
12. We will use wine/food pairing charts and flyers to make people more comfortable with their wine selections and realize the power of suggestive selling.
13. We will make available wine publication ratings, because an educated consumer

is our best customer.

14.   We will define specific sections and signage within our store that are either type of product or brand established.
15.   We will use shelf talkers to describe product.
16.   We will prominently feature wine club specials to encourage membership.
17.   We will use bottle neckers to identify items featured at wine tastings or club events.
18.   We will display small inventories using promotional bins supplied by distributors.
19.   We will make baskets readily available throughout the store to make shopping easier.
20.   We will allocate our best store real estate to a chilled wine cooler to facilitate impulse sales.
21.   We will set-up a permanent booth within the store to conduct regular wine tasting events and wine club sign-ups, with the help of our distributor reps.
22.   We will install a sign that specifies the various varietals and their characteristics.
23.   We will cluster the best wines into approachable groupings.

The décor of the merchandising area is extremely important to sales. Display units are primary, but lighting, furniture, wall surfaces, window treatments, carpeting, accessories and countertops will all play important supporting roles. We will monitor our sales figures and data to confirm that products in demand are well-stocked and slow moving products are phased-out. We will improve the telephone skills of employees to boost phone orders. We will attach our own additional business labels to all products to promote our line of services and location.

Video Displays

We will use video displays as effective marketing and merchandising tools. Actually seeing the product or service people in action will provide much needed information and incentive to buy. We will place a large flat-screen television with a DVD player in the display area and use the instructional and educational videos, provided by the manufacturer or produced by our staff, to demonstrate the effectiveness of the items or the results of our service.

Themed Displays

We will create compelling and interactive themed displays. We will incorporate products our retail store is already selling to create holiday themed displays. This will increase our sales and help move our most profitable products. Creating holiday-themed merchandising displays will also help our store avoid costly leftovers that must be sold at highly discounted prices.

Interactive Displays

Providing free samples and creating a "try me" section in our retail store, will serve to create a place where customers can try out the latest products and buy only the ones they like the most. Creating a sample section will generate excitement and buzz among our existing customers, encouraging them to return to sample the latest products. A sample section will also build trust with new customers, since it shows that we are willing to let browsers sample products before making a purchase, and provide an opportunity to solicit immediate feedback. On the back end, providing free samples will reduce costly returns, since customers can make sure the item is what they need prior to purchase.

We will use the following devices for in-store merchandising purposes: (select)
1.   Assortment display: a display designed to offer the consumer an array of sizes, colors, or types of merchandise
2.   Audiovisual display: a display in which audiovisual technology is used to stimulate purchases
3.   Case stacking: a display constructed by piling up product in its shipping cases, usually with its top row or front side cut open to display the product
4.   Display stock: usually, durable goods that are placed on various display fixtures so they can be examined by consumers
5.   Dump display: goods that are casually collected on a table or in a box to suggest a bargain to customers
6.   End-aisle display or end-cap display: a display placed at the end of a row of shelving to attract attention to a featured item
7.   Environmental setting: a display set up, usually with a variety of coordinated merchandise, in a setting that is meant to resemble a shopper's home
8.   Floor pyramid: a product display in which the items are stacked in a stepped pyramid.
9.   Floor stand: a display unit, usually of corrugated cardboard, that elevates products that are too small or too expensive to be stacked in the usual manner
10.   Gondola: a display stand with shelves open on all sides both to display goods and provide space for back-up stock
11.   Island display: a freestanding display in a store's aisle or other open space that is accessible from all sides
12.   Shelf-extender: a small tray, designed to fasten on the shelf and project from it, extending the space of the shelf
13.   Showcase: a glass display case in which products can be viewed, but not handled unless removed by a salesperson
14.   Tie-in display: a joint display with a non-competing product
15.   Theme display or setting display: a retail display in which products are presented in a setting or environment having a specific theme
16.   Vignette: a display that shows a product in use

To avoid confusing customers when they enter your store, we will direct them to their desired product by hanging signs for each type of alcohol, using "Rum," "Tequila," "Wine" and "Vodka" signs. We will also place items that are usually bought in pairs together, such as tequila and margarita mix.

Point-of-Purchase Displays (POP)
The term point-of-purchase, or POP, typically refers to the promotional graphics focused on influencing consumer behavior at the moment of the purchasing decision. These graphics serve to impact a buying decision in favor of a specific brand or product in-store where the purchase is imminent. POP is increasingly becoming one of the more important aspects of advertising and promotion, because of its efficiency in targeting the consumer

in the actual buying environment, the decline of network television viewership and newspaper readership, and the stark reality of recession-sized ad budgets.

Pricing Strategy

Product pricing will be based on competitive parity guidelines. Prices will be consistent with those of the retail stores in our area, with the exception of very high-volume operations who have more powerful pricing leverage. Pricing will be monitored continuously against neighborhood and other competitive sources who we can readily research. Our plan is to discount thematically, that is, tied to an event theme.

Our pricing strategy will take into view the following factors: (State Dependent)
1. The distiller's, brewer's or vintner's price to the Board.
2. Federal taxes: excise tax on all liquor & custom duty rates on imported liquor.
3. Freight costs: From the suppliers to the Distribution Center and to the stores.
4. Mark-up: As established by the State Board.
5. State sales and liter taxes as established by the State Legislature.

We are not interested in being the low price leader, as our pricing strategy plays a major role in whether we will be able to create and maintain customers for a profit. Our revenue structure must support our cost structure, so the salaries we pay to our staff are balanced by the revenue we collect.

The number of competitors in the area largely determines what type of pricing we will have. We don't want to be known as the highest price place in town but it is equally important not to be the cheapest.

Cost control is important. Beer, and to a lesser extent liquor, goes on sale periodically (also known as postoff). It will be vital to try to time our purchases correctly so that we are always able to buy on sale. This means we have to carefully track sales and make accurate forecasts on how much inventory we will need. We will try to aim for two months of inventory when an item is on sale, and two to three weeks if it is not.

Profit margins will depend on the competition and how well we buy. In our particular area, I will aim for ____ (25)% profit margin for liquor, ___ (20)% beer, ___ (40_% on wine, soda, water, and snacks. We will pick some well known items and make them cheap. People know these high profile items and will think our store is pricy or cheap based on a few items. We will use Smirnoff as our lower price item. On lesser known items we will be able to get away with charging a higher price because people don't necessarily know what the item should cost.

We will continuously try to expand our selection. If a customer asks for something that we don't have, we will write it down and get it for them the next week. Friendliness, product knowledge and convenience are what will keep people coming to our liquor store instead of the cheaper stuff at the grocery store.

Price List Comparison

Competitor	Service/Product	Our Price	Competitor Price	B/(W) Competitor

Determining the costs of servicing business is the most important part of covering our expenses and earning profits. We will factor in the following pricing formula:

Product Cost + Materials + Overhead + Labor + Profit + Tax = Price
Materials are those items consumed in the delivering of the service.
Overhead costs are the variable and fixed expenses that must be covered to stay in business. Variable costs are those expenses that fluctuate including vehicle expenses, rental expenses, utility bills and supplies. Fixed costs include the purchase of equipment, service ware, marketing and advertising, and insurance. After overhead costs are determined, the total overhead costs are divided among the total number of transactions forecasted for the year.
Labor costs include the costs of performing the services. Also included are Social Security taxes (FICA), vacation time, retirement and other benefits such as health or life insurance. To determine labor costs per hour, keep a time log. When placing a value on our time, we will consider the following: 1) skill and reputation; 2) wages paid by employers for similar skills and 3) where we live. Other pricing factors include image, inflation, supply and demand, and competition.
Profit is a desired percentage added to our total costs. We will need to determine the percentage of profit added to each service. It will be important to cover all our costs to stay in business. We will investigate available computer software programs to help us price our services and keep financial data for decision-making purposes. Close contact with customers will allow our company to react quickly to changes in demand.
We will develop a pricing strategy that will reinforce the perception of value to the customer and manage profitability, especially in the face of rising inflation. To ensure our success, we will use periodic competitor and customer research to continuously evaluate our pricing strategy. We intend to review our profit margins every six months.

Differentiation Strategies

We will use differentiation strategies to develop and market unique products for different customer segments. To differentiate ourselves from the competition, we will focus on the assets, creative ideas and competencies that we have that none of our competitors has. The goal of our differentiation strategies is to be able to charge a premium price for our unique products and services and/or to promote loyalty and assist in retaining our customers.

1. Due to the increase in two-income families, many service-oriented businesses are leaning toward differentiating themselves on the basis of convenience. We plan to have two shifts, an early morning shift and an evening shift in which the store will be fully functional from ___ (5) A.M. to ___ (12) A.M. or later on various days of the week.
2. We will utilize software systems that will enable us to personalize each customer's buying experience, including easy access to customer transaction history, preference profile and information about all the products of interest to that client.
3. Wide aisles and the open floor design will make it easier not only to navigate the many offerings, but to see them from afar, a feature that will speed up service for customers looking to get in and out quickly.
4. We will offer a comfortable seating area for wine tasting events.(if permitted?)
5. We will add a range of financial services, including money transfers, check cashing and bill payments, to become a one-stop destination.
6. We will enable the online and fax ordering of our products and services.
7. We will install kiosks to connect customers with various vendors, including the ability to order movie and theater tickets, download ring tones, book hotel rooms and redeem credit card points.

Other differentiation strategies include the following:
1. Private label and designer branded products and services.
2. We will offer mobile bartending services.
3. We will build an extensive profile on customers to capture information about their lifestyle, taste preferences and key occasion reminder dates.
4. We will develop a referral program that turns our clients into referral agents.
5. We will use regular client satisfaction surveys to collect feedback, improvement ideas, referrals and testimonials.
6. We will promote our "green" practices, such as establishing a recycling program, purchasing recycled-content office goods and responsibly handling hazardous wastes.
7. We will customize our offerings according to the language, cultural influences, customs, interests and preferences of our local market to create loyalty and increase sales.
8. We will develop the expertise to satisfy the needs of targeted market segments with customized and exceptional support services.

Milestones   (select)

The Milestones Chart is a timeline that will guide our company in developing and growing our business. It will list chronologically the various critical actions and events that must occur to bring our business to life. We will make certain to assign real, attainable dates to each planned action or event.

_____ (company name) has identified several specific milestones which will function as goals for the company. The milestones will provide a target for achievement as well as a mechanism for tracking progress. The dates were chosen based on realistic delivery times and necessary construction times. All critical path milestones will be completed within their allotted time frames to ensure the success of contingent milestones. The following table will provide a timeframe for each milestone.

Table: Milestones

Milestones	Start Date	End Date	Budget	Responsibility
Business Plan Completion				
Secure Permits/Licenses				
Locate & Secure Space				
Obtain Insurance Coverage				
Secure Additional Financing				
Get Start-up Supplies Quotes				
Obtain County Certification				
Purchase Office Equipment				
Renovate Facilities				
Define Marketing Programs				
Install Equipment/Displays				
Technology Systems				
Set-up Accounting System				
Develop Office Policies				
Develop Procedures Manual				
Arrange Support Service Providers				
Finalize Media Plan				
Create Facebook Brand Page				
Conduct Blogger Outreach				
Develop Personnel Plan				
Develop Staff Training Programs				
Hire/Train Staff				
Implement Marketing Plan				
Get Website Live				
Conduct SEO Campaign				
Form Strategic Alliances				
Purchase Start-up Inventory/Supplies				
Press Release Announcements				
Advertise Grand Opening				
Kickoff Advertising Program				

Join Community Orgs./Network _____

Conduct Satisfaction Surveys _____

Evaluate/Revise Plan _____

Devise Growth Strategy _____

Monitor Social Media Networks _____

Respond to reviews _____

Measure Return on Marketing $$$ _____

Revenues Exceed $_____ _____

Reach Profitability _____

Totals: _____

Website Plan Summary

_____ (company name) is currently developing a website at the URL address www. (company name).com. We will primarily use the website to promote an understanding of the distilled spirits and wines we offer, and to enable online product ordering and catering scheduling. Supplying the visitors to our websites with this information will make a huge difference in turning our website visitors into new customers.

To improve the readability of our website, we will organize our website content in the following ways.

1.	Headlines	2.	Bullet points
3.	Callout text	4.	Top of page summaries

To improve search engine optimization, we will maximize the utilization of the following;

1.	Links	2.	Headers
3.	Bold text	4.	Bullets
5.	Keywords	6.	Meta tags

This website will serve the following purposes:

About Us	How We Work/Our Philosophy
Contact Us	Customer service contact info
Our Services	Event Planning Services/Catering
Our Product Catalog	Online Ordering/Shopping Cart
Gift Baskets	Gourmet Foods/Wines
Gift Certificate	Order Form
New Arrivals	New Releases/Pre-Sales
Wine Pairings	Articles
Frequently Asked Questions	FAQs
Club Membership	Sign-up
Newsletter Sign-up	Join Mailing List
Newsletter Archives	Foot Care Articles
Upcoming Events	Wine Tasting Schedule
Customer Testimonials	Letters w/photos
Referral Program	Details
Directions	Location directions.
Customer Satisfaction Survey	Feedback
Hours of Operation	
Press Releases	Community Involvement
Strategic Alliance Partners	Links
Resources	Professional Associations
Our Blog	Center diary/Accept comments
Refer-a-Friend	Viral marketing
YouTube Video Clips	Seminar Presentation/Testimonials
Guarantees/Code of Ethics	

Website Marketing Strategy

Our online marketing strategy will employ the following distinct mechanisms:

1. Search Engine Submission

    This will be most useful to people who are unfamiliar with _____ (company name), but are looking for a local liquor store. There will also be searches from customers who may know about us, but who are seeking additional information.

2. Website Address (URL) on Marketing Materials

    Our URL will be printed on all marketing communications, business cards, letterheads, faxes, and invoices and product labels. This will encourage a visit to our website for additional information

3. Online Directories Listings

    We will make an effort to list our website on relevant, free and paid online directories and manufacturer website product locators.

    The good online directories possess the following features:

    Free or paid listings that do not expire and do not require monthly renewal.

    Ample space to get your advertising message across.

    Navigation buttons that are easy for visitors to use.

    Optimization for top placement in the search engines based on keywords that people typically use to find liquor stores.

    Direct links to your website, if available.

    An ongoing directory promotion campaign to maintain high traffic volumes to the directory site.

4. Strategic Business Partners

    We will use a Business Partners page to cross-link to prominent _____ (city) area dance web sites as well as the city Web sites and local recreational sites. We will also cross-link with brand name suppliers.

5. YouTube Posting

    We will produce a video of testimonials from several of our satisfied clients and educate viewers as to the range of our services and products. Our research indicates that the YouTube video will also serve to significantly improve our ranking with the Google Search Engine.

6. Exchange of links with strategic marketing partners.

    We will cross-link to non-profit businesses that accept our gift certificate donations as in-house run contest prize awards.

7. E-Newsletter

    Use the newsletter sign-up as a reason to collect email addresses and limited profiles, and use embedded links in the newsletter to return readers to website.

8. Create an account for your photos on flickr.com

    Use the name of your site on flickr so you have the same keywords and your branded.

9.   Geo Target Pay Per Click (PPC) Campaign

Available through Google Adwords program. Example keywords include wine, liquor store, alcoholic beverages, party, beer, vodka, and _____ (city).

10.   Post messages on Internet user groups and forums.

Get involved with liquor store related discussion groups and forums and develop a descriptive signature paragraph.

11.   Write up your own MySpace.com and Facebook.com bios.

Highlight your background and professional interests.

12.   Facebook.com Brand-Building Applications:

As a Facebook member, we will create a specific Facebook page for our business through its "Facebook Pages" application. This page will be used to promote who we are and what we do. We will use this page to post alerts when we have new articles to distribute, news to announce, etc. Facebook members can then become fans of our page and receive these updates on their newsfeed as we post them. We will create our business page by going to the "Advertising" link on the bottom of our personal Facebook page. We will choose the "Pages" tab at the top of that page, and then choose "Create a Page." We will upload our logo, enter our company profile details, and establish our settings. Once completed, we will click the "publish your site" button to go live. We will also promote our Page everywhere we can. We will add a Facebook link to our website, our email signatures, and email newsletters. We will also add Facebook to the marketing mix by deploying pay-per-click ads through their advertising application. With Facebook advertising, we will target by specifying sex, age, relationship, location, education, as well as specific keywords. Once we specify our target criteria, the tool will tell us how many members in the network meet our target needs.

13.   Blog to share our success stories

Blogging will be a great way for us to share information, expertise, and news, and start a conversation with our customers, the media, suppliers, and any other target audiences. Blogging will be a great online marketing strategy because it keeps our content fresh, engages our audience to leave comments on specific posts, improves search engine rankings and attracts links. In the blog we will share fun drink recipes and party tips. We will also provide a link to our Facebook.com page.   Resource: www.blogger.com

Development Requirements

A full development plan will be generated as documented in the milestones. Costs that _____ (company name) will expect to incur with development of its new website include:

Development Costs

User interface design	$_____.
Site development and testing	$_____
Site Implementation	$._____

Ongoing Costs

Website name registration	$_____ per year.
Site Hosting	$_____ or less per month.

Site design changes, updates and maintenance are considered part of Marketing.

The site will be developed by _____ (company name), a local start-up company. The user interface designer will use our existing graphic art to come up with the website logo and graphics. We have already secured hosting with a local provider, _____ (business name). Additionally, they will prepare a monthly statistical usage report to analyze and improve web usage and return on investment.

The plan is for the website to be live by ___(date). Basic website maintenance, including update and data entry will be handled by our staff. Site content, such as images and text will be maintained by _____ (owner name). In the future, we may need to contract with a technical resource to build the trackable article download and newsletter capabilities.

Sample Frequently Asked Questions

The following frequently asked questions will enable us to convey a lot of important information to our clients in a condensed format. We will post these questions and answers on our website and create a hardcopy version to be included on our sales presentation folder.

Do you offer gift cards?
Yes we offer a variety of gift cards in our store.
Do you deliver or do mail orders?
Sorry, at this time we do not handle deliveries or mail orders.
Do you make suggestions on wine and food pairings?
Yes, we are trained to do wine and food pairings. We work closely with local chefs that offer catering and provide them with informed decisions on how to properly pair food and wine. We also handle wine tastings, and our staff includes former chefs with great insight on proper pairings.
Do you help with party and or/reception planning?
Yes, we offer a variety of event related services, please contact us for more information.
Do you offer wine gift baskets?
We make custom order gift baskets throughout the year. During the holidays we ask that you give at least 72 hours notice due to the large quantity of baskets made during that time of year.
Is there a discount for bulk purchases of wine?
Yes, we offer a 10% discount on full cases of wine, excluding wines that are already offered at a discount price.
Do you offer local wine from _____?
Yes, we are proud to offer a variety of local wines.

Improve the Total Customer Experience

Definition: The emotional response of a customer when interacting with a company, over the course of a business transaction.

Objectives: To use the customer experience as a differentiating strategy. To make a memorable first impression.

Fact: A unique customer experience can establish a competitive advantage that is difficult, if not impossible, to overcome.

Methodology: Status

1. Exceed Customer Expectations.   _____
2. Provide excellent customer service.   _____
3. Improve the consistency of your offerings   _____
4. Provide a full-range of stimulating sensory experiences.   _____
5. Make your offering user friendly.   _____
6. Encourage and facilitate customer feedback.   _____
7. Promptly respond to customer problems.   _____
8. Make it a hassle-free experience.   _____
9. Remember customer names.   _____
10. Provide personal service advisors.   _____
11. Keep records of customer personal preferences.   _____
12. Reward loyalty.   _____
13. Train employees to be knowledgeable and helpful consultants.   _____
14. Hire employees who can be friendly and caring.   _____
15. Arrange for childcare while shopping.   _____
16. Enable express transaction processing.   _____
17. Educate customers on new trends.   _____
18. Facilitate competitor comparisons.   _____
19. Reduce wasted search time.   _____
20. Extend your hours of availability   _____
21. Give customers more plan options.   _____
22. Offer customers more customized solutions.   _____
23. Structure the customer needs analysis study.   _____
24. Perform quality assurance prior to delivery.   _____
25. Provide more post-consumption support.   _____
26. Give customers more payment and term options.   _____
27. Make refreshments available.   _____
28. Enable more interaction with displays.   _____
29. Find creative and informative ways to stay in touch with frequent correspondence and progress updates.   _____
30. Ask staff to learn client names and offer a friendly greeting.   _____
31. Adorn the walls with mood-setting artwork.   _____
32. Paint the wall with warm colors.   _____
33. Hire a salespersons with a warm engaging smiles.   _____

Operations Plan

We will open accounts with liquor distributors in our state. Every state has liquor wholesalers who warehouse and sell alcohol to businesses that hold a liquor license. We will obtain a complete list of these companies from the Alcoholic Beverage Control Board or the equivalent office in our state.

Security Measures

Because liquor stores are often a direct target of armed robbery, we will take the following precautions:

1.   Installation of a bulletproof glass window.
2.   Restrict access inside at night, requiring customers to go to a walk-up window specifically for such situations to make purchases.
3.   Installation of a cash drop slot into a time-delay safe so clerks may limit the amount of cash on hand.
4.   Installation of security cameras to help prevent robberies and shoplifting.
5.   Maintain a friendly relationship with the local police.
6.   Limit the height of store shelving to allow clerks to watch customers at all times.

Control Costs

We will implement the following cost of goods profit controls and manage them consistently to have a profound impact on the profitability of the business.

1.   **Systematize Ordering** This means that the operation has an organized practice of procuring products each day. Components of that system include order guides, par levels, count sheets, inventory counts, a manager in charge of all procurement and a prime vendor relationship to reduce price and product fluctuations.
2.   **Check It In.** We will assign a teammate to check in every product that comes through the door using an organized process of time and date specific delivery windows. We will not only check product count but also vigorously demand and inspect the consistency of product quality and product price.
3.   **Store it well.** We will manage against profit erosion through theft, spoilage and other mishandling issues. We will ensure that each product has a specific home, that each product is labeled, that products are stored using the first-in, first-out storage method to ensure quality rotation and that products are locked and put away until they are needed.
4.   **Standardize.** We will create process standards that can be duplicated through consistent training and management of staff members.
5.   **Manage the Cash Flow.** We will follow a strict process whereby every item that is sold is accounted for and paid for by the end-user. We will carefully manage voided checks.

Supply Chain Relationships

We will seek to establish good working relationships with our vendors and encourage suppliers to provide more special deals to help improve sales of products. We will also encourage our suppliers to provide in-store merchandising/marketing ideas, lower prices and other types of promotional support.

The store will be run as a team, with each employee playing an integral part in the success or failure of the business. Employees will be given whatever tools and training is deemed necessary to carry out their assignments. An emphasis on process improvement will be instilled in each of the "teammates" by offering bonuses or special privileges. Teammates will be rewarded both monetarily and non-monetarily for jobs well done. Effective communication will be stressed in the business. This will cut down on misunderstandings and miscommunications among customers, employees, and managers. Weekly meetings will be held to discuss the weekly agenda, and to give a report of last week's happenings. Teammates will be given the opportunity to add input at these meetings in the form of suggestions, comments, and complaints. Teammates will have defined tasks, but are to be open to doing whatever requests outside of their set guidelines need to be done to bring success to the business. Finally, we plan to offer perks to employees to keep them satisfied and willing to give the business 100 percent.

We will consolidate the number of suppliers we deal with to reduce the volume of paperwork and realize volume discounts.

We will conduct a quality improvement plan, which consists of an ongoing process of improvement activities and includes periodic samplings of activities not initiated solely in response to an identified problem. Our plan will be evaluated annually and revised as necessary. Our client satisfaction survey goal is a ___ (98.0)% satisfaction rating.

We also plan to develop a list of specific interview questions and a worksheet to evaluate, compare and pre-screen potential suppliers. We will also check vendor references and their rating with the Hoovers.com.

Operations include the business aspects of running our business, such as conducting quality assessment and improvement activities, auditing functions, cost-management analysis, and customer service. We plan to write and maintain an operations manual and a personnel policies handbook. We will also develop a personnel manual. Its purpose is to set fair and equal guidelines in print for all to abide. It's the playbook detailing specific policies, as well as enforcement, thereby preventing any misinterpretation, miscommunication or ill feelings. This manual will reflect only the concerns that affect our personnel. A companion policy and procedure manual will cover everything else.

We plan to develop and install a computerized customer tracking system that will enable us to target customers who are likely to have an interest in a particular type of store promotional event.

Resource:
Liquor Store POS Software   http://paygopos.com/profile_bottlerocket.html

Set-up an Advisory Board

Objective: To secure valuable input on your business idea before you start the business and continuous mentoring support after the business opens.

Advisor Qualifications Checklist

		Yes/No
1.	Possess relevant business knowledge and experience?	_____
2.	Can be trusted with financial information?	_____
3.	Can provide honest and unbiased opinions and feedback?	_____
4.	Possess contacts to your local business community?	_____
5.	Respect expressed opinions?	_____

Methodology:

		Status
1.	Conduct regular monthly or quarterly meetings.	_____
2.	Develop alternative feedback methods (email, conference calls)	_____
3.	Decide on ideal number of members (3 to 5)	_____
4.	Define the role of and expectations for advisory board.	_____
5.	Review business plan milestone tracking.	_____
6.	Prepare meeting agenda.	_____
7.	Email agenda to advisors prior to meeting.	_____
8.	Provide a meal to express gratitude.	_____
9.	Consider a stipend ($100/meeting)	_____
10.	Listen to feedback and suggestions.	_____
11.	Assess business strengths and challenges.	_____
12.	Propose business plan updates/changes.	_____
13.	Make informed final business decisions.	_____
14.	Keep board members updated.	_____
15.	Use advisors to help evaluate the results.	_____

Advisory Board Worksheet

Possible Member Name/Affiliation	Expertise Offered	Role/Expectations	Status

Management Summary

At the present time _____ (owner name) will run all operations for _____ (company name). _____ (His/Her) background in _____ (business management?) indicates an understanding of the importance of financial control systems. There is not expected to be any shortage of qualified staff from local labor pools in the market area.

Owner Personal History

The owner has been working in the _____ industry for over _____ (#) years, gaining personal knowledge and experience in all phases of the industry. _____ (owner name) is the founder and operations manager of _____ (company name). The owner holds a degree from the University of _____ at _____ (city).

_____ (owner name) also earned a Higher Certificate with Distinction from the Wine and Spirit Education Trust, and a Certified Sommelier degree from the Sommelier Society of America. He/she began his/her career as a _____ .

Over the last _ (#) years, ____ (owner name) became quite proficient in a wide range of management activities and responsibilities, becoming an operations manager for ____ (former employer name) from __ to _ (dates). There he/she was able to achieve _____. For _____ years he/she has managed a business similar to _____ (company name). _____ (His/her) duties included _____. Specifically, the owner brings _____ (#) years of experience as a _____ , as well as certification as a _____ from the _____ (National _____ Association). He/she is an experienced entrepreneur with _____ years of small business accounting, finance, marketing and management experience. Education includes college course work in business administration, banking and finance, investments, and commercial credit management. The owner will draw an annual salary of $____ from the business although most of this goes to repay loans to finance business start-up costs. These loans will be paid-in-full by _____ (month) of _____ (year).

Management Team Gaps

The Board of Advisors will provide continuous mentoring support on business matters. Expertise gaps in legal, tax, marketing and personnel will be covered by the Board of Advisors. The owner will actively seek free business advice from SCORE, a national non-profit organization with a local office. This is a group of retired executives and business owners who donate their time to serve as business counselors to new business owners.

Advisory Resources Available to the Business Include:

	Name	Address	Phone
CPA/Accountant			
Attorney			
Insurance Broker			
Banker			
Business Consultant			

Wholesale Suppliers   _____

Trade Association   _____

Realtor   _____

SCORE.org   _____

Other   _____

Management Matrix

Name	Title	Credentials Functions	Responsibilities

Outsourcing Matrix

Company Name	Functions	Responsibilities	Cost

Job Descriptions

Job Description— Store Manager

This position plans, organizes, and directs the operations of a liquor store. Incumbents monitor sales and inventory trends to forecast sales and maintain adequate stock levels. They order supplies, monitor and evaluate cost effectiveness and efficiency of store operations, prepare and balance daily reports and maintain and balance inventory records on a computerized point-of-sale system. Incumbents provide customer service and specialized information regarding liquor products and laws, policies, and procedures governing liquor related issues. Incumbents utilize effective public relations to provide services to customers, respond to inquiries, handle complaints or resolve problems. This position is responsible for the efficient operations of the store. Incumbents determine staffing needs, prepare work schedules, establish and implement work procedures and priorities, and recommend changes to policies. They supervise staff including hiring and training employees, assigning work, preparing and conducting performance evaluations, and handling employee problem solving issues. The store manager must possess proven management skills, and the ability to drive sales in the store. Must have a passion for people development and delivering excellent customer service. Must be capable of delivering performance through their teams and drive customer service through high retail standards, availability and presentation.

Key Accountabilities:

Exceptional customer focus.

Excellent Interpersonal skills.

Effective planning and organizational skills.

Influencing and negotiation skills.

Budget management

Supportive and persuasive management style.

Tactical and strategic planning and implementation skills are a must.

Clear vision and a determination to succeed.

Job Description -- Assistant Store Manager

Assists in management of liquor store by performing the following duties:

1. Assist in planning and preparing work schedules and assignments of employees to specific duties.
2. Assists and supervises employees engaged in sales work, taking of inventories, reconciling cash with sales receipts, keeping operating records and preparing daily record of transactions or performs work of subordinates, as needed.
3. Ensures compliance of employees with established security, sales, and record keeping procedures and practices.
4. Orders merchandise or prepares requisitions to replenish merchandise on hand.
5. Ensures all reports, such as purchase, inventory and sales, are accurate and timely.
6. Monitors and verifies vendor activity in store.
7. Monitors and maintains proper store cleanliness, appearance and maintenance as per company guidelines.
8. Ensures all store employees are trained properly.
9. Coordinates sales promotion activities and prepares, or directs workers preparing, merchandise displays and advertising copy.
10. Maintains a customer service oriented operation.
11. Performs all shift duties as required.
12. Able to perform daily duties of Store Manager in his/her absence.
13. Assists with overall operations improvement such as increasing customer base.
14. Assists in pricing adjustments, if necessary.

Job Description Format

Our job descriptions will adhere to the following format guidelines:

1.	Job Title	2.	Reports to:
3.	Pay Rate	4.	Job Responsibilities
5.	Travel Requirements	5.	Supervisory Responsibilities
6.	Qualifications	7.	Work Experience
8.	Required Skills	10.	Salary Range
11.	Benefits	12.	Opportunities

Personnel Plan

1. We will develop a system for recruiting, screening and interviewing employees.
2. Background checks will be performed as well as reference checks and drug tests.
3. We will develop an assistant training course.
4. We will keep track of staff scheduling.
5. We will develop client satisfaction surveys to provide feedback and ideas.
6. We will develop and perform semi-annual employee evaluations.
7. We will "coach" all of our employees to improve their abilities and range of skills.
8. We will employ temporary employees via a local staffing agency to assist with one-time special projects.
9. Each employee will be provided an Employee Handbook, which will include detailed job descriptions and list of business policies, and be asked to sign these documents

as a form of employment contract.
10. Incentives will be offered for reaching quarterly financial and enrollment goals, completing the probationary period, and passing county inspections.
11. Customer service awards will be presented to those employees who best exemplify our stated mission and exceed customer expectations.

Our Employee Handbook will include the following sections:
1. Introduction to the Company
2. Organizational Structure
3. Employment and Hiring Policies
4. Performance Evaluation and Promotion Policies
5. Compensation Policies
6. Time Off Policies
7. Training Programs and Reimbursement Policies
8. General Rules and Policies
9. Termination Policies.

Staffing Plan

The following table summarizes our personnel expenditures for the first three years, with compensation costs increasing from $__ in he first year to about $__ in the third year, based on __(5?) % payroll increases each year and 100% enrollment. The payroll includes tuition reimbursement, pay increases, vacation pay, bonuses and required certifications.

Table: Personnel Plan			Annual Salaries		
	Number of Employees	**Hourly Rate**	**2017**	**2018**	**2019**
Owner/Director					
Store Manager					
Assistant Stores Manager					
Sales Associate					
F/T Stock/Deliver					
Seasonal Stock/Delivery					
Cashier					
P/T Marketing Coordinator					
P/T Bookkeeper					
P/T Janitor					
Other					
Total People: Headcount					
Total Annual Payroll					
Payroll Burden (Fringe Benefits)		(+)			
Total Payroll Expense		(=)			

Basic Hiring Practices

Do's

1. Do only hire for identified expertise requirements, operating need, and the can-do attitude to accomplish great things. _____
2. Do track revenue and cost per employee. _____
3. Do consider a combination compensation package with a low base salary component and substantial pay-for-performance incentives. _____
4. Do have trigger thresholds for when to add or subtract staff. _____
5. Do realize that human efficiency and innovation is what creates value. _____
6. Do share the dream and the overhead burden by offering a low base salary and a large pay-for-performance or commission compensation component. _____
7. Do check with support team and advisory board members for possible good hiring candidate leads. _____
8. Do investigate the appropriateness of asking selective employees to sign non-compete agreements.   Resource: www.ahipubs.com/ _____
   1. Do create detailed performance standards and goal-setting job descriptions that can also serve as employment contracts. _____
   2. Do pre-determine if you want to hire independent thinkers or obedient followers. _____
   3. Do setup an employee disciplinary and performance review process. _____
   4. Do secure signed permission from the applicant before conducting a background check. _____
   5. Do create a formal training program. _____
   6. Do create and implement a cross-training matrix. _____
   7. Do maintain a file of possible job candidates. _____
   8. Do hire people from outside your industry with a fresh perspective and the courage to express their opinions. _____
   9. Do focus on staff retention, because training is costly. _____
   10. Do check with your industry trade association or Chamber of Commerce to help establish pay rates for employees. _____
   11. Do prepare a basic list of interview questions. _____

Don'ts

1. Don't hire out of the goodness of your heart or friendship. _____
2. Don't hire anyone who you are not genuinely thrilled about. _____
3. Don't tolerate mediocre employees. _____
4. Don't downgrade tasks and expectations to suit employee abilities. _____
5. Don't build out your staff or infrastructure in the expectation of rapid growth. _____
6. Don't over delegate to consultants, accountants, or lawyers as even the good ones are only as good as the standards and guidance you provide. _____

Basic Interview Questions

Instruction: Consider the following interview questions and
adding questions of specific value to your business.

Possible Menu of Interview Questions:
1. What are your duties and responsibilities in your current job?
2. What do like most about your current job?
3. What do you like least about your current job?
4. Talk about an important prior goal and how you worked with your manager to achieve that goal.
5. Give an example of when you went beyond the call of duty on your job.
6. How do you deal with job responsibilities that do not match your abilities?
7. How do you handle multiple tasks?
8. Under what conditions do you do your best work?
9. How do you know when you are doing a good job?
10. How do you handle problems with co-workers?
11. What is your process for solving problems?
12. Give me an example of a good decision you made in a difficult situation.
13. What are your strengths?
14. How are your strengths important to customers?
15. What specific certifications have you earned and how have they improved your performance?
16. What performance rewards have you received in the recent past?
17. What is your number one weakness?
18. What is your plan to overcome that weakness?
19. How do you get others to help you with a task?
20. What kinds of decisions do you make rapidly?
21. What was your most recent creative problem solution?
22. What kind of experience do you have in dealing with customers?
23. What is your process for handling angry customer complaints?
24. How do you handle difficult customers?
25. How do you deal with unforeseen circumstances?
26. What made you want to apply for this job?
27. Why do you want to work for this small company?
28. What are your interests, hobbies and favorite participation sports?
29. What are your goals?
30. What have you recently done to improve your skill set?

Business Risk Reduction Strategy

We plan to implement the following strategies to reduce our start-up business risk:

1. Implement our business plan based on go, no-go stage criteria.
2. Develop employee cross-training programs.
3. Regularly back-up all computer files/Install ant-virus software.
4. Arrange adequate insurance coverage with higher deductibles.
5. Develop a limited number of prototype samples.
6. Test market offerings to determine level of market demand and appropriate pricing strategy.
7. Thoroughly investigate and benchmark to competitor offerings.
8. Research similar franchised businesses for insights into successful prototype business/operations models.
9. Reduce operation risks and costs by flowcharting all structured systems & standardized manual processes.
10. Use market surveys to listen to customer needs and priorities.
11. Purchase used equipment to reduce capital outlays.
12. Use leasing to reduce financial risk.
13. Outsource manufacturing to job shops to reduce capital at risk.
14. Use subcontractors to limit fixed overhead salary expenses.
15. Ask manufacturers about profit sharing arrangements.
16. Pay advertisers with a percent of revenues generated.
17. Develop contingency plans for identified risks.
18. Set-up procedures to control employee theft.
19. Do criminal background checks on potential employees.
20. Take immediate action on delinquent accounts.
21. Only extend credit to established account with D&B rating
22. Get regular competitive bids from alternative suppliers.
23. Check that operating costs as a percent of rising sales are lower as a result of productivity improvements.
24. Request bulk rate pricing on fast moving supplies.
25. Don't be tempted to tie up cash in slow moving inventory to qualify for bigger discounts.
26. Reduce financial risk by practicing cash flow policies.
27. Reduce hazard risk by installing safety procedures.
28. Use financial management ratios to monitor business vitals.
29. Make business decisions after brainstorming sessions.
30. Focus on the products with biggest return on investment.
31. Where possible, purchase off-the-shelf components.
32. Request manufacturer samples and assistance to build prototypes.
33. Design production facilities to be flexible and easy to change.
34. Develop a network of suppliers with outsourcing capabilities.
35. Analyze and shorten every cycle time, including product development.
36. Develop multiple sources for every important input.
37. Treat the business plan as a living document and update it frequently.
38. Conduct a SWOT analysis and use determined strengths to pursue opportunities.

Reduce Customer Perceived Risk Tactics

We will utilize the following tactics to help reduce the new customer's perceived risk of starting to do business with our company.

Status

1. Publish a page of testimonials. _____
2. Secure Opinion Leader written endorsements. _____
3. Offer an Unconditional Satisfaction Money Back Guarantee. _____
4. Long-term Performance Guarantee (Financial Risk). _____
5. Guaranteed Buy Back (Obsolete time risk) _____
6. Offer free trials and samples. _____
7. Brand Image (consistent marketing image and performance) _____
8. Patents/Trademarks/Copyrights _____
9. Publish case studies _____
10. Share your expertise (Articles, Seminars, etc.) _____
11. Get recognized Certification _____
12. Conduct responsive customer service _____
13. Accept Installment Payments _____
14. Display product materials composition or ingredients. _____
15. Publish product test results. _____
16. Publish sales record milestones. _____
17. Foster word-of-mouth by offering an unexpected extra. _____
18. Distribute factual, pre-purchase info. _____
19. Reduce consumer search costs with online directories. _____
20. Reduce customer transaction costs. _____
21. Facilitate in-depth comparisons to alternative services. _____
22. Make available prior customer ratings and comments. _____
23. Provide customized info based on prior transactions. _____
24. Become a Better Business Bureau member. _____
25. Publish overall customer satisfaction survey results. _____
26. Offer plan options that match niche segment needs. _____
27. Require client sign-off before proceeding to next phase. _____
28. Document procedures for dispute resolution. _____
29. Offer the equivalent of open source code. _____
30. Stress your compatibility features (avoid lock-in fear). _____
31. Create detailed checklists & flowcharts to show processes _____
32. Publish a list of frequently asked questions/answers. _____
33. Create a community that enables clients to connect with each other and share common interests. _____
34. Inform customers as to your stay-in-touch methods. _____
35. Conduct and handover a detailed needs analysis worksheet. _____
36. Offer to pay all return shipping charges and/or refund all original shipping and handling fees. _____
37. Describe your product testing procedures prior to shipping. _____
38. Highlight your competitive advantages in all marketing materials. _____

Break-even Analysis

Break-Even Analysis will be performed to determine the point at which revenue received equals the costs associated with generating the revenue. Break-even analysis calculates what is known as a margin of safety, the amount that revenues exceed the break-even point. This is the amount that revenues can fall while still staying above the break-even point. The two main purposes of using the break-even analysis for marketing is to (1) determine the minimum number of sales that is required to avoid a loss at a designated sales price and (2) it is an exercise tool so that we can tweak the sales price to determine the minimum volume of sales we can reasonably expect to sell in order to avoid a loss.

Definition: Break-Even Is the Volume Where All Fixed Expenses Are Covered.

Three important definitions used in break-even analysis are:
- **Variable Costs** (Expenses) are costs that change directly in proportion to changes in activity (volume), such as raw materials, labor and packaging.

- **Fixed Costs** (Expenses) are costs that remain constant (fixed) for a given time period despite wide fluctuations in activity (volume), such as rent, loan payments, insurance, payroll and utilities.

- **Unit Contribution Margin** is the difference between your product's unit selling price and its unit variable cost.
  Unit Contribution Margin = Unit Sales Price - Unit Variable Cost

For the purposes of this breakeven analysis, the assumed fixed operating costs will be approximately $ _____ per month, as shown in the following table.

Averaged Monthly Fixed Costs:		**Variable Costs:**	
Payroll	_____	Cost of Inventory Sold	_____
Rent	_____	Labor	_____
Insurance	_____	Supplies	_____
Utilities	_____	Direct Costs per Patient	_____
Security.	_____	Other	_____
Legal/Technical Help	_____		
Other	_____		
Total:	_____	Total	_____

A break-even analysis table has been completed on the basis of average costs/prices. With monthly fixed costs averaging $_____ , $_____ in average sales and $_____ in average variable costs, we need approximately $_____ in sales per month to break-even.

Based on our assumed ____ % variable cost, we estimate our breakeven sales volume at around $_____ per month. We expect to reach that sales volume by our

_____ month of operations. Our break-even analysis is shown in further detail in the following table.

Breakeven Formulas:

Break Even Units = Total Fixed Costs / (Unit Selling Price - Variable Unit Cost)

· _____ = _____ / (_____ - _____)

·

·BE Dollars = (Total Fixed Costs / (Unit Price – Variable Unit Costs))/ Unit Price

_____ = (_____ / (_____ - _____)) / _____

·BE Sales = Annual Fixed Costs / (1- Unit Variable costs / Unit Sales Price)

_____ = _____ / (1 - _____ / _____)

Table: Break-even Analysis

Monthly Units Break-even	_____
Monthly Revenue Break-even	$ _____
Assumptions:	
Average Per-Unit Revenue	$ _____
Average Per-Unit Variable Cost	$ _____
Estimated monthly Fixed Cost	$ _____

Ways to Improve Breakeven Point:
1. Reduce Fixed Costs via Cost Controls
2. Raise unit sales prices.
3. Lower Variable Costs by improving employee productivity or getting lower competitive bids from suppliers.
4. Broaden product/service line to generate multiple revenue streams.

Projected Profit and Loss

Pro forma income statements are an important tool for planning our future business operations. If the projections predict a downturn in profitability, we can make operational changes such as increasing prices or decreasing costs before these projections become reality.

Our monthly profit for the first year varies significantly, as we aggressively seek improvements and begin to implement our marketing plan. However, after the first ___ months, profitability should be established.

We predict advertising costs will go down in the next three years as word-of-mouth about our practice gets out to the public and we are able to find what has worked well for us and concentrate on those advertising methods, and corporate affiliations generate sales without the need for extra advertising.

Our net profit/sales ratio will be low the first year. We expect this ratio to rise at least _____ (15?) percent the second year. Normally, a startup concern will operate with negative profits through the first two years. We will avoid that kind of operating loss on our second year by knowing our competitors and having a full understanding of our target markets.

Our projected profit and loss is indicated in the following table. From our research of the alcoholic beverage industry, our annual projections are quite realistic and conservative, and we prefer this approach so that we can ensure an adequate cash flow.

Key P & L Formulas:

Gross Profit Margin = Total Sales Revenue - Cost of Goods Sold

Gross Margin % = (Total Sales Revenue - Cost of Goods Sold) / Total Sales Revenue
This number represents the proportion of each dollar of revenue that the company retains as gross profit.

EBITDA =Revenue - Expenses (exclude interest, taxes, depreciation & amortization)

PBIT = Profit (Earnings) Before Interest and Taxes = EBIT
A profitability measure that looks at a company's profits before the company has to pay corporate income tax and interest expenses. This measure deducts all operating expenses from revenue, but it leaves out the payment of interest and tax. Also referred to as "earnings before interest and tax ".

Net Profit = Total Sales Revenues - Total Expenses

Pro Forma Profit and Loss

	Formula	2017	2018	2019
Gross Revenue:				
Liquor Sales				
Wine Sales				
Beer Sales				
Related Grocery Sales				
Catering Services				
Other Revenue				
Total Revenue	A			
Cost of Sales				
Cost of Goods Sold				
Other				
Total Costs of Sales	D			
Gross Margin	A-D=E			
Gross Margin %	E / A			
Operating Expenses:				
Payroll				
Payroll Taxes				
Sales & Marketing				
Conventions/Trade Shows				
Depreciation				
License/Permit Fees				
Dues and Subscriptions				
Rent				
Utilities				
Deposits				
Repairs and Maintenance				
Janitorial Supplies				
Office Supplies				
Classroom Supplies				
Leased Equipment				
Buildout Costs				
Insurance				
Van Expenses				
Professional Development				
Merchant Fees				
Bad Debts				
Misc.				
Total Operating Expenses	F			
Profit Before Int. & Taxes	E - F = G			
Interest Expenses	H			
Taxes Incurred	I			
Net Profit	G - H - I = J			
Net Profit / Sales	J / A = K			

Projected Cash Flow

The Cash Flow Statement shows how the company is paying for its operations and future growth, by detailing the "flow" of cash between the company and the outside world. Positive numbers represent cash flowing in, negative numbers represent cash flowing out. We are positioning ourselves in the market as a medium-risk concern with steady cash flows. Accounts payable is paid at the end of each month while sales are in cash and short-term credit card collectibles. Cash balances will be used to reduce outstanding line of credit balances, or will be invested in a low-risk liquid money market fund to decrease the opportunity cost of cash held. Surplus cash balances during the critical first year of operations will function as protection against unforeseen changes in the timing of disbursements required to fund operations.

The first year's monthly cash flows are will vary significantly, but we do expect a solid cash balance from day one. We expect that the majority of our sales will be done in cash or by credit card and that will be good for our cash flow position. Additionally, we will stock only slightly more than one month's inventory at any time. Consequently, we do not anticipate any problems with cash flow, once we have obtained sufficient start-up funds.

A __ year commercial loan in the amount of $_____, sought by the owner will be used to cover our working capital requirement. Our projected cash flow is summarized in the following table, and is expected to meet our needs. In the following years, excess cash will be used to finance our growth plans.

Cash Flow Management:
We will use the following practices to improve our cash flow position:
1.   Perform credit checks and become more selective when granting credit.
2.   Seek deposits or multiple stage payments.
3.   Reduce the amount/time of credit given to clients.
4.   Reduce direct and indirect costs and overhead expenses.
5.   Use the 80/20 rule to manage inventories, receivables and payables.
6.   Invoice as soon as the project has been completed.
7.   Generate regular reports on receivable ratios and aging.
8.   Establish and adhere to sound credit practices.
9.   Use more pro-active collection techniques.
10.   Add late payment fees where possible.
11.   Increase the credit taken from suppliers.
12.   Negotiate purchase prices and extended credit terms from vendors.
13.   Use some barter arrangements to acquire goods and service.
14.   Use leasing to gain access to the use of productive assets.
15.   Covert debt into equity.
16.   Regularly update cash flow forecasts.
17.   Defer projects which cannot achieve acceptable cash paybacks.
18.   Require a 50% deposit upon the signing of the contract and the balance in full, due five days before the event.
19.   Speed-up the completion of projects to get paid faster.

20. Ask for extended credit terms from major suppliers.
21. Put ideal bank balances into interest-bearing (sweep) accounts.
22. Charge interest on client installment payments.
23. Check the accuracy of invoices to avoid unnecessary rework delays.
24. Include stop-work clauses in contracts to address delinquent payments.

Cash Flow Formulas:

Net Cash Flow = Incoming Cash Receipts - Outgoing Cash Payments
Equivalently, net profit plus amounts charged off for depreciation, depletion, and amortization. (also called cash flow).

Cash Balance = Opening Cash Balance + Net Cash Flow
We are positioning ourselves in the market as a medium risk concern with steady cash flows. Accounts payable is paid at the end of each month, while sales are in cash, giving our company an excellent cash structure.

Pro Forma Cash Flow

	Formula	2017	2018	2019
Cash Received				
Cash from Operations				
Cash Sales	A			
Cash from Receivables	B			
Subtotal Cash from Operations	A + B = C			
Additional Cash Received				
Non Operating (Other) Income				
Sales Tax, VAT, HST/GST Received				
New Current Borrowing				
New Other Liabilities (interest fee)				
New Long-term Liabilities				
Sales of Other Current Assets				
Sales of Long-term Assets				
New Investment Received				
Total Additional Cash Received	D			
Subtotal Cash Received	C + D = E			
Expenditures				
Expenditures from Operations				
Cash Spending	F			
Payment of Accounts Payable	G			
Subtotal Spent on Operations	F+G = H			
Additional Cash Spent				
Non Operating (Other) Expenses				
Sales Tax, VAT, HST/GST Paid Out				
Principal Repayment Current Borrowing				
Other Liabilities Principal Repayment				
Long-term Liabilities Principal Repayment				
Purchase Other Current Assets				
Dividends				
Total Additional Cash Spent	I			
Subtotal Cash Spent	H + I = J			
Net Cash Flow	**E - J = K**			
Cash Balance				

Small Business Control Costs Tips

1. Always get multiple supplier bids in writing.
2. Personally authorize all purchase orders.
3. Track all expenses against a budget plan.
4. Set-up a good inventory tracking system, either a manual unit-control/bin ticket system or computerized point-of-sale system.
5. Perform regular energy consumption audits to reduce energy bills and make Power Company recommended changes.
6. Use space organizers to maximize vertical space usage.
7. Use garage sales and auctions to move stale inventory.
8. Enable some employees to telecommute their services.
9. Turn some staff into independent contractors to save benefits package costs.
10. Buy used furniture or remanufactured equipment.
11. Lease rather than buy outright.
12. Recycle paper into notepads.
13. Comparison shop and negotiate everything, including landlord leasehold improvements and several free rent months.
14. Barter for services.
15. Use email instead of mail.
16. Consolidate and schedule shipping or mailings to take advantage of special rates.
17. Monitor office supply usage.
18. Take advantage of trade association negotiated discounts
19. If possible, start-up in your garage, den or attic space.
20. Take advantage of low-cost marketing techniques such as press releases, non-profit seminar giving, networking events, referral programs, testimonials, sampling, blogs, article writing and commissioned sales reps.
21. Pay employees a nominal base salary plus a pay-per-performance commission.
22. Check out Vonage as a telecommunication provider.
23. Check all invoices and bank statements for errors.
24. Use instant messaging instead of telephone calls.
25. Institute security procedures to control employee and customer theft.
26. Utilize a virtual consulting team of experts to contract out specific pieces of projects.
27. Set-up intern and temp alternative employee programs.
28. Build your own website. (**www.smallbusiness.officelive.com**).
29. Sublet some of your space.

Helpful Resources:

Associations:

The Distilled Spirits Council of the United States	http://www.discus.org
International Centre for Spirits and Liquors	http://www.ciedv.org
National Retail Federation	http://www.nrf.org
National Association of C-Stores	www.nacsonline.com
Alcohol and Tobacco Tax & Trade Bureau	www.ttb.gov/wine/control_board.shtml

Publications:

Beverage Dynamics	www.beveragedynamics.com

Miscellaneous:

Vista Print Free Business Cards	www.vistaprint.com
Free Business Guides	www.smbtn.com/businessplanguides/
Open Office	http://download.openoffice.org/
US Census Bureau	www.census.gov
Federal Government	www.business.gov
US Patent & Trademark Office	www.uspto.gov
US Small Business Administration	www.sba.gov
National Association for the Self-Employed	www.nase.org
International Franchise Association	www.franchise.org
Center for Women's Business Research	www.cfwbr.org

Some sites for USA business:
http://sbinformation.about.com/
http://www.business.gov/
http://www.sba.gov/regions/states.html
http://freeadvice.com/
http://www.government-grants-101.com/
http://www.pueblo.gsa.gov/
http://www.smallbusinessnotes.com/sitemap.html

State Liquor Boards Directory:

Alabama Alcoholic Beverage Control Board	334/271-3840
Alaska Revenue Department Control Board	(907) 269-0350
Arizona Department of Liquor Licenses and Control	602/542-5141
Arkansas Alcohol Beverage Control	501/ 682-1105
California Department of Alcoholic Beverage Control	(916) 419-2500
Canada Liquor Control and Licensing Branch (LCLB)	250/356-9596
Colorado Department of Revenue-Liquor	303/205-2300
Connecticut Department of Consumer Protection	860/713-6200
Delaware Department of Public Services	302/577-5210
DC Alcoholic Beverage Regulation Administration	202/442-4423
Florida Department of Professional Business Regulations	850/488-3227
Georgia Department of Revenue Alcohol & Tobacco Tax Division	404/417-4900
Hawaii Liquor Commission	808/523-4458
Idaho State Liquor Dispensary	208/947-9400
Illinois Liquor Control Commission	312/814-2206
Indiana Alcohol and Tobacco Commission	317-233-2430
Iowa Alcoholic Beverages Division	515/281-7400
Kansas Department of Revenue Alcohol Beverage Control	785/296-7015
Kentucky Alcoholic Beverage Control Department	502/564-4850
Louisiana Department of Revenue	225/925-4041
Main Department of Public Safety Control Board	207/624-7220
Maryland Office of the Comptroller of the Treasury	410/260-7314
Massachusetts Alcoholic Beverages Control Commission	617/727-3040
Michigan Liquor Control Commission	517/322-1345
Minnesota Department of Public Safety Liquor Control Division	651/296-6979
Mississippi (Control State) Alcoholic Beverage Control Office	601/856-1301
Missouri Division of Alcohol and Tobacco Control	573/751-2333
Montana Liquor License Bureau (Control State)	406/444-0700
Nebraska Liquor Control Commission	402/471-2571
Nevada Department of Taxation	775/687-4892
New Hampshire State Liquor Commission (Control State)	603/271-3134
New Jersey Department of Law and Public Safety	609/984-2830
New Mexico Regulation & Licensing Department	505/827-7066
New York State Liquor Authority	212 961-8385
North Carolina Alcoholic Beverage Control Commission	919/779-0700
North Dakota Office of the State Tax Commissioner	701-328-2702
Ohio (Control State) Division Of Liquor Control	614/644-2411
Oklahoma Alcoholic Beverage Law Enforcement Commission	405/521-3484
Oregon Liquor Control Commission (Control State)	503/872-5000
Pennsylvania Liquor Control Board (Control State)	717/783-9454
Rhode Island Division of Commercial Licensing and Regulation	401/222-2562
South Carolina Department of Revenue & Taxation	803/737-5000
South Dakota Department of Revenue	605/773-3311
Tennessee Alcoholic Beverage Commission	615/741-1602
Texas Alcoholic Beverage Commission	512/206-3333

Utah Department of Alcoholic Beverage Control	801/977-6800
Vermont Department of Liquor Control	802/828-2345
Virginia Department of Alcoholic Beverage Control	804/213-4413
Washington Business License Services (Control State)	360/586-2784
West Virginia Alcohol Beverage Control Commission	304/558-2481
Wisconsin Alcohol & Tobacco Enforcement	608/266-2776
Wyoming Liquor Commission (Control State)	307/777-7231

A list of Washington DC Liquor Stores authorized to open on Sundays.
Source:
www.washingtonian.com/blogs/capitalcomment/images/2013-6-21-liquor-stores2.pdf
www.washingtonian.com/blogs/capitalcomment/local-news/the-full-list-of-dc-liquor-
stores-approved-for-sunday-sales.php

Advertising Plan Worksheet

Ad Campaign Title: _____

Ad Campaign Start Date: _____ End Date: _____

What are the features (what product has) and hidden benefits (what product does for consumer) of my products/services?

Who is the targeted audience?

What problems are faced by this targeted audience?

What solutions do you offer?

Who is the competition and how do they advertise?

What is your differentiation strategy?

What are your bullet point competitive advantages?

What are the objectives of this advertising campaign?

What are your general assumptions?

What positioning image do you want to project?
  ___ Exclusiveness   ___ Low Cost   ___ High Quality
  ___ Speedy Service   ___ Convenient   ___ Innovative

What is the ad headline?

What is the advertising budget for this advertising campaign?

What advertising methods will be used?
  ___ Radio   ___ TV/Cable   ___ Yellow Pages
  ___ Coupons   ___ Telemarketing ___ Flyers
  ___ Direct Mail   ___ Magazines   ___ Newspapers
  ___ Press Release ___ Brochures   ___ Billboards
  ___ Other

When will each advertising method start and what will it cost?
  Method   Start Date   Frequency   Cost

_____

Indicate how you will measure the cost-effectiveness of the advertising plan?
Formula: Return on Investment (ROI) = Generated Sales / Ad Costs.

YouTube Marketing Tips

Definition: An online video destination to watch and share original video clips. (World-wide approx. 55 million unique users/month)

1. Focus on something that is funny or humorous, so that people will feel compelled to share it with friends and family.
2. Make the video begin and end with a black screen and include the URL of your originating website to bring traffic to your site.
3. Put your URL at the bottom of the entire video.
4. Clearly demonstrate how your product works.
5. Create how-to videos to share your expertise and develop a following.
6. Build contests and events around special holidays and occasions.
7. Run a search on similar content by keyword, and use the info to choose the right category and tags for your video.
8. Make sure the video is real, with no gimmicks or tricks.
9. Add as many keywords as you can.
10. Make sure that your running time is five minutes or less.
11. Break longer videos into several clips, each with a clear title, so that they can be selectively viewed.
12. Encourage viewer participation and support.
13. Take advantage of YouTube tags, use adjectives to target people searching based on interests, and match your title and description to the tags.
14. Use the flexibility provided by the medium to experiment.
15. Use the 'Guru Account' sign-up designation to highlight info videos and how-to guides.
16. Create 'Playlists' to gather individual clips into niche-targeted context so viewers can easily find related content.
17. Use 'Bulletins' to broadcast short messages to the world via Your YouTube Channel.
18. Email 'The Robin Good YouTube Channel' to promote a new video release.
19. Join a 'YouTube Group' to post videos or comments to the group discussion area and build your network of contacts.
20. Use 'YouTube Streams' to join or create a room where videos are shared and discussed in real-time.
21. Use 'Active Sharing' to broadcast the videos that you are currently watching, and drive traffic to your profile.
22. Use the 'Share Video' link found under each video you submit and then check the box 'Friends' to send your video to all your friends.
23. Create your own YouTube Channel when you sign-up for a new YouTube account.

Track Ad Return on Investment (ROI)

Objective: To invest in those marketing activities that generate the greatest return on invested funds.

Medium	Cost	Calls Received	Cost/Call	No. Act. New Clients	Cost/New Client
Formula:	A	B	A/B=C	D	A/D=E
Newspaper					
Classified Ads					
Yellow Pages					
Billboards					
Cable TV					
Magazine					
Flyers					
Posters					
Coupons					
Direct Mail					
Brochures					
Business Cards					
Seminars					
Demonstrations					
Sponsored Events					
Sign					
Radio					
Trade Shows					
Specialties					
Cold Calling					
Door Hangers					
T-shirts					
Coupon Books					
Transit Ads					
Press Releases					
Word-of-Mouth					
_____					
Totals:					

Sample Thank-you and Referral Letter

Dear _____ (client name)

I wanted to take this opportunity to thank you for your business once again. If I can be of service to you in the future, I hope you will not hesitate to call.

In the meantime, I have enclosed a few business cards and referral cards. I would very much appreciate your passing them along to anyone in need of our services. As usual, I will mail you a referral fee for any business that comes my way from your efforts.

I have also enclosed a 'Customer Satisfaction Survey' with a self-addressed and stamped return envelope. Your feedback is invaluable in helping us to improve the services that we offer and we very much appreciate the time you will spend in completing the survey.

I hope you are enjoying your new surroundings and we look forward to serving you and your family in the future.

Please call me if I can be of any help. Thanks again.

Sincerely,

Beverage Inventory Recap

Date Range: _____ Prepared By: _____

Revenue Category	Usage Cost	Potential Sales	Actual Sales	Sales Variance	Sales Variance Percentage	Cost Percentage
Liquor						
Wine						
Bottle Beer						
Draft Beer						
Misc. Items						

Formulas:

Sales Variance = Actual Sales - Potential Sales

Sales Variance Percentage = Sales Variance / Potential Sales

Cost Percentage = Usage Cost / Actual Sales

Liquor Inventory Worksheet

Period: _____ Prepared by: _____

Brand	Bottle Size	Beginning Inventory	Purchased Bottles	Ending Inventory	Comments

Time Management Tips

Objective: To optimize your time in order to allocate more time to grow your business.

Methodology:

Check

1. Create a daily short 'to-do' list of tasks with prioritized time slots. _____
2. Narrow your focus to a fewer number of priorities in any given week. _____
3. Schedule regular meetings with the people that you interact with the most and use these meetings to address non-emergency issues. _____
4. Create a weekly detailed time plan, which can be modified on a daily basis, if needed. _____
5. Do not over-schedule each day. _____
6. Learn how to say 'No' to the requests from others. _____
7. Get organized to improve your productivity. _____
8. Focus your time on priorities, such as bringing in money, selling more products/services and hiring the right people. _____

Action Log

Name: _____ Date: _____

Item No.	Task	Person Resp.	Today's Date	Estimated Complete Date	Required Actions	Comments	Complete Date

Improving Your Credit-Worthiness

Objective: To improve credit-worthiness to be able to apply for either a personal loan or personally guaranteed business loan.

Key: Credit experts recommend that consumers review their credit reports at least once a year to check for accuracy, errors, and any signs of identity theft.

Note: A credit score of 680+ is workable.

Fact: Credit scores range from 300 to 850 with 850 being a perfect score. A difference of 100 points in your credit score could equate to several hundred dollars per month in added mortgage costs.

Key: Get a copy of your credit report early in the process so you have sufficient time to correct errors, and then request a second report (45 days later) to confirm the changes requested have been made. You will need to show at least 4 trade lines that have been open for 24 months.

Ways to Improve Your Credit Score

1. Keep your credit card balances down to less than 50 percent of your credit limit within each account.
2. Make sure the information on your credit report(s) is accurate, and dispute incorrect, outdated and misleading info in your credit file, by submitting supporting documentation with a detailed letter via certified mail.
3. Do not hesitate to send follow-up letters with documentation copies to the same address as the original letters, requesting confirmation of their corrective actions.
4. If the matter is not resolved to your satisfaction contact the Federal Trade Commission's Bureau of Consumer Protection (FTC.org) or your local Better Business Bureau (BBB.org)
5. If all other methods have failed, utilize the Fair Credit Laws and initiate a small claims action against any creditors or credit bureaus who are reporting negative and/or incorrect information on your credit reports. (If you win, the Judge awards a court order to remove the negative credit from your file.)
6. Only close totally inactive old accounts, as long credit relationships are viewed positively.
7. Do not apply for many new accounts within a short period of time.
8. If you are hunting for a mortgage or car loan, file all of your applications within 14 days of one another, so that these multiple credit inquiries are treated as one inquiry.
9. Do not let anyone pull an inquiry of your credit reports unless you are actually ready to buy something today.
10. Try not to apply for any new credit if you already have five or more open lines of credit or open loans.
11. Pay all bills by their due date, especially property taxes.
12. Clear all collections, tax liens, judgments and other charge-offs from your credit reports before starting the loan process.

13. Try to pay off debt rather than moving it around.
14. Do not open new accounts, change jobs, lease a new car or take on new debt while applying for a loan.
15. Only carry between two and four major credit cards.
16. Get your credit grantors to report your account information and on-time monthly payment history to credit reporting agencies by sending them a recent account statement and copies of paid checks.
17. Open a bank savings account to establish reserves to repay debts, and a checking account to provide evidence you pay your bills (cancelled checks).
18. Get the credit bureau to include a short statement of explanation in your report concerning negative information, such as a disagreement over whether you owe a debt or the product was defective as received.
19. Know that under the Fair Credit Reporting Act, a credit bureau has 30 days in which to investigate your claim of inaccuracy or they must delete the item from your report.
20. Avoid identity theft by only dealing with businesses that adhere to strict privacy policies and protect sensitive customer information.
    Warning: Never give personal info over the phone.
21. Make absolutely certain to pay all mortgage loans on time, and, if possible, sign-up for an automatic payment withdrawal from your bank account to ensure timely payments.
22. Always have an ex-spouse expunged from your credit card accounts, cancel all joint accounts, and send letters to all 3 credit bureaus requesting that your credit information be maintained in separate files..
23. Resist the temptation to be a co-signer on family loans, as these loans will show up on your credit report.
24. Ask a family member or a trusted friend, with a good credit standing, to request a secondary credit card be issued to you as a co-applicant, and ask them to guarantee the payment on this account.
25. Reduce the potential for error in your credit file by using the exact same name every time you fill out a credit application, including your middle name and always specify if you are a junior or senior.
26. Rebuild your credit by applying for a couple of secured credit cards, guaranteed
by a savings account. But, first check with Bankcard Holders of America or CardTrak of America (800-344-7714) to verify their legitimacy, and the fact that they report their information to the credit bureaus.
27. Try to rebuild your credit by applying for department store credit cards with a low initial credit limit.
28. Add a 100 word statement of explanation or clarification to your credit report.
29. If you can't make a payment on time, call the creditor to work out a payment plan that will keep your credit in good standing.
30. If you make an isolated late payment, send a letter of apology with a plausible explanation of the one time event.
31. Try to negotiate a settlement agreement with a delinquent creditor and get a signed guarantee of the removal of entire items from all three credit bureaus before releasing any money.

32. Continually work to resolve any discrepancies between the information you provide on a credit application and the information on your credit report with timely updates on life changes. Especially add background information that shows stability of employment, savings and residence.

33. Specifically, request that credit bureaus delete accounts or inquiries from your credit report that do not belong to you, it is an outdated account (> 7 years) or bankruptcy (>10 years) or inquiry (>2 yrs old) and/or the account no longer exists.

34. Secure a copy of "The Complete Guide to Credit Repair" by Bill Kelly Jr., published by Adam Media Corp., for copies of standard letters and forms that can used to help repair your credit.

35. Do not treat a bankruptcy on your credit report as a death sentence. Only a Chapter 7 bankruptcy signals a total inability to handle payments. Use your right to annotate your file with a brief explanation of the verifiable factors that contributed to the bankruptcy filing, and start to rebuild your financial health, as some lenders will consider making a loan after 2 years.

36. As your Mortgage Broker if he/she subscribes to an agency that offers 'rapid rescoring', and submit a letter from the creditor acknowledging that your account was reported as late when you were in fact on time.

Credit Score Calculation Weighting:
- 35% based on payment history
- 30% based on amount owed
- 15% based on length of credit history
- 10% for new credit
- 10% for types of credit used.

Helpful Resources:
Free Credit Report	www.annualcreditreport.com	877-322-8228
My Fico	www.myfico.com	

Opening a Liquor Store in Delaware

Resource: http://date.delaware.gov/dabcpublic/index.jsp

1.   Contact the alcohol commission and present a certificate of compliance from city or county where the establishment will be selling liquor. This requires showing the establishment has been properly zoned, all permits are in place and the other licenses have been approved by the local governments.

2.   Submit the names and addresses of everything within 200 feet of the properties where they will be selling the liquor. There are some exceptions, including an establishment inside a mall or alongside an ocean, lake or river. The rules for those properties are different concerning the radius of the required addresses.

3.   Submit a floor plan of the proposed establishment. The commission will be looking to see how and where the business is going to be set up and if it meets the rules set forth by the commission. The rules will be provided by the commission upon request.

4.   Applicants must acquire a copy of the ABC's rules for selling liquor in the state of Delaware. This costs $50 and can be obtained through the ABC.

5.   All documents must be taken to the commission and presented for what is called preview. Gather up and recheck that all documents are in place and are valid before scheduling a review. It is also wise to know the date the establishment is opening. This will help determine the right time to file for a license and aid with other legal issues such as notifying the public.

Opening a Liquor Store in Connecticut

1.	Request an application from the Connecticut Department of Consumer Protection. Resource: http://www.ct.gov/DCP/cwp/view.asp?a=1622&q=288378 Application requires owner information, building plans, photos of the building, a copy of the lease, tax number, authorization for release of financial history, statement of personal history and approval from local officials.

2.	Take several photographs of the selected property and attach the required photographs to the application for a liquor license in Connecticut. Take photographs to show the outside of the building and the neighborhood , as well as the inside where alcohol will be sold or stored.

3.	Make sketches of the property, complete with measurements to define the space where alcohol will be sold or stored. If the location is part of a larger complex, include sketches that identify where your portion of the building fits in relation to the rest of the property.

4.	Determine the type of liquor license you need. Manufacturers, distributors, bars and restaurants all operate under different licenses. Review more information about available license types on the Liquor Control Division's website.

5.	File an application for a liquor license. The application must be accompanied by a check or money order for the filing fee, which will vary depending on the type of license selected in the previous step. The address is 165 Capitol Avenue, Hartford, Connecticut. Questions can be answered by the Liquor Control Division by calling (860) 713-6210. An assigned liquor control agent will help you get started in your liquor service and will help you understand the terms of the permit.

6.	Await public reaction from the public notices posted on the property and carried in the legal notices section of the local newspaper. These notices are intended to alert the general public to the fact that a business in their area has applied for a liquor license. The public will then have an opportunity to voice an objection and any objections received will be taken into consideration when the commission makes a ruling on your application.

7.	Each person listed on the liquor license application will need to undergo an extensive background investigation to make sure that they meet the minimum qualifications to obtain a liquor license. It is important to list all legal infractions on your application, because the Liquor Control Division considers even something as minor as a speeding ticket to be a conviction. Failure to disclose any convictions may complicate the license application process.

8.	After your license has been issued by the Liquor Control Division, you will need to file a copy of the license with the local city clerk in the town where you operate the business.

Resource: Connecticut Liquor Law Library   www.jud.ct.gov/lawlib/Law/liquor.htm

How to Get a Liquor License in New Jersey

The state's liquor laws are enforced by the Division of Alcoholic Beverage Control, which is a division of the Department of Law and Public Safety, under the direction of the state Attorney General.

Liquor laws in New Jersey limit the number of liquor licenses granted based on population. A given municipality may issue only one license for on-premise consumption (bar or restaurant) per 3,000 residents and one for off-premise consumption (liquor store) per 7,500 residents. Consequently, few new licenses are issued, but if you want to open a restaurant or other establishment in the state that will serve alcoholic beverages, it is possible to get a license.

Most restaurant and club owners, retail store owners and others seeking a retail New Jersey liquor license must submit an application for a Class C license to the Alcoholic Beverage Control Board. Fees vary depending on the size of the venue, anticipated volume and whether the applicant will be using vehicles to transport alcohol. Retail liquor outlets are prohibited within 200 feet of a church or school entrance unless the license applicant gets a variance approval from a local municipal official.
Resource: http://www.nj.gov/oag/abc/downloads/abchandbook02.pdf

Procedure:
1.   Decide on the type of liquor license required. If opening a restaurant or bar, a Plenary Retail Consumption Liquor License is required. If you are opening a liquor store, you will need a Plenary Retail Distribution License. These licenses are subject to population restrictions, but other types, such as for theaters, private clubs and hotels are not.
Resource: http://www.nj.gov/oag/abc/downloads/retail-license-app-06.pdf

2.   Consider location, because the population guidelines make it very significant for liquor licenses in New Jersey. A city with a growing population offers the best chance to apply for a new license. Older communities might have more than their share of liquor establishments because of a "grandfather clause" that allows businesses in existence before passage of the 1948 legislation to remain in operation, even if they exceed the limit.

3.   Contact the Alcoholic Beverage Control Board for the city or town where you want to establish your business. Find out if a new license is an option or whether an existing one is available for purchase.
Resource: http://www.nj.gov/oag/abc/licensing-files.html

4.   Contact the current owner of the license for sale and negotiate a deal. Once you've reached a deal for transfer of ownership, file a person-to-person transfer application with the board.
Resource: Liquor License Brokers   http://www.liquorlicense.com/

5. Publish a notice of the impending sale in a local newspaper. Wait for the city to conduct a background investigation on you and the purchase you are proposing.

6. Pay the purchase price and fees upon approval. The annual renewal fee for a Plenary Retail Consumption Liquor License in New Jersey was $200 in 2010. Resource: http://www.nj.gov/oag/abc/downloads/state_licensing_fees.pdf
        (609) 984-2830

Types of NJ Liquor Licenses

According to New Jersey's Division of Alcoholic Beverage Control, there are three types of liquor licenses available in the state: retail, wholesale and manufacturing.

Plenary Retail Consumption License

Bars and restaurants that wish to serve alcohol to be consumed on the premises need a plenary retail consumption licenses. Additionally, licensees may sell alcoholic beverages, unopened and in their original packaging, for consumption off the premises. No additional commercial activity may take place on the premises outside of those activities associated with bars or restaurants. Only one of these licenses may be issued in a municipality for every 3,000 residents, though this rule does not apply to licenses obtained before 1947. Exceptions to the population restriction exist for hotels and motels, theaters, and businesses that wish to obtain a seasonal license.

Plenary Retail Distribution License

Plenary retail distribution licenses permit retail establishments such as liquor stores, beer distributors or, in limited cases, grocery and convenience stores to sell alcoholic beverages in their original, unopened containers for consumption off the premises. Only one of these licenses may be issued in a municipality for every 7,500 residents, though this rule does not apply to licenses obtained before 1947. Additional commercial activity may take place on the premises unless it's prohibited by a municipal ordinance.

Club License

A club license permits a non-profit club operating for benevolent, fraternal, social or recreational purposes to serve alcoholic beverages for consumption on the premises. No population limits are associated with this license, though a municipality may limit the number of licenses issued.

Plenary Retail Transit License

Plenary retail transit licenses permit the sale of opened alcoholic beverages for consumption on trains, airplanes, limousines and boats while the vehicle is in transit. The license is required for vehicles that are traveling through or stopping in New Jersey, whether the alcoholic beverages are sold per drink or included in the price of transportation. This is the only retail license that is issued by the director of the Division of Alcoholic Beverage Control rather than a municipality.

Wholesale License

Wholesale licenses permit the sale of large quantities of alcoholic beverages to licensed bars, restaurants and retail distribution establishments. These licenses are issued by the director of the Division of Alcoholic Beverage Control.

Manufacturing License

This license is granted to breweries, wineries, distilleries and bottling facilities in New Jersey. Licensing depends on what type of beverage is being manufactured or bottled. Licenses are granted by the director of the Division of Alcoholic Beverage Control.

How to Get a Liquor License in Arkansas

1.   Contact the Alcohol Beverage Control Administration Division in Little Rock, Arkansas, to inform the group that you want to apply for a liquor license. In summary, the mission of the Alcoholic Beverage Control Division is to exercise supervision and control over a system which allows for the legal distribution of alcoholic beverage products in the State of Arkansas.
Resource: www.dfa.arkansas.gov/offices/abc/rules/Pages/title1SubtitleC.aspx

Office	Address	Phone	Fax
Alcoholic Beverage Control Administration	1515 Building 1515 W 7th St, Ste 503 Little Rock, AR 72201	501-682-1105	501-682-2221
Alcoholic Beverage Control Enforcement	PO Box 2259 Little Rock, AR 72203	501-682-8174	501-682-3874

The mission of the Alcoholic Beverage Control Enforcement Division is to enforce all Arkansas Code Annotated Laws of the State Control Act, cigarette, sales, Rules and Regulations adopted by the Alcoholic Beverage Control Board, and the training and assistance for all law enforcement agencies as well as other organizations regarding alcoholic beverages. In addition to enforcement, the Alcoholic Beverage Control Enforcement Division conducts investigations of those persons, businesses and organizations who apply for licenses under the Alcoholic Beverage Control Act. The Alcoholic Beverage Control agents conduct inspections and report on permit applications in addition to the investigations of violations and apprehensions of violators. The agents also answer complaints and perform other special assignments; such as food stamp fraud when used to purchase alcoholic beverages. All Alcoholic Beverage Control Enforcement agents must be certified law enforcement officers.

2.   Ensure that you meet all the requirements of the state before you apply. Arkansas requires that those applying for a liquor license be free of criminal convictions, that their location has the ability to seat at least 50 people at one time and that you meet certain financial requirements.

3.   Determine which category you fall under, since Arkansas has several categories of liquor licenses. The licenses aren't the same, but rather are based on the type of business operated. For example, those opening a restaurant inside a motel fall under a different category than those operating a private club or a liquor store.

4.   Ask for an application from the ABC office in Little Rock. In some situations, you may be able to have the application sent to you if you live a significant distance away from the office. Otherwise, request an application from the head office.

5.   Complete your application using all information required by the state of Arkansas, and include any other information they need. You'll probably need to include a copy of your state ID such as a driver's license, and you may need to undergo a background or fingerprint check.

How to Obtain a Liquor License in Michigan

1.   Determine what type of license you need. There are many types available--for example, for liquor stores, clubs, taverns, hotels and golf clubs, and most categories have "classes" within them.

2.   Determine if you are seeking a liquor store license in a city that is already at its state-mandated limit. Michigan has 1,721 liquor stores as of June 2015, and the state limits licenses to one per every 3,000 people in each municipality.

3.   Inquire at your local municipality or attend a city, township or village board meeting to inquire about local laws, limits and restrictions on new liquor licenses.

4.   The process of obtaining a Michigan liquor license involves the Michigan Liquor Control Commission (MLCC) and obtaining local recommendations from the local municipality in support of your application.

5.   Before spending money applying for the liquor license, perform the research with the MLCC and your municipality to find out about your chances of acquiring a license.

6.   Be aware that most municipalities limit permits according to proximity to other bars, restaurants, schools and churches, and they thoroughly research the applicant's background, including long ago misdemeanor offenses.

7.   Consider hiring an attorney.

8.   Be particularly aware of parking issues at your establishment, including adequacy of handicapped parking, access and exit venues and capacity.

9.   Be prepared for police and fire inspectors, who will visit the place of business to look closely at the parking issue and other safety factors, inside and outside of the building.

10.   Collect the documentation needed to apply for a liquor license, which includes location photos (inside and outside) and real estate documents of the establishment, building or site plans if the facility isn't complete, documents of individual or partner status, a spousal application, money for investigation fees and a host of other individual background and business identification documents.

11.   Request an application from the MLCC, by calling, writing to the commission's Lansing office or making the request online.

12.   Complete the application, which will include an application fee of up to $1,000 and a required $70 investigative fee.

13.   Be prepared for the application process to take 90 to 180 days, although local

obstacles at the investigative stage will often cause added delays.

14.   If denied a license, appeal the ruling within 20 days of the judgment.

Resources:
Michigan Department of Consumer & Industry Services
MICHIGAN LIQUOR CONTROL COMMISSION (MLCC)
7150 Harris Drive, P.O. Box 30005 - Lansing, Michigan 48909-7505

INDIVIDUAL OR PARTNERSHIP REQUEST FOR APPLICATION
http://www.michigan.gov/documents/CIS_Cis_LCC_lc-2096_27070_7.pdf

CORPORATION / LIMITED LIABILITY COMPANY REQUEST FOR
APPLICATION
http://www.michigan.gov/documents/CIS_Cis_LCC_lc-2097_27072_7.pdf

Frequently Asked Questions
http://www.michigan.gov/dleg/0,1607,7-154-10570_16941-40899--,00.html#lic

Retail Liquor Licenses
http://www.michigan.gov/documents/cis_lcc_mlccpub2_150372_7.pdf

Application for New Licenses
http://www.michigan.gov/documents/dleg/LC687_233944_7.pdf

How to Get a Liquor License in Missouri

1. Determine the type of liquor license needed. There are several types of licenses available. The most common types are By-The-Drink, Package, Wholesaler and Manufacturer. If you have a retail, or By-The-Drink license, you will be further classified as either Tavern, Place of Entertainment, Place of Amusement, Restaurant/Bar or Caterer.

2. Identify the District that your business operates in, because liquor licenses are managed and enforced on a district level. Each district has its own office for applications, fees, questions and complaints. You can identify the district that relates to your business by visiting the website for the Missouri Division of Alcohol and Tobacco Control.

3. Contact the Agent of your district to obtain the necessary application forms. The agent will need to read and sign the application to help prevent any oversights before it reaches the ATC office. You will also need to attach a passport size photo of yourself to the application, as well as a postcard sized photograph of the location where you intend to sell liquor.

4. Submit the completed application, along with a check or money order for the required fees. The typical application fee for a liquor license in St. Louis is $230; fees vary depending on the type of license you need. This will need to be submitted directly to the Supervisor of Liquor Control, Jefferson City, MO, 65101. The amount of the fees may vary from one district to another, so check with your agent to determine the appropriate fee to send with your application. The liquor license application fee is nonrefundable.

5. The Missouri Division of Alcohol and Tobacco Control will review your application, the history of your property, and any city ordinances that may affect your license. If you have reason to believe that you are not a person of "good moral character," they may request fingerprints, which will be used in a criminal history search. A liquor license will not be issued if the surrounding neighborhood does not support the issuance of the license. Additionally, many towns in Missouri have a City Ordinance preventing the sale of alcohol within 300 feet of a school or church. If your establishment falls within these boundaries, you will be required to submit, with your application, written consent from the majority of members on the board of the school or church you are near

6. Upon successfully reviewing your application, assuming there is no reason for them to deny the application, a license will be issued directly to you from the Supervisor of Liquor Control.

Missouri Division of Alcohol and Tobacco Control

http://www.atc.dps.mo.gov/index.asp

The liquor control laws and the state's system of alcoholic beverage regulations are designed to ensure the public health and safety as affected by alcoholic beverages. ATC supervises the collection of state revenue derived from alcoholic beverage excise taxes and license fees. Additionally, state statutes mandate that ATC protect the consumer from tainted alcoholic beverages and the liquor industry from infiltration and exploitation by the criminal element.

Missouri has no specific state limitations on the places where alcohol may be sold "off-premises" (i.e. for consumption elsewhere). As a result, Missouri is famous in the region for grocery stores, drug stores, and even gas stations throughout the state which sell a wide variety of beer, wine, and liquor. As long as it is not located within 300 feet of a school or church, virtually any retail business, including a vague and undefined "general merchandise store", which obtains the proper licenses from the Division of Alcohol and Tobacco Control and local authorities may sell any type of alcohol. State law even forbids a local option and prohibits cities and counties from banning the off-premises sale of alcohol.

Missouri does, however, limit the hours of retail alcohol sales to between 6:00 AM and 1:30 AM Monday through Saturday, and - for an additional license fee - between 9:00 AM and midnight on Sunday. Most municipalities, including St. Louis and Kansas City have enacted local laws following the state law, which prohibit the retail sale of liquor between 1:30 AM and 6:00 AM Tuesday through Saturday, and between midnight on Sunday and 9:00 AM the following morning.

No Missouri law prohibits establishments from holding both off-premises and on-premises licenses. As a result, some businesses are licensed to sell liquor both "by the drink" (individually for consumption on premises) and "by the package" (by the container for consumption off premises). Effectively, these are bars which double as liquor stores. In these places, off-premises sales are allowed until 1:30 a.m., even in those in St. Louis and Kansas City specially licensed to serve liquor by the drink until 3:00 a.m. (on-premises sales may continue until 3:00, but off-premises sales must cease by 1:30).

On-premises sales

Generally, the hours for sales of liquor by the drink (for consumption on the premises) are the same as liquor by the package: between 6:00 AM and 1:30 AM Monday through Saturday, and - again for an additional fee - between 9:00 AM and midnight on Sunday. State law allows incorporated cities to prohibit the on-premises sale of liquor by public referendum, although no city in Missouri ever has held such a referendum. The on-premises sale of liquor is allowed throughout the state, without any limitation except for the hours when sale is permitted.

Shipping

Except for wine, Missouri places no limitations on the interstate shipping of alcohol into the state, as long the alcohol is in a quantity less than five gallons, has been lawfully manufactured in its source jurisdiction, and is shipped to a person who is at least 21 years of age. There are no quantity limits whatsoever for shipments which are entirely within Missouri or which are made by licensed Missouri alcohol retailers.

Bulk shipments

To ship alcohol into Missouri in quantities greater than five gallons, both the commercial carrier doing the shipping and the sender itself must obtain a "transporter's license" from the Missouri Department of Revenue and pay the necessary licensing fees. Additionally, for such shipments, the commercial carrier must be generally licensed to do business by the Department of Economic Development. In practice, ordinary commercial shippers like FedEx and UPS have the necessary licenses.

Special regulations for wine shipments

An alcohol retailer licensed in Missouri or in any other state which has similar, "reciprocal" wine-shipping laws may ship up to two cases of wine each year to any Missouri resident over the age of 21, provided that the wine is for personal use and not for resale. Such a delivery is deemed not to be a sale in Missouri. Otherwise, for direct shipments of wine from a winery, a wine manufacturer licensed in Missouri or any other state can obtain a "wine direct shipper license" from the Division of Alcohol and Tobacco Control which lets that manufacturer ship up to two cases of wine per month to any person in Missouri who is at least 21 years of age. Unlike shipments under the "reciprocal" provision, for shipments under this provision, the wine manufacturer must use a licensed alcohol carrier.

How to Get a Liquor License in Colorado

In order to obtain a liquor license in Colorado, retailers are required to first get approval at the local government level. After the local licensing authority has approved the license, it is passed onto the state's Liquor Enforcement Division for approval. Because this process can take several months, it is important to communicate with the local licensing authority well in advance of the opening date.

Resources: www.colorado.gov/cs/Satellite/Rev-Liquor/LIQ/1206696331368
www.colorado.gov/cs/Satellite?c=Page&cid=1210151340944&pagename=Rev-Liquor%2FLIQLayout

The applicant must fill out a liquor license application for the Colorado Department of Revenue and submit it to selected Colorado County. The form can be downloaded from their website. Besides the application, the applicant will need to provide information for a background check of each person in the business partnership, LLC or corporation. For the background check, he or she can download an Individual History Record form from the Department of Revenue website. The applicant must also submit their fingerprints to the sheriff's office as part of the background check process.

Resource: http://www.colorado.gov/revenue/liquor

The applicant must file the application materials, along with checks to cover the County and Colorado Department of Revenue liquor license fees, to the County Clerk and Recorder's Office. Besides the filled-out forms and the checks, he or she will also need to submit copies of their articles of incorporation or partnership agreement; certification that the corporation is in good standing with the Secretary of State's Office; a certificate of residency if the business will be in a new or newly-remodeled building; and a diagram of the premises where liquor will be served. If leasing the property, the applicant will need to supply a copy of the lease that shows authorization to serve liquor. If a manager other than a partner or officer of the corporation will be responsible for the business, he or she will need to submit a copy of the management agreement.

While at the courthouse, the applicant should also schedule a public hearing for their license. It cannot be less than 30 days after submitting the relevant information and fees, and a legal ad must be run 10 days prior to the hearing.

Process Overview:

1. The applicant must meet basic requirements and qualifications. Background investigations will be performed to review the applicant's criminal history, liquor license violation history, ownership interests in other liquor industry members, and tax payment history.

2. The applicant must determine the type of alcohol he or she would like to sell and to whom the liquor is going to be sold. There are many types of liquor licenses: brew pub, beer and wine, club license, race track, tavern license, special events permit, retail liquor store, hotel and restaurant license, and more. Applications for each license type differ.

3. In order to apply for the alcohol license, the applicant must contact the clerk for the town or city in which he or she wants to do business in. The clerk will supply the appropriate application and information about legal requirements.

4. After making application, the clerk will publish the application in the local newspaper to see whether there are any objections in the community. The licensing authority then will vote on the application for approval.

5. The next step is to pay the licensing fee, which is set by local municipalities. The applicant must contact the local clerk of the selected city or town for specific fees.

How to Get a Liquor License in New Hampshire

The New Hampshire Liquor Commission controls all liquor licensing in the state of New Hampshire. In order to obtain a liquor license in New Hampshire, the applicant must be over 21 and a U.S. citizen or registered alien, and not have any felony convictions. The application process starts at the New Hampshire Liquor Commission website.

Resources: http://www.nh.gov/liquor/applicantprocess.shtml
Fee Schedule: http://www.gencourt.state.nh.us/rsa/html/XIII/178/178-29.htm
Application: http://www.nh.gov/liquor/License_application_form.shtml

1.   The applicant must go to the New Hampshire Liquor Commission website and read the retail application process page. After reading the page, select the type of liquor license wanted.

2.   To complete the online application, the applicant must have all of their business and personal information on hand before starting the application. He or she will be asked to choose the type of application, which is determined by how the liquor will be sold. The information required on the application will differ based on the application type. Print the completed the application.

3.   The applicant must mail the application along with the nonrefundable processing fee. As of April 2015, the fee is $100 and can be paid by check or money order. There may be other fees depending on the type of liquor license applied for.

4.   After the application has been processed, the licensing commission will ask for additional paperwork and permits.
        Mail to: NHSLC, Division of Enforcement
                         P.O. Box 1795
                         Concord, NH 03302

5.   Gather together all paperwork and permits that the New Hampshire Liquor Commission request. Call the Licensing Help Desk 603-271-3521. Someone there will contact an investigator to inspect the location where liquor will be sold. The investigator will contact you directly to set up an appointment; it is important that you provide a valid phone number where you can be reached.

6.   After the inspection is complete the investigator will give a recommendation of licensing to the Help Desk.

7.   After the investigator has approved your premises and sent her report to the Help Desk, call to schedule the final appointment. The Help Desk representative will tell you what documents and information is needed for this final appointment, and will be able to answer any additional questions you have. If you have met all requirements and provided all requested information, after final appointment the liquor license will be issued.

Opening a Liquor Store in Texas

There are basically three types of liquor licenses in the state of Texas: on premises, off premises and temporary. The requirements vary for each. An additional license is required for any liquor with an alcohol content greater than 15.5 percent. The liquor must be sold in a county or municipality that is considered "wet."

On-Premise Permits

Business owners applying for a liquor license in Texas which allows for on-site alcohol consumption must fill out and submit Form L-ON, published by the TABC. All on-premise liquor license applications must include a certificate for late hours operation from either the county or city clerk, whichever is appropriate. On-premise retailer permits for excursion boats, buffets or club cars offering wine and beer must include a county clerk certificate verifying the alcohol content of the drinks offered. Food and dining establishments, as well as the previously mentioned retailers, must also obtain a county or city clerk certificate verifying that the business for which the on-premise permit is awarded is in a wet area for legal alcohol consumption.

Off-Premise Permits

Applications for the retail sale of alcohol which isn't consumed on the business premises must fill out Form L-OFF and submit it to the Texas Alcoholic Beverage Commission. Retail stores selling alcohol for off-site consumption must also obtain certification from the city or county clerk that the area within which business is being operated is considered a wet area. Package stores, which can only sell sealed alcoholic containers, must publish notice of their opening in a qualified local newspaper.

Temporary Permits

Festivals, fairs or any other short-term event where alcohol will be sold must apply for a temporary TABC liquor license. Temporary alcohol permits in Texas are awarded either to current liquor license holders who want to hold an event at a site other than their business facilities or to civic, charitable or religious organizations holding a special event. Temporary liquor license applications can be downloaded from the TABC website or are available at local TABC offices. Temporary licenses are not required for events where alcohol is offered free to adults.

The Texas Alcoholic Beverage Commission

TABC is responsible for enforcing requirements and laws pertaining to the sale of alcoholic beverages---whether at a restaurant, convenience or grocery store, liquor store, or nightclub---in the state of Texas. The state issues about 100,000 licenses and permits each year, according to the TABC. The TABC also issues temporary permits for fundraising events. Anyone who manufactures, distributes or sells alcohol in the state of Texas must have the necessary licenses and permits from the TABC.

Types of Liquor Licenses

There are three types of liquor licenses in the state of Texas: on premises, off premises and temporary. The requirements vary for each. An additional license is required for any liquor with an alcohol content greater than 15.5 percent. The liquor must be sold in a county or municipality that is considered "wet."

Eligibility

Any U.S. resident who is 21 years or older and law-abiding qualifies for a retail liquor license or permit in the state of Texas, according to the TABC.

Fees

Fees for a liquor license in Texas range from $1,426 for a package store to $6,512 mixed beverage provider, with licenses for each lasting up to two years. There also may be other fees paid to the municipality in which the business exists.

Initial Requirements

An application must be filled out, and certification from the state comptroller, city secretary and county clerk must be obtained. The county judge must hold a hearing or the provider must obtain a waiver. Permit bonds may be required as well as anything else requested by the TABC. The application for both on-premises and off-premises businesses is available at http://www.tabc.state.tx.us/licensing/index.asp.

Additional Requirements

The Alcoholic Beverage Code in Texas includes notification requirements for municipalities that include hospitals, public and private schools, and day care centers. Requirements vary from city to city but generally fall within 300 to 1,000 feet.

TABC Contacts

The TABC has five regional divisions that serve major cities as well as their surrounding areas: West, which serves Lubbock, Amarillo, El Paso, Odessa, Abilene and the surrounding area; Northeast, which serves Dallas, Fort Worth, Longview and Nacogdoches; Southeast, which serves Houston, Beaumont, Conroe and Huntsville; Central, which serves Austin, Waco, Victoria and Brazoria; and South, which serves San Antonio, Corpus Christi and the Rio Grande Valley. Contact the office in your area to request application materials or call the TABC's main switchboard at 512-206-3333.

License Acquisition Steps

1.   Establish a business by registering as a corporation, sole proprietorship or partnership. Secure a federal employer identification number from the Internal Revenue Service and a sales tax permit from the Texas Comptroller of Public Accounts. Contact the office in your area to request application materials or call the TABC's main switchboard at 512-206-3333. Before 2007, only state residents could obtain alcoholic beverage licenses. That law has changed, but U.S.

citizenship or legal permanent resident status is still required. Only corporations registered by the state may qualify for licensing.

2.   Find a suitable location, preferably one in a high-traffic area. The Alcoholic Beverage Code in Texas includes notification requirements for municipalities that include hospitals, public and private schools, and day care centers. Requirements vary from city to city but generally fall within 300 to 1,000 feet. Locations farther than 1,000 feet from a public school must be bonded for $5,000, while those closer must be bonded for $5,000.
Resource: www.tabc.state.tx.us/licensing/bonds.asp

3.   Sign a lease or purchase contract for your chosen location. If possible, make the lease or contract contingent upon receiving a liquor license.

4.   Schedule a pre-licensing interview with the Texas Alcoholic Beverage Commission (TABC). Your partners and other investors should be present at the interview, which will outline your responsibilities as a liquor retailer while explaining and providing materials necessary to your application.
Resource: www.tabc.state.tx.us/publications/licensing/GuideRetailers.pdf

5.   Post provided notices prominently in the windows of the location for 60 days before receiving your liquor license, if the location hasn't sold liquor for the past two years. This 60-day sign must be prominently displayed so it notifies the public about the upcoming licensing hearing. At this time, arrange for inspectors from the TABC to inspect the location, as required by law.

6.   Obtain a small-business loan or other financing if necessary. Most lenders will require you to present your business plan and personal credit rating, so they can be certain you're not likely to default on your investment.

7.   Pay fees and other charges necessary to obtain a liquor license. In Dallas, Harris and Tarrant counties, total fees amount to $2,470 for retailers, as of 2015. In all other counties, fees total $820. Fees for a liquor license in Texas range from $1,426 for a package store to $6,512 mixed beverage provider, with licenses for each lasting up to two years.

8.   Locate a suitable beer, wine and liquor distributor to serve your store. Larger companies, such as the major breweries, may handle their own distribution rather than working through a third party, so you may need to work with several vendors. Distributors can be located online or in the phone book under "alcoholic beverage distributors."

9.   Attend a licensing hearing at your county courthouse. Your application must be approved in court, and members of the public are allowed to raise objections to the licensing at this time.

10.   Contact your chosen distributors and place your initial orders. Many distributors may be able to guide first-time orders to ensure you select a variety of brands that are most likely to sell.

11.   The Texas Alcoholic Beverage Code issues temporary permits in two scenarios:
     TABC retail permit holders may be eligible to obtain a temporary permit to sell or serve alcoholic beverages at an event taking place at a location separate from their TABC-licensed premises.
     Civic, religious or charitable organizations may be eligible to obtain a temporary permit to sell or serve alcoholic beverages at a special event not being held on

TABC-licensed premises.
Resource: www.tabc.state.tx.us/licensing/fundraising_and_temporary_permits.asp
12.   Stock your store and open it for business.

Types of Texas Liquor Permits

BQ Permit

Retailers that sell both beer and wine that will not be consumed on the property of the establishment require a liquor license called a BQ permit. The volume of alcohol in the beverages sold may not exceed 17% by volume.

Q Permit

Q permits only allow a retailer to sell wine that is to be consumed off the premises of the seller. Stores with this permit are allowed to sell wine that has an alcohol content of 24%.

BF Permit

BF permits are very similar to the Q permit and are often authorized in combination as a BF/Q permit. The BF permit, however, pertains to beer rather than wine. Again, this permit is only for beverages that will be consumed off premises.

BF/P Permit

The BF/P permit is issued to liquor stores in Texas. This permit authorizes the liquor store to sell liquor, beer and wine to be consumed off premises.

MB Permit

An MB permit allows a bar or restaurant to sell mixed drinks, beer, wine and liquor. The beverages served in the establishment with an MB permit may be consumed on site. This permit falls under a special category since they are figured at a different tax rate.

BG Permit

BG permits authorize a restaurant or bar to sell beer and wine that can be consumed on and off site. There are areas in Texas that allow individuals to purchase a drink, walk down the street and enter another bar. These businesses would carry a BG permit.

BE Permits

Permits that allow a restaurant or bar to sell beer for consumption on site while also allowing them to sell beer to go must apply for a BE permit. In order to leave the establishment with alcohol, the beer must remain unopened.

Other Permits

Besides the more common licenses listed above, there are brewer permits, airline permits, caterers permits, warehousing permits, manufacturers permits, distillers permits, mini-bar permits, passenger train permits, and the list keeps going. The Texas Alcoholic Beverage Commission website provides a large list of the available permits..

How to Get a Liquor License in Illinois

1. Request and fill out the necessary forms to get an Illinois liquor license. Request these forms from the State of Illinois Liquor Control Commission.
    Resource: www.state.il.us/lcc/licensediv.asp
    Forms: www.state.il.us/lcc/viewall.asp

2. In order to qualify for the Illinois liquor license, the applicant must have the completed retail liquor license application, pay the $500 fee for the license, have their local liquor license, Bulk Sales Release Order, Vender Employer Identification Number, Illinois Business Tax Number and a Federal Employer Identification Number. The applicant will also need to show a photocopy of a Certificate of Insurance for the place of business.
    Resource: www2.illinois.gov/business/Pages/default.aspx

3. Research all of the permits needed or if any additional types of liquor licenses are required. This can be determined by calling the State of Illinois Liquor Control Commission at 312-814-2206 or 217-782-2136. The applicant can also find the information about the permits and applications on the State of Illinois Liquor Control Commission's website.

4. Send the application to the Illinois Liquor Control Commission at the following address:
    100 W Randolph St., Suite 7-801, Chicago, IL 60601

5. Study the rules and regulations of the Illinois Liquor Control Commission as posted on their website. Make sure to follow the liquor laws, or else the applicant will risk getting the liquor license fined, suspended or revoked.

6. The applicant should get familiar with the Industry Education Division. They work together with the Illinois Liquor Control Commission to educate the liquor industry about the various liquor laws in the state of Illinois. They also publish informative literature and conduct alcohol presentations in many cities and counties throughout Illinois.

How to Get a Liquor License in Illinois

1. Request and fill out the necessary forms to get an Illinois liquor license. Request these forms from the State of Illinois Liquor Control Commission.
    Resources: www.state.il.us/lcc/licensediv.asp
                  www.springfield.il.us/license/default.htm
    Forms: www.state.il.us/lcc/viewall.asp

2. In order to qualify for the Illinois liquor license, the applicant must have the completed retail liquor license application, pay the $500 fee for the license, have their local liquor license, Bulk Sales Release Order, Vender Employer Identification Number, Illinois Business Tax Number and a Federal Employer Identification Number. The applicant will also need to show a photocopy of a Certificate of Insurance for the place of business.
    Resource: www2.illinois.gov/business/Pages/default.aspx

3. Research all of the permits needed or if any additional types of liquor licenses are required. This can be determined by calling the State of Illinois Liquor Control Commission at 312-814-2206 or 217-782-2136. The applicant can also find the information about the permits and applications on the State of Illinois Liquor Control Commission's website.

4. Send the application to the Illinois Liquor Control Commission at the following address:
    100 W Randolph St., Suite 7-801, Chicago, IL 60601

5. Study the rules and regulations of the Illinois Liquor Control Commission as posted on their website. Make sure to follow the liquor laws, or else the applicant will risk getting the liquor license fined, suspended or revoked.

6. The applicant should get familiar with the Industry Education Division. They work together with the Illinois Liquor Control Commission to educate the liquor industry about the various liquor laws in the state of Illinois. They also publish informative literature and conduct alcohol presentations in many cities and counties throughout Illinois.

7. The Beverage Alcohol Sellers and Servers Education and Training (BASSET) program is the state of Illinois' seller/server training program. The program is an educational and training tool to sellers/servers of alcoholic beverages to serve responsibly and stay within the law. The BASSET Certification Program serves as a preventive measure to discourage over consumption and keep drunk drivers off the roads.
    Resources: www.bassetcertification.org/
                  www.servercertificationcorp.com/state.php?statecode='il'

Steps in the Liquor License Application Process

The liquor license application process is outlined below. Please note that a Business Consultant will assist and guide you through the application process.

Step 1:   **Getting Started**

You must request an appointment to meet with a Business Consultant. A pre-scheduled appointment is required for any liquor or amusement license applications. We are located at: Department of Business Affairs and Consumer Protection
     121 N. LaSalle St., City Hall, Room 800, Chicago, IL 60602
     312-74-GOBIZ (744-6249)

The Department of Business Affairs and Consumer Protection is open Monday–Friday 8:30 A.M-4:30 P.M. You can schedule an appointment by calling 312-74-GOBIZ (744-6249) or request an appointment online. Your appointment will be confirmed via email within one (1) business day from receipt of the original request.

At your first meeting, your Business Consultant will ask you a series of questions regarding the ownership of your business, what type of business you want to open and the exact location you wish to do business. You should be prepared to answer these questions and provide the information requested in the Business License Information Form. Please complete the BIS form and bring it with you to your meeting. During this meeting a Business Consultant will explain the entire application process in detail. You will be given an application and a checklist of required documents that must be submitted within 30 days after you have filed your written license application. This information is also available in this guide and on the city's website. Please prepare as much of this information as possible and bring it with you to your meeting.

If you are purchasing an existing business with a liquor license, you may need to request a Type III Change of Ownership/Shareholders application.

Step 2:   **Determine if your business is located in a restricted area**

You are strongly encouraged to determine if a liquor license is permitted in a location before investing in any business. There are several different types of restrictions that may prevent you from obtaining a liquor license in the City of Chicago. On your first visit, a business consultant will help determine if your proposed business location is in a restricted area. Precincts that have been voted dry do not permit the sale of any alcohol. Moratorium areas, located throughout the City, also prohibit the issuance of new Tavern, Packaged Goods, Incidental Consumption on Premises, and Club licenses in certain areas in each ward. A liquor license of any type is not permitted within 100 ft. of a school, church, daycare center or library.

Step 3:   **Complete the Written Application/Zoning Review**

To begin the liquor license application process, you are required to complete the written application. You should also be prepared to submit a detailed floor and business site plan to your case manager. The Department of Zoning will review your written application and floor and site plans to determine if liquor sales are allowed at your business location. Your case manager will present your application and floor and site plans to the Department of Zoning on your behalf.

You may review the zoning classification of your proposed business location at http://www.cityofchicago.org/zoning.

Step 4:   File the Written Application
Once you have secured approval from the Department of Zoning, you are permitted to file your application with the Department of Business Affairs & Consumer Protection (BACP) and pay the required license application fees. The date you file your application is known as your application file date. You will have 30 days from your application file date to submit all of the Required Documents.
Once you have filed your written application, your business consultant will provide you a list of all required documents, schedule all required inspections, and prepare all required public notifications, including notice to all legal voters residing within 250 feet of your business location.

Step 5: Task Force Inspections
Liquor license applicants are required to pass inspections from the Departments of Health, Fire and Buildings, plumbing and ventilation. These inspections are also known as "Task Force Inspections." Your case manager will schedule these inspections at a time convenient for you. A representative of the business must be available at the scheduled time. You should be prepared for an inspection when you file your written application.

Step 6: Police Background Check
All liquor license applicants are required to undergo a police background check. Your case manager will schedule an appointment for the business owner(s) and officers to meet with a police officer. During this meeting, each person who owns 5% or more interest in the business will be fingerprinted. The corporate officers, authorized manager, and any other person loaning or giving more than 10% interest in the business will also be fingerprinted. Spouses of owners with a 5% or greater share of the business are required to submit a completed Spousal Affidavit. The police may also conduct an interview with the license applicants.

The police officer will review the financial and business information provided in the application file, and the results of the criminal background check, to determine if the owners/officers of the business are eligible to hold a liquor license. The Illinois Liquor Control Act prohibits the issuance of a liquor license to persons who have been convicted of a felony and some types of misdemeanors.

The police will also conduct an inspection of your establishment to determine if your business is located within 100 feet of a church, school, library or home of the aged, or library.

Step 7: Public Notifications

Within 5 days of the application file date, the Department of Business Affairs and Consumer Protection is required to notify all of the registered voters residing within 250 ft. of the proposed business location by mail. The notification informs the public that an application for liquor license has been filed. The public has the opportunity to provide comments or submit written objections to the Department of Business Affairs and Consumer Protection. The public has 40 days to submit comments and/or written objections. Negative community response may result in the denial of a liquor license. No liquor license will be issued until the public comment period has expired. The public comment period ends 45 days after the application is filed.

The Department of Business Affairs and Consumer Protection is responsible for sending notice to the alderman and the police district commander. The notification informs the alderman and police commander that an application for liquor license has been filed. Finally, the Department of Revenue will publish a legal notice in a daily newspaper of general circulation in the city, four times over a two-week period.

Step 8: Submit Required Documents

Once you have filed your written application with the Department of Business Affairs and Consumer Protection, you will have 30 days in which to submit all applicable Required Documents. Your business consultant will provide a list of required documents. You will be sent a weekly reminder notice indicating all of the outstanding documents that are required to complete your application. You will receive this notice once per week until the expiration of your 30-day document submission time period.

During this 30-day document submission period, you should be working closely with your case manager to submit all required documents. Please be aware that the Department of Business Affairs and Consumer Protection must review all documents for accuracy and cannot guarantee that the 30-day deadline will be met unless all required documents are received for review within 25 days of your application file date. You are strongly encouraged to submit all required documents as soon as possible, as application fees are not refundable due to failure to meet the 30-day timeline.

Failure to submit all of the required documents within 30 days of your application file date, will suspend further processing of your application. Applicants will have the option to reactivate the application by submitting a $500 reactivation fee. You will have up to six months from your application file date to reactivate your application. If you fail to reactivate your application within 6 months, you will forfeit your license application fee. In order to apply for a liquor license after the 6-month period has lapsed, you must submit a new application and start the process over again. You will not be eligible for a refund of any previously paid application fees.

Step 9: Application Review

Once the entire application and all its contents have been submitted, the Department of Business Affairs and Consumer Protection / Local Liquor Control Commission is required to review the application materials, as well as any community objections, and issue a decision on the license application within a maximum of 60 days from the date you submitted all required documents. A license can be issued as early as 45 days from your application file date. If you are denied a license you have the right to file an appeal before the License Appeal Commission within 20 days of the denial.

Resource: www.cityofchicago.org/city/en/depts/bacp/supp_info/steps_in_the_
                    liquorlicenseapplicationprocess.html

The Procedures for Obtaining a Liquor License in Illinois

By *Article provided by Ciesla and Ciesla, PC.*

In the state of Illinois, there are number of steps an applicant must take in order to obtain a liquor license. However, before the process begins, an applicant will have to determine what type of liquor license it needs, and if any additional related licenses are needed. There are a number of different types of liquor licenses, including those for taverns, packaged goods (mainly for liquor stores), caterers, or private clubs. Related licenses may include those for food service, live entertainment, late hours or even gaming equipment, such as pinball machines, pool tables, etc. Each type of license involves different fees and requirements.

After determining what type of liquor license best suits their business, the applicant must request the application or applications for the city, district or municipality in which the license is intended for use. In some cases, municipalities may not even issue an application until the applicant makes a presentation before the Board of Trustees or Village staff. It is often helpful for the applicant to meet with the city's business license department, economic development director, or other municipal staff member who will explain the application process and any other requirements.

In many cases the initial meeting is informal, as the applicant may be required to provide answers to standard questions on a pre-printed form, in other cases, an applicant may need to make a thorough presentation, including the businesses' value to the community (economic impact, job creation), size, hours of operation, floor plan, target market, menu, managerial experience, etc.

As part of the process, the applicant should investigate the types of restrictions that may impede or prevent a business from obtaining a liquor license, as license restrictions and special regulations are set by both cities and the State of Illinois. In Chicago, there are some areas of City wards which have a moratorium, a prohibition on the issuance of a particular class of liquor license, for example packaged goods or a tavern license, while that area may permit a restaurant with an incidental liquor sales license. In the entire State of Illinois, a liquor license will not be issued to a business that is located within 100 feet of a school, church, hospital, daycare, library, or nursing home.

As part of the license application, the city's zoning department or its municipal equivalent may require the applicant to submit a floor plan and business site plan. In most cases, liquor license applicants will be required to pass scheduled inspections from the plumbing and ventilation department, fire department and health department and undergo a police background check. Chicago and many municipalities require the owner, manager and even staff to be trained to be a responsible server – or present proof that he/she is BASST trained.

Once the applicant has been issued a liquor license from the city or municipality, the business must file an application with the Illinois Liquor Control Commission and pay the required fees. Applicants are also required to register with the Alcohol Tobacco Tax and Trade Bureau of the United States Department of Treasury.

After receiving all necessary licenses and permits, the business must comply with the rules and regulations of the both the municipality and the ILCC. Any violation of these rules could result in a fine, or a suspension or revocation of the liquor license. Businesses that develop a reputation for harboring violent behavior or require constant police presence due to violence or other lawbreaking practices also risk revocation of the their liquor licenses.

It is important that a business with a liquor license is pro-active and has policies and procedures in place to prevent violations, including service to minors and over service. Many companies use ID scanning technology, install digital security cameras, use cash register software that prevents a sale unless an ID is checked, offer regular training to employees, require employees to sign contracts when they are hired explaining the business' alcohol policies, and more. Once your business receives the licenses, you need to do all you can to protect it.

Resource: http://library.findlaw.com/2009/Feb/2/247304.html

How to Get a Liquor License in Massachusetts

1. Determine if liquor licenses are available in the selected area. Nearly all of Massachusetts issues liquor licenses, but there are 14 cities that do not. The following cities will not issue a liquor license: Alford, Chilmark, Dunstable, Gay Head, Gosnold, Hawley, Montgomery, Mount Washington, Tisbury, West Tisbury, Westhampton and Weston.
    Resource: http://www.mass.gov/abcc/faqs.htm

2. Select the type of license that is appropriate for the business venture, as there are a number of licensing options. Bars need a very different license than distributors. The Alcoholic Beverages Control Commission (ABCC) has information on its website about what kind of license is required for each type of business.
    Resources:
    Alcoholic Beverages Control Commission   www.mass.gov/abcc/
    License Types: www.mass.gov/abcc/licensing/lic_type.htm

3. Apply for an on-site retail license if you plan to open a restaurant, bar or other establishment that serves liquor on the premises. This license entitles you to sell liquor, but your customers may not carry the liquor off the property. Apply for an off-site retail license if you intend to sell liquor for consumers to use elsewhere (e.g., a liquor store).

4. Start by submitting the application for a liquor license at the local city level. Contact your local mayor's office for more specific details about the address for submitting a license and the hours that applications are accepted. Be ready for a brief interview at the time that the application is submitted.

5. After your application is approved at the local level, city officials will forward the application to the ABCC. The ABCC will conduct a criminal history check and make a final ruling as to whether a liquor license will be issued.

6. After final approval from the ABCC, the liquor license will be sent back to the city office where the applicant made their initial application. All fees related to the issuance of the license will be made at, and payable to, the city office at the time the license is picked up. As of 2010, the application fee for Massachusetts is $200.

MA Liquor Laws

No individual, partnership, or corporation may have more than three off-premises licenses in the state, nor more than two in any city, nor more than one in any town.

On-premises regulations: No discounts at specific times (i.e. no "Happy Hour" discounts) or for specific individuals, no fixed-price open bar or all-you-can-drink (except at private functions), no more than two drinks per individual at any one time, no pitchers for fewer than two people, no drinking contests, no drinks as prizes, no free drinks.

Off-premises sale of alcohol is prohibited on the last Monday in May (Memorial Day), Thanksgiving Day, Christmas Day, and the day after Christmas if Christmas falls on a Sunday. Sale of alcohol is prohibited during polling hours on election days (subject to local exceptions).
"Malt beverages" defined as having not more than 12% alcohol by weight.

Alcohol Sales Hours
On Premises:
8:00 a.m.–2:00 a.m. by state law, although individual cities and towns may prohibit sales before 11:00 a.m. and after 11:00 p.m Not before noon on Sunday.

Off Premises:
8:00 a.m.–11:00 p.m., or 8:00 a.m.–11:30 p.m. on the day before a holiday. Not before noon on Sunday.

Beer Sales: No

How to Get a New York Liquor Store License

The New York State Liquor Authority requires that all applicants be a U.S. citizen or permanent resident alien. In addition, you must be at least 21 years old. Applicants must not be a law enforcement officer with powers to arrest. Felons are not allowed to apply unless they have a Certificate of Release from Civil Disabilities. If you fail to meet any of these criteria, you will be denied a liquor license in New York.

1. Make sure your establishment is not within 200 feet of a church, school, synagogue or any other place of worship if you're looking to get a liquor license.

2. Download the application form at the New York State Liquor Authority website. You can also contact the Licensing Division and request the liquor license application by mail.

3. Complete an application in its entirety and include the application fee. Be sure that you submit the application to the Zone Office that supports the county where your business will be located. There are four zones: Zone 1, Zone 2, Zone 3 and Syracuse District.
    Resource: http://www.abc.state.ny.us/contact-directory#zone_offices

4. The application requires the disclosure of a great amount of detail regarding your intended operation and it's owners, managers, lenders, donors and investors. Additionally, you will be required to submit a Certificate of Occupancy for the Premise (or a letter of no objection from the Department of Buildings), the original certified mailing card, penal bond, photographs of all rooms and the exterior, the lease for the premise, proof of citizenship, diagrams, bank statements, certificate of authority to collect sales tax, workers compensation and disability insurance policies and a proposed menu (if a restaurant).
    New York Search Resources:
    www.trans.abc.state.ny.us/JSP/query/PublicQueryNameSearchPage.jsp
    www.trans.abc.state.ny.us/JSP/query/PublicQueryPrincipalSearchPage.jsp

5. In September of 2009, the NYSLA initiated an Attorney Self Certification Program. This program allows attorneys to self certify an application that they file by requiring the attorney to verify and attest as to accuracy of the information and the documentation contained in the application. This allows the NYSLA to bypass the lengthy investigation and grant the approval of the liquor license application in just weeks as opposed to six months. Hire an experienced liquor license attorney to prepare and file your liquor license application so you can take advantage of this NYSLA self certification process. Most attorneys charge $3,000.00 and up to prepare and file the liquor license application but that amount is nominal when compared to the money saved in rent (and the money made in revenue) by getting the license and opening the establishment many months earlier.

Resources: http://www.newyorklawyers.org/
http://www.ny-liquor-license.com/

6.   Check the status of your liquor license application on the New York State Liquor Authority website. If your application has been processed, you will see the status as pending, active, expired or inactive. If you are in active status, you should receive your liquor license in the mail within a few weeks.

7.   In 2020, a liquor store's average license fee was approximately $4,000 and additional filing fees can cost about $200.

Arizona Liquor Licenses

Arizona Department of Liquor Licenses and Forms
http://www.azliquor.gov/forms.html

Arizona Liquor Laws
http://www.azliquor.gov/law.html

Frequently Asked Questions
http://www.azliquor.gov/faq.html
http://www.azliquor.gov/forms/lic_appfaq.pdf

Who must apply for a liquor licenses?
Any person who intends to manufacture, sell or deal in liquor in the state of Arizona. An application for an original license or transfer of ownership for an existing license must be filed with the Department of Liquor Licenses and Control along with an application fee of $100 which is not refundable.

What are different types of liquor license ownership?
a) When the applicant is an individual (not an entity), this person must be a U.S. citizen or a legal resident alien, and a bona fide Arizona resident. The license must be held in the name of a designated agent who meets the requirements of an individual licensee.
b) When the applicant is a general partnership (not an individual), each partner must be a U.S. citizen or a legal resident alien, and a bona fide Arizona resident. The license must be held in the name of a designated agent who meets the requirements of an individual licensee.
c) When the applicant is a limited partnership (not an individual), all general partners are required to meet the qualifications for an individual. All limited partners are not required to be Arizona residents. The license must be held in the name of a designated agent who meets the requirements of an individual licensee.
d) When the applicant is a corporate general partnership (not an individual), each corporate partner must be qualified to do business in Arizona. The license must be held in the name of a designated agent who meets the requirements of an individual licensee.
e) When the applicant is a corporation (not an individual), it must be qualified to do business in Arizona. The license must be held in the name of a designated agent who meets the requirements of an individual licensee.
f) When the applicant is a limited liability company, it must be qualified to do business in Arizona. The license must be held in the name of a designated agent who meets the requirements of an individual licensee.
g) When the applicant is a club, the license must be held in the name of a designated agent who meets the requirements of an individual licensee.
h) When the applicant is a joint tenancy (J.T.W.R.O.S.), each person must meet the requirements of an individual licensee (A.R.S. §4-202).

What information will I need to complete the application?
a) the type of ownership,
b) the type of license,
c) the applicants name,
d) the name of all partners for corporate general partnerships,
e) a list of officers, directors and stockholders who own 10% or more of the business if applicant is a corporation,
f) the designation of the person who will manage the licensed premises (this person must meet the requirements of an individual licensee),
g) a questionnaire completed by the applicant(s), manager(s), and controlling person(s) and the fingerprinting fee,
h) a fingerprint card completed by the applicant(s), manager(s), and controlling person(s) and the fingerprinting fee,
i) floor plans and diagrams designating areas where liquor will be produced, stored, and provided on the licensed premises,
j) the retail applicant's sworn statement that the premises, at the time the license application is received by the director, is not within three hundred (300) horizontal feet of a church, within three hundred (300) horizontal feet of a public or private school building with kindergarten programs or grades one (1) through twelve (12) or within three hundred (300) horizontal feet of a fenced recreational area adjacent to such school building.
The above paragraph DOES NOT apply to:
a) Restaurant license (A.R.S.§4-205.02) c) Government license (A.R.S.§4-205.03)
b) Hotel/motel license (A.R.S.§4-205.01) d) Fenced playing area of a golf course (A.R.S.§4-207 (B)(5))
k) license transfer and interim permit applications must include a license surrender authorization signed by the current licensee. In addition, the current, valid (not expired) liquor license must be attached to the application (A.R.S. §4-202).

Who cannot be issued a liquor license in Arizona?
The Department of Liquor Licenses and Control will conduct a background investigation of all applicants. A license will not be issued or renewed to any person who;
a) within five (5) years prior to application, has been convicted of a felony or of any offense in another state that would be a felony in Arizona,
b) within one (1) year prior to application has had a liquor license revoked,
c) at the director's request, fails to provide complete financial disclosure statement(s) for financial holdings for them self and/or any other person with interesting the license which includes all co-signers on financial holdings, land, buildings, leases and/or other forms of indebtedness which the applicant has incurred (A.R.S. §4-202).

What other documents will be required for me to complete the application process?
a) the interim permit if you wish to continue business operations at the same location

during the application process,

b) all paperwork included in the application kits created by license type,

c) if you are born outside of the United States, include one of the following forms which proves your citizenship or alien status:

• Certificate of Naturalization,

• U.S. Passport,

• Permanent Resident Alien card,

• Other proof of legal alien residency.

d) proof of Arizona residency (driver's license or voter registration card),

e) the ability to verify corporate status with the Arizona Corporation Commission,

f) a menu and restaurant operation plan for restaurant (series 12) and hotel/motel with restaurant (series 11) applications,

g) recommendation from the local government (city, town or municipality),

h) payment of local government licensing fees,

i) satisfactory completion of background investigation(s),

j) payment of final issuance fees.

What mistakes commonly interfere with the application process?

a) retail liquor license will not be issued for any premises which do not comply with A.R.S. §4-202,

b) liquor licenses will not be issued for a location which was rejected within twelve (12) months of the date on the document stating rejection,

c) an application which is incomplete.

What are the steps and timeframes in the approval process?

The approval process normally takes sixty-five (65) to one hundred five (105) days once a

complete application has been filed. The Department of Liquor Licenses and Control files your application once it is deemed complete. When an application is not complete, it is returned to the applicant with specific instructions to assist in the satisfactory completion the application.

Once an application is filed, the approval process steps are as follows:

a) the Department of Liquor Licenses and Control will send two (2) copies of the completed application to one of the following local governing bodies;

• the clerk of the city or town in which the proposed licensed premises will be located,

• the clerk of the County Board of Supervisors if the proposed business will be located outside of a city or town, the copies will be sent to,

• the governing body of the reservation and an "information only" copy to clerk of the County Board of Supervisors for that county if the proposed business will be located on a sovereign Indian reservation,

b) the clerk of the local governing body will post one (1) copy of the application on the front of the proposed licensed premises for twenty (20) days,

c) the appropriate local governing body will hold a meeting and must either approve, disapprove or offer a "no recommendation" decision on the application. This action must take place within sixty (60) days of the filing of the application. While the local governing body is processing the application, the Department of Liquor Licenses and Control conducts the background check(s),

d) if the application is:

• approved at the appropriate local governing body level, and

• no written protests have been received by the Department of Liquor Licenses and Control, and

• there is not objection by the director of the Department of Liquor Licenses and Control,

the application will be approved.

e) if the local governing body;

• disapproves the application, or

• offers a "no recommendation", or

• if protests have been filed with the Department of Liquor Licenses and Control,

the application must be set for a hearing before the State Liquor Board.

f) hearings may be conducted by the board or a designated hearing officer. The purpose of a hearing is to consider all evidence and testimony in favor of or opposed to the granting of a liquor license. The applicant for a new license bears the burden of demonstrating his or her "capability, qualification, and reliability". In addition, the applicant for a new license bears the burden of demonstrating that the granting of a license is in "the best interest of the community". In a person-to-person transfer of a liquor license, the applicant of a new liquor license need only prove his or her "capability, qualification, and reliability". In a location-to-location transfer of a liquor license, the applicant of a new liquor license need only prove that the license is in "the best interest of the community".

The decision by the board to grant or deny an application will normally take place within one-hundred five (105) days after the application has been filed unless the director of the Department of Liquor Licenses and Control deems it necessary to extend the time period.

Wisconsin Liquor Laws

What does an alcohol beverage license allow?

It allows persons to sell alcohol beverages to individual retail customers, from a particular place (premises). Licenses are issued by municipalities (cities, villages, towns) after the governing body (city council, town board, etc.) determines that the applicant is qualified for the license. No one can sell alcohol beverages (or give away for a commercial purpose) or allow consumption in a public place without getting the appropriate license.

Are licenses and permits the same thing?

No. Licenses are issued by the municipality where the business is conducted; permits are issued by the state. While there is some functional overlap, retailers are usually covered by licenses and wholesale and production tiers of the industry are generally covered by permits.

What types of alcohol beverage licenses are there?

Class "A" fermented malt beverage licenses allow retail sale of fermented malt beverages (beer) for consumption off the premises. Examples: grocery or convenience stores.

"Class A" liquor licenses allow retail sale of intoxicating liquor (including wine) for consumption off the premises. Examples: liquor stores or grocery stores with full liquor sales sections.

Class "B" fermented malt beverage licenses allow retail sale of fermented malt beverages (beer) for consumption on or off the premises. Examples: restaurants, "beer bars."

"Class B" liquor licenses allow retail sale of intoxicating liquor (including wine) for consumption on the premises, and wine in original containers for consumption off the premises. If the community elects to, it may also permit sale of not more than four liters of intoxicating liquor (there are no limits on wine), in the original container, for consumption off the premises. Check local ordinances for the allowance. State law also allows carryout of a single, opened (resealed) bottle of wine if sold with a meal. Examples: taverns and restaurants with full alcohol service.

"Class C" wine licenses allow the sale of wine for consumption only on the premises and allow the carryout of a single opened (resealed) bottle if sold with a meal.

Temporary Class B licenses (often called picnic licenses) allow retail beer and/or wine sales, at temporary events like fairs and festivals. Only certain organizations qualify for such a license. They must be bona-fide clubs, county or local fair associations, churches, lodges, or societies that have been in existence for at least six months.

There are several other locally issued licenses or state issued permits that allow retail sale of alcohol beverages under certain circumstances. The licenses listed above are the most common, however.

I've heard that some licenses are very expensive. Is that true?

It depends. Fees are set by local municipalities, with limits set by state law. Certain "Class B" liquor licenses are considered "Reserve Licenses" and are subject to a one-time fee of not less than $10,000. "Class B" liquor licenses are restricted by a population based quota.

How are quotas and reserve licenses determined?

The municipality is responsible for determining quotas and reserve fees, based on formulas in state law. Quotas are based on population and the number of licenses in effect in the community as of December 1, 1997.

I want specific information about licensing. Where do I go?

Licensing decisions, quotas, reserve fees, etc., are all controlled by the municipality. This is not a responsibility of the Department of Revenue, and Department employees cannot give accurate and timely information about municipal licensing. For more information regarding the quotas and fees for "Class B" licenses, please contact the clerk of the municipality where the license is issued or will be applied for.

Municipal clerks who need information about quota and reserve license law should seek advice from their municipal attorney or from the appropriate municipal organization that serves them. Cities and villages can contact the League of Wisconsin Municipalities, 1-800-991-5502, and towns can contact the Wisconsin Towns Association, (715) 526-3157.

How do I apply for an alcohol beverage license?

Contact the clerk for the city, village, or town where you wish to do business. The clerk will give you applications and information about legal requirements. After you apply, the clerk will publish the application three consecutive days in a local daily newspaper, or once in a weekly newspaper, to see if there are objections in the community. The licensing authority (city council, council licensing board, town board, etc.) will vote on the application. The license may not be granted until at least fifteen days after the application is filed with the clerk.

What are the basic qualifications for a person to get a license?

The basic qualifications are:

You must be of legal drinking age (21).

You must have resided continuously in Wisconsin for at least 90 days prior to the application date.

You must have a seller's permit issued by the Department of Revenue. Call (608) 266-2776.

You must have completed a responsible beverage server training course. Call your local Vocational, Technical and Adult Education (VTAE) school, or see "Training" on the Department of Revenue web site.

A criminal record may prevent you from getting a license, as explained below.

Can I get a liquor license if I have a criminal record?

That will largely be up to the municipality to determine. A criminal record is not an automatic bar to getting a license. The municipality must determine whether the violation is something related to the business of selling alcohol beverages. Violations such as selling liquor without a license, tax evasion, etc., are closely related to this business and might well be a bar to licensing. A record of auto theft may not. The municipality will weigh the nature of the violation, the time that has elapsed since the violation, the person's overall record in the community, etc., in making that determination.

Are licensing qualifications different if I incorporate?

A corporation /LLC must meet the seller's permit and criminal offense requirements. The officers must be of legal drinking age and may be affected by a criminal record as described above. The officers and directors need not be residents of Wisconsin, or attend server training, but the agent does. You must appoint a (single) agent, and the agent must meet all the qualifications of an individual applicant. The agent has the authority of a licensee who is a natural person. The agent, like an individual licensee, is in control of the premises and of the business conducted there.

Does the licensee or the agent always have to be at the premises when it is open for business?

No. There must be one or more licensed operators in charge of the premises. An operator's license is often called a "bartender's license." Not all bartenders must hold operator's licenses, but there must be at least one licensed operator in charge of the premises. If the premise is large, with several serving areas, bar areas, etc., licensed operators must be in charge of each discrete area, in order to supervise and direct unlicensed persons who may be selling/serving.

How do I qualify for an operator's license?

To qualify for an operator's license, you must
> be at least 18 years old,
> meet criminal record requirements, and
> have completed a responsible beverage server course. Call your local Vocational, Technical and Adult Education (VTAE) school, or see "Training" on the Department of Revenue web site.

The last requirement can be waived if it is a renewal application or if you held an alcohol beverage license, including an operator's license, within the past two years. The municipality may issue you a provisional operator's license if you are enrolled in a responsible beverage server course when you apply. An operator's license is only good in the municipality that issues it. For instance, if you are issued an operator's license in the City of Milwaukee, you may not use it in a suburban municipality, like Franklin.

What are responsible beverage server training courses?

These courses are required to hold alcohol beverage licenses, with some exceptions. They cover alcohol beverage laws, signs of intoxication, safe serving of alcohol beverages, etc. These courses are most often offered by local technical colleges. For further information, contact your local Vocational, Technical and Adult Education (VTAE) school.

Not all responsible beverage server courses are taught by technical colleges. Other courses (see "Training" on the Department of Revenue web site) may be substituted for those taught at VTAE schools, as long as they have been approved by the Department of Revenue or the educational approval board. Make sure of this approval **before enrolling** in a responsible server course not offered at a VTAE school.

What exceptions are there to the server training course requirement?

The exceptions to this requirement are

> if you are renewing a Wisconsin retail or an operator's license,
>
> if you were the agent of a corporation that held a Wisconsin retail license within the past two years,
>
> if you held a Wisconsin retail or operator's license within the past two years, or
>
> if you completed a Wisconsin approved server training course within the past two years.

FOR MORE INFORMATION CONTACT:

WISCONSIN DEPARTMENT OF REVENUE
Alcohol & Tobacco Enforcement
Mail Stop 6-40
P.O. Box 8933
Madison, WI 53708-8933
Phone: (608) 266-2772
Fax: (608) 261-6240
Resources: www.revenue.wi.gov/faqs/ise/atlicns.html
            www.revenue.wi.gov/faqs/ise/atonprm.html#onprm4

Note: Wisconsin permits the consumption of alcohol by minors, provided they are being supervised by parents/guardians/spouses. Most municipalities have a uniform 9 p.m. restriction on all alcohol sales. Notable exceptions: La Crosse, Maple Bluff (near Madison), Baraboo (near the Dells). Supermarkets, liquor stores, and gas stations may sell liquor, wine, and beer. Law changed effective 12/7/2015 to allow all liquor sales to begin at 6 a.m.

Wisconsin Alcohol Beverage and Tobacco Laws for Retailers

http://www.dor.state.wi.us/pubs/pb302.pdf

How to Obtain a Georgia Liquor License

License Application
https://etax.dor.ga.gov/ctr/TSD_State_Alcohol_License_Application_CRF009.pdf

General Alcohol and Tobacco Forms
https://etax.dor.ga.gov/alcohol/alc_forms.aspx

Contact: Howard A. Tyler, Director
1800 Century Blvd, N.E. Room 4235, Atlanta, GA 30345
Phone: 404-417-4900   Fax: 404-417-4901
Email: ATDIV@dor.ga.gov

Frequently Asked Questions

Which license do I get first, the local or the State?

In order to operate a business dealing in alcohol, you must have a local alcohol license, a State alcohol license and a Federal Basic Permit. Georgia is a local option license state, which means the local licenses must be issued before the State may issue a license or permit. Revenue Regulation 560-2-2-.26

Can I sell wine through the internet in such things as gift baskets?

An entity licensed as a wine producer by the United States Alcohol and Tobacco Tax and Trade Bureau may apply for a Special Order Shippers license. If your business has not been issued a Special Order shippers license, shipping wine out of or within the State is prohibited. Official Code of Georgia Annotated § 3-6-31 (2008)

GA Process Overview

Check the State of Georgia's requirements before putting an application for a liquor license in your name. Requirements include being at least 21 years old, being a U.S. citizen or permanent resident, and being a resident of the city or county where you are applying for the license.

Get fingerprinted at the local police station. License applicants will need to undergo a background check, which can take up to 4 months to complete.

Visit the Georgia Department of Revenue at www.dor.ga.gov and download the appropriate application forms to apply for a liquor license. In Georgia, you can apply for a Certificate of Residence for Retail Liquor License, which is an ATT-14 form; fill out a State Beverage Alcohol Personnel Statement, which is an ATT-17; or fill out a Retailers and a Consumption on Premises Liquor License, which is an ATT-59. There is also an application for an alcohol permit (ATT-15). You can also visit your local City Hall to obtain most of these applications and documents.

Be sure that you can afford both the state and city liquor licenses. A city license can cost thousands of dollars a year.

Attend the NPU (Non Plus Ultra) hearing or city council meeting. If you are approved, the mayor will sign your liquor license within 90 days.

Business Requirements

In order to qualify for a liquor license in Georgia, your business must have a name registered with the state as well as a physical address. The Alcohol and Tobacco Unit must confirm and approve the physical location of the business as part of the application process. The business also must have a state tax identification number. As of 2011, the application fees for a liquor license in Georgia cost $100 plus an additional $100 fee for a background check.

Individual Requirements

Individual qualifications for a liquor license in Georgia include having United States citizenship or permanent resident status, being a resident of the county in which the license will be issued and being at least 21 years old. Liquor license applicants must submit to a Federal Bureau of Investigation fingerprint-based, in-depth background check that may take up to four months to complete.

Restrictions

Applicants for a Georgia liquor license must agree not to sell liquor within 600 feet of a school property or within 300 feet of a church building. In addition, qualified applicants must not sell liquor within 300 feet of any alcohol treatment center owned and operated by the local, state or federal government. Establishments selling liquor packages must be at least 500 yards apart. Other state-wide restrictions for obtaining a liquor license pertain to the license applicant, members of their immediate family and employees. Whether the license is for a retail dealer or retail consumption dealer, no person listed may have any ownership, interest or association with a liquor manufacturer, producer, shipper, wholesaler, broker or importer.

Hearing

Another qualification for a Georgia liquor license involves a hearing with the applicable county board of commissioners at a monthly scheduled meeting. Hearing requirements vary by county and often include additional investigation fees, advertising fees, license fees and inspection fees that can total several thousand dollars. The fees must be submitted at the time of the application in most counties. The applicable county also may require a certified surveyor's plot indicating the distance between the closest public school, church building, private residence, public library and school bus stop.

Annual License Renewal

Businesses that have been granted a license to sell liquor are required under Georgia law to renew their license each year. The state Revenue Department allows businesses to file their renewal application and fees online. The renewal process begins in September every year and closes in December. Those wishing to renew their liquor license should check the dates carefully, as they change every year slightly, and make sure to have their application in and fees paid before the cut-off date.

Local Liquor License Application

In Georgia, retailers of alcohol are required to be licensed at the local government level and pay local excise taxes. Local governments must issue a license before an establishment may register to sell or serve alcohol with the state government. This local license will be submitted with the state alcohol license application. Local jurisdictions have their own application procedures, deadlines and fees, which vary.

Local Licensing Fees

Local governments charge different fee schedules to license in their jurisdictions. Douglas County charges $5,000 to register or renew a liquor license. In DeKalb County, the fee is $333 per month of operation, plus an a $200application fee. This license can be renewed annually for $4,000 per year. In Fulton County, the fees are different according to the type of liquor business being operated. Those that serve liquor on premises pay $3,200 annually for a license, while those who sell packaged liquor pay $3,800. Both service and retail businesses are also subject to a $855 background investigation fee.

Requirements of Licensees

Those granted a liquor license in Georgia must be eligible under both state and local requirements regarding their business location, age and regulatory compliances. Businesses can lose their liquor license at the discretion of local authorities for repeated alcohol-related violations like over service and neighborhood disturbances. To be eligible, a retail business must be located at least 600 feet from a school property, church building or alcohol treatment center, and their employees must be at least 18 years of age. Managers must be at least 21.

How to Get A Liquor License in Nevada

Retail Liquor Store: (Specific NRS 369.090)
An establishment (tavern, lounge, package sales store, restaurant, grocery store, etc.) where alcoholic beverages are sold to the consumer.

Nevada state law specifically requires each county's board of county commissioners to allow liquor licenses and follow the provisions of state liquor law. As a result, there can be no dry cities or counties in Nevada, except that a few rural jurisdictions are grandfathered into the ability to still be partially or totally dry.

Nevada has very liberal alcohol laws. Bars are permitted to remain open 24 hours, with no "last call". Liquor stores, convenience stores and supermarkets may also sell alcohol 24 hours per day, and may sell beer, wine and spirits.
Source: http://en.wikipedia.org/wiki/Nevada

NEVADA THREE TIER SYSTEM
1. Supplier (Certificate of Compliance Holder) may ship/sell only to Nevada importers and holders of a permissible person permit.
2. Importer/Wholesaler may sell only to retailers and other wholesalers.
3. Retailer may purchase from wholesaler only and cannot legally sell to or buy from other retailers. Sales must be at the retail level to the general public only.

RETAILERS
Retail liquor store operators should be advised to consult city or county clerks regarding licensing requirements. Other than sales and use tax obligations, the Department of Taxation is not involved in the licensing of retail liquor establishments.

Development Services Center
City Hall, 240 Water Street, Henderson, NV 89015
Days and Hours of Operation: Monday-Thursday, 7:30 am-4:30 pm
General Information - License Technicians 702-267-1730
Business License Fax 702-267-1704
Business License Officers - Enforcement 702-267-1724
License Officers - Enforcement Fax 702-267-1701

www.clarkcountynv.gov/Depts/business_license/lg/Pages/LiquorApplicationForms.aspx

Application Form for Liquor License:
www.clarkcountynv.gov/Depts/business_license/lg/Documents/Liq%20App.pdf

Liquor License Summary Information
www.clarkcountynv.gov/Depts/business_license/lg/Documents/Liq%20Summary.pdf

Meeting Dates

www.clarkcountynv.gov/depts/business_license/lg/Pages/LiquorandGamingLicensingBo
a   rdMeetings.aspx

Resource: www.cityofhenderson.com/finance/business_license_common_questions.php
Examples:

What is a "Privileged" license and how long is the process for a privileged license?
A privileged license represents an industry that has been declared privileged by the
Nevada State Legislation and is governed by the Nevada Revised Statutes and the Clark
County Code. These businesses may require an investigation by the State Gaming
Control Board and /or an in depth investigation by the Las Vegas Metropolitan Police
Department for determination of the owner's suitability to hold such a license. On
average, license processing, investigation and issuance takes about six months depending
upon the type of license being sought.
Resource: http://www.clarkcountynv.gov/depts/business_license/lg/Pages/faq.aspx

Can I sell or serve alcohol at a special event?
Any public event using any public street or right-of-way requires a special events permit.
Applications for special events permits must be submitted to the Henderson Police
Department not less than sixty (60) or more than one hundred twenty (120) days before
the event. In addition, if alcohol will be sold or served for consumption on the premises a
Special Events Liquor Permit must be obtained from the Business License Division. A
request for the Special Events Liquor Permit must be submitted in writing to the Business
License Division prior to the event along with the appropriate fee.

Fees for the Special Events Liquor Permit are as follows:
Non-profit organizations
  $50.00 per day for alcoholic liquor
  $25.00 per day for beer, wine and spirit-based products only
Others
  $100.00 per day for alcoholic liquor
  $50.00 per day for beer, wine and spirit-based products only
Once the request has been reviewed and approval has been obtained from the
Administrator of Licensing, the permit will be issued.

When do I need a sales tax permit?
Every business operating in the State of Nevada requires a Sales Tax or Use Tax Permit,
or exemption, issued by the State of Nevada Department of Taxation. To apply or for
questions regarding sales or use tax, contact the State of Nevada, Department of
Taxation, 2550 Paseo Verde Parkway, Suite 180, Henderson, Nevada 89074, (702) 486-
2300.

When do I need a State of Nevada Business License?
Every business operating in the State of Nevada is required to obtain a State of Nevada
Business License through the Office of the Nevada Secretary of State. To apply or for
questions regarding the State Business License, contact the Secretary of State, 555 E

Washington Avenue, Suite 400, Las Vegas, Nevada 89101, (702) 486-2880; or visit the Secretary of State website at www.sos.state.nv.us.
Resource: http://tax.state.nv.us/faq.htm

Application Process

1. Determine which of the three types of Nevada liquor licenses to apply for. The retail license is for bars, restaurants and grocery stores that intend to sell alcohol directly to individual patrons. A wholesaler license is for a business that intends to sell alcoholic beverages to retail establishments. Finally, the supplier license is for businesses that intend to sell liquor and other alcoholic beverages to wholesalers.

2. Obtain an application for the type of liquor license that your business requires. Wholesale and supplier license applications can be obtained through the Nevada Department of Taxation. Retail liquor license applications can be obtained through your county's business license center.

3. Complete the liquor license application that's relevant to your business and submit it to the appropriate regulatory authority. Wholesale and supplier license applications should be submitted to the Nevada Department of Taxation with the appropriate fees; fees vary for each business depending upon the types of alcohol that they sell or supply. Retail applications should be submitted to the licensing authority in the county in which the retail establishment is located. Each county has its own fee structure for retail liquor licenses.

Pennsylvania Liquor Control Board

The Pennsylvania Liquor Control Board is firmly committed to regulating the sale of alcohol, educating consumers on the responsible use of alcohol and working to prevent underage alcohol use while ensuring convenient access to a wide array of competitively-priced products and impeccable customer service at stores throughout the commonwealth.

http://www.lcb.state.pa.us/PLCB/About/index.htm

http://www.lcbapps.lcb.state.pa.us/app/retail/Storeloc.asp

The Battle for Liquor Store Privatization
http://paindependent.com/2011/07/liquor-store-privatization-battle-begins-again/

The Commonwealth of Pennsylvania has run the liquor stores for eight decades, a relic of the post-Prohibition era, when government thought controlling the sale of alcohol would limit consumption.
Source: www.nytimes.com/2011/01/01/us/politics/01transitionpa.html

Liquor Store License in Oklahoma

Any beverage containing more than 3.2% alcohol by weight or 4% alcohol by volume, that is, most liquors, wines, and typical beer, may only be sold in licensed liquor stores at room temperature. To circumvent the alcohol content restrictions, beer distributors in Oklahoma primarily sell low-point beer. This allows the beer to be sold not only in convenience stores and supermarkets, but in refrigerated form. The law defines low-point beer as any beverage containing between 0.5% and 3.2% alcohol by weight. Minors under the age of 21 are not permitted to possess or purchase alcohol; however, consumption in a "private setting" is not prohibited by Oklahoma law. Minors may not have a blood alcohol level of more than .02%.

Licensing
The owner of a liquor store in the state of Oklahoma, over the age of 21 by definition, must obtain licenses to sell and serve alcohol from the Alcoholic Beverage Laws Enforcement (ABLE) Commission.

Regulations
All liquor store employees must be 21 years of age or older. All customers must have their license of other picture form of identification checked to confirm that they are also 21 or over. Any violations may result in the loss of the store's liquor licenses, a hefty fine and possible jail time.

Hours of Operation
To maintain a license, any liquor store in the state of Oklahoma must be closed between 9 p.m. and 10 a.m., when rates of drunken drivers are highest. Additionally, alcohol cannot be sold on the holidays of Christmas, Thanksgiving, Memorial Day, Labor Day and Fourth of July.

Alcohol Guidelines
Any beverage that is more than 3.2 percent alcohol cannot be sold chilled in the state of Oklahoma. This is to discourage consumption while operating a motor vehicle. Only liquor stores may serve liquor and high-point beer in the state of Oklahoma.

Criminal Record
Felons cannot obtain a liquor license, thus prohibiting them from owning and operating a liquor store. A liquor store owner can also not knowingly hire a felon.

Off-premises
It is illegal to sell packaged liquor (off-premises sales) on Sundays. Sales also are prohibited on Memorial Day, Independence Day, Labor Day, Thanksgiving Day, and Christmas Day.[5] Low-point beer for consumption off-premises may not be sold between 2:00 a.m. and 6:00 a.m.   People who have been convicted of a felony or any alcohol-related crime may not obtain a license to sell packaged alcohol.

On-premises

In Oklahoma, each county decides for itself whether it will permit the sale of alcohol by the glass. Low-point beer may not be sold for consumption on-premises or allowed to be consumed in places licensed to sell alcohol between 2:00 a.m. and 7:00 a.m. This crime is punishable by a fine of up to $500 and up to 6 months imprisonment. Licensed vendors may not advertise happy hours, serve more than two beverages at a time to a customer, give a discount to a person or group of persons, or permit the play of games that involve drinking.

Resources:

Alcoholic Beverage Laws Enforcement Commission
3812 N. Santa Fe, Suite 200
Oklahoma City, Oklahoma 73118
Main Office: (405) 521-3484 Fax (405) 521-6578
TOLL FREE NUMBER: 1-866-894-3517
http://www.ok.gov/able/

How to Obtain a Liquor Store License in Tennessee

REQUIRED DOCUMENTS FOR RETAIL (OFF-PREMISE)
LICENSE FEE - $850 (ANNUAL FEE)
$300 APPLICATION FEE – NON REFUNDABLE

All documentation must first be submitted to and reviewed by the local TABC Office. Then, the completed application and related documentation will be forwarded to the Nashville TABC office for final review.

To be placed on the agenda for the next Commission meeting, all documentation must have been reviewed by the local TABC Office and submitted to the Nashville TABC Office two weeks prior to the date of the Commission Meeting.

The following documentation is required to be submitted in conjunction with a retail store application:

1. APPLICATION FORM. *Form #AB-0015.* This application should be notarized and filled out completely. See Commission Meeting Schedule.

2. QUESTIONNAIRES. *Form #AB-0009.* Owners, partners, officers, managers and/or any person who owns five percent (5%) or more in the corporation or the business, should complete these forms. All questionnaires should be filled out **completely.**

3. CERTIFICATE OF COMPLIANCE. The Certificate of Compliance may be obtained from the local municipality Mayor's office. Please contact the local Mayor's office in the jurisdiction in which the store will be located for additional information.

4. CERTIFICATE OF OCCUPANCY. The Certificate of Occupancy is issued by the local municipality's Codes Department. Please contact the local Codes Department in the jurisdiction in which the store will be located for additional information.

5. PROOF OF POSSESSION. A copy of the lease must be furnished to this office. Along with the lease, a copy of the **Deed** (registered with the Registrar of Deed's Office) must be furnished also. If the application is for a change of ownership, a copy of the Bill of Sale or Purchase Agreement must be provided.

6. CHARTER FROM THE STATE OF TENNESSEE. (This document is required only if the applicant is a corporation, a limited liability company (LLC) or a formal partnership). A copy of the Tennessee charter must be furnished to this office and it may be obtained from the Tennessee Secretary of State's Office, 6th Floor, William Snodgrass Building, 7th Avenue North between Charlotte Avenue and Union Avenue, Nashville, Tennessee, telephone (615) 741-2286.

7. LIST OF OFFICERS AND/OR OWNERS OF CORPORATION. A separate list of officers (with their titles) and owners with five percent (5%) or more of ownership, indicating amount of percentage of ownership, must be furnished with the application. Please use form AB-0099.

8. COPY OF NEWSPAPER NOTICE and SWORN STATEMENT REGARDING THE PUBLICATION. Prior to the Certificate of Compliance hearing date, a newspaper notice must be published in the local newspaper for three (3) consecutive issues. Further, an affidavit from the local newspaper should be provided verifying publication. For the affidavit, please see Public Forms.

9. WAIVER OF ANY RIGHT TO AN ADMINISTRATIVE HEARING BY APPLICANT. See ABC Rule #0100-3-.09(10).

10. Tax Numbers: A Tennessee sales tax number can be obtained from the Tennessee

Department of Revenue, 3rd Floor, Andrew Jackson Building, 500 Deaderick Street, Nashville, Tennessee 37242.

    i. SALES TAX: telephone (615) 253-0600

    ii. LIQUOR–BY–THE-DRINK TAX: telephone (615) 532-4552

    iii. FRANCHISE AND EXCISE: telephone (615) 253-0700.

11. ABC INSPECTION. An inspection will be conducted by a TABC agent after the application has been reviewed by the local TABC office.

12. COPY OF ALL LOAN CONTRACTS.

13. FINANCIAL BACKGROUND CHECK OF APPLICANT.

14. CREDIT CHECK FROM BANKING/LENDING INSTITUTION.

15. EMPLOYEE PERMITS. *Form AB-0014.* All employees must obtain an employee permit card. See Retail Employee permit (blue card) information.

Source: TN Alcoholic Beverage Commission

www.tn.gov/abc/licensing%20-%20retail%20package%20store%20lead%20page.shtml

OFF-PREMISE CONSUMPTION LICENSES (RETAIL)

    Retail liquor store license is for liquor stores selling liquor by the bottle to individuals for off-premise consumption. See how to obtain the Retail package store license.

    Retail Employee permit (blue card) is required for individuals selling liquor in a TABC licensed retail liquor store. Please see Retail Employee permit.

    Consumer Educational Seminars are permitted by the TABC and conducted by the designated retail establishment, or package store. An application requesting permission to conduct an educational seminar may be submitted by the retail establishment. See how to obtain a Consumer Education Seminar application.

Source: http://www.tn.gov/abc/llicensing%20-%20lead%20page.shtml

Resource: http://license.org/tennessee/liquor-license

Minnesota Liquor Laws

Minnesota Liquor Laws are stricter than many other states. The legal drinking age in Minnesota is 21.

Off sales of liquor are restricted to licensed liquor stores. Liquor is only sold in liquor stores. Not supermarkets as you may be used to from other states, or gas stations as Wisconsin does. Some supermarkets operate their own liquor store right next door to their food supermarket, notably Trader Joe's.

You can't buy alcohol from a liquor store on a Sunday in Minnesota. Liquor stores are closed on Sundays, and also Thanksgiving Day, Christmas Day, and liquor stores must close at 8 p.m. on Christmas Eve.

Liquor stores can only open from 8 a.m. until 10 p.m., Monday through Saturday. Some cities restrict liquor store opening hours further - Minneapolis liquor stores may open these hours, but St. Paul liquor stores close at 8 p.m. Monday through Thursday, and are open until 10 p.m. on Friday and Saturday.

Some cities in Minnesota don't permit privately owned liquor stores. Instead, the city operates one or more liquor stores, and uses the profits for public projects. Among the Cities in the Minneapolis-St. Paul Metro Area with only city-run liquor stores are Brooklyn Center and Edina.

3.2 beer is less strictly regulated. It can be sold in grocery stores, and it can be sold on Sundays. High alcohol spirits like Everclear are illegal in Minnesota.

Procedure

1. Contact the Alcohol and Gambling Enforcement Division of the Minnesota Department of Public Safety (MDPS) at 651-201-7507 for the appropriate liquor license applications. Different applications may be required depending on the type of business you wish to obtain the license for, such as a grocery store, restaurant or bar.

2. Download the required applications through the MDPS website at www.dps.state.mn.us under the "Alcohol & Gambling Enforcement."

3. Obtain liquor liability insurance. Many counties in Minnesota require proof of liquor liability insurance along with the liquor license application. Contact a Minnesota state insurance agent to acquire liquor liability insurance. If your business is incorporated, the insurance must be in the corporate name. If the business is unincorporated, the insurance must be in the individual's name. The liquor liability insurance must cover the entire liquor license period.

4. Receive a sales and use tax ID number. A sales and use tax ID number is required

for any business wishing to obtain a liquor license. To obtain a sales and use tax ID number, contact the Minnesota Department of Revenue at 651-296-618 for an application.

5.   Acquire a special occupational tax stamp. Producers and sellers of alcohol must obtain a special occupation tax stamp. Contact the Minnesota Bureau of Alcohol, Tobacco , and Firearms at 800-937-8864 for an application to receive your tax stamp.

6.   Submit the liquor license application to the MDPS Alcohol and Gambling Enforcement Division along with all required documents, including proof of liquor liability insurance, the sales and use ID number, and occupational tax stamp.

7.   After the department reviews your liquor license application, it will send government officials to inspect the business establishment. Once the liquor license is approved, you will receive it by mail.

How to Get a Liquor Store License in California

Liquor License Auctioneers
www.liquorlicenseauctioneers.com/?gclid=CMDUwf-wxbUCFQLqnAodOSgALA

California Bureau of Alcoholic Beverage Control
Resource: http://www.abc.ca.gov/AboutUs.html
The mission of the Department of Alcoholic Beverage Control is to administer the provisions of the Alcoholic Beverage Control Act in a manner that fosters and protects the health, safety, welfare, and economic well being of the people of the State.
Forms: http://www.abc.ca.gov/forms/PDFlist.html

CA Liquor Licenses and Permits
Process Overview Topics:
    Leasing a Business Location
    Obtaining Local Zoning Permit Approval
    Finding a California Liquor License
    Filing a California Liquor License Application
Resource:
www.licensesandpermits.com/how-to/how-to-buy-a-california-liquor-license.aspx

Types of CA ABC Licenses and their privileges
Resource: http://www.abc.ca.gov/forms/abc616.pdf

License Type 20 - Off-Sale Beer & Wine
If a liquor store or other retail establishment chooses to limit its stock to just beer, wine and malt beverages, it can obtain an Off-Sale Beer and Wine license from California's Department of Alcoholic Beverage Control. Also referred to as a "package store" license, it only allows the store to sell alcohol for consumption off the premises.

License Type 21 - Off-Sale General
The type 21 Off-Sale General license offers the same rights as the type 20 license, but allows the store to sell any type of alcoholic spirit in addition to beer, wine and malt liquor. A store needs this license to sell gin, whisky, vodka, tequila, liqueur or any other type of spirit, distilled or not.

Licensing Costs
The off-sale beer and wine license is $100 to obtain and $254 to renew. The cost of transferring a license from one person to another is $50. The off-sale general license is significantly more expensive, at $12,000 for a new issue, $582 to renew and $1,250 for a transfer to a different licenseholder.

Licensing Limitations

California started limiting the number of licenses that can be outstanding in 1939. The current law allows one off-sale general license per 2,500 people per county and an additional off-sale beer and wine license per 2,500 people per county. In other words, a county with 250,000 people can have only 100 general licenses and an additional 100 beer and wine licenses outstanding at any given time.

A liquor store license, also known as an "off sale" license, is not permitted to cater alcoholic beverages and not able to apply for ABC event permits.

How to Get a Liquor Store License in Florida

To sell liquor, beer or wine in Florida, you must apply for a license from the Florida Division of Alcoholic Beverages and Tobacco Bureau of Licensing. Alcohol sales in Florida require one of two main licenses. The first is a quota license, which is only for a full-service alcohol establishment. A quota liquor license in Florida is only offered once a year on a lottery, and more licenses become available yearly as population increases. The second liquor license Florida offers is an SRX, a special restaurant license that can be applied for year-round if 51 percent or more of sales at an establishment is food. There are 55 subcategories of licenses based on the type of business you own
Resource: www.myfloridalicense.com/dbpr/abt/rules_statutes/license_types.pdf

Division of Alcoholic Beverages and Tobacco

The Division of Alcoholic Beverages and Tobacco licenses the alcoholic beverage and tobacco industries, collects and audits taxes and fees paid by the licensees, and enforces the laws and regulation of the alcoholic beverage and tobacco industries, pursuant to Chapter 210, Chapters 561-565 and Chapters 567-569 of Florida Statutes. Florida has approximately 75,000 active alcoholic beverage and tobacco license holders. The division generates over $1.9 billion in license fees, taxes, fines, etc. With 328.25 employees, these responsibilities are carried out through three bureaus within the division: Licensing, Auditing and Enforcement.
Source: http://www.myfloridalicense.com/dbpr/abt/index.html

Division of Alcoholic Beverages and Tobacco
1940 North Monroe Street
Tallahassee, FL 32399
Customer Service Phone: 850.487.1395   Fax: 850.922.5175

Steps:
1. Check with the local city zoning board to determine whether the location you want to purchase a Florida liquor license for is zoned for serving alcohol.
2. Get a zoning approval document and include it in your liquor license application. Obtain the signature of your local zoning office to complete Section 6 of the application. The zoning office will confirm that your proposed location is properly zoned to allow for the sale of alcoholic beverages.
3. Get health approval for safety and sanitation from either the Division of Hotels and Restaurants if you are serving food or the County Health Authority or Department of Health if you are not serving food. Obtain the signature of the local county health department on Section 8 of the application. You will need to contact the county health department to schedule an inspection. The health department will confirm that your business location complies with the Florida Sanitary Code.
4. Fingerprinting is required for a liquor license in Florida. Florida contracts with PearsonVue to handle this. Turn in your receipt from PearsonVue with your application. Be sure to make a copy for yourself.
5. Collect the social security numbers for anyone who will be on the liquor license

application.

6. Make sure your business is properly registered with the state of Florida. Obtain the signature of the Florida Department of Revenue on Section 7 of the application. The Department of Revenue will confirm that your business has registered to collect sales and use tax and that you are current on all taxes.

7. Obtain a federal employer's identification number.

8. Prepare a sketch of the business to submit with your application. Architectural renderings are not accepted. Draw a sketch of the premises that you are seeking to license as indicated in Section 5 of the application. The state requires that drawings include all doors, restrooms, storage rooms, counters and sales areas, so it is important to be familiar with the building prior to completing the application.

9. Get a certified copy of arrest disposition if necessary (only if you answered yes to any questions on the application about your criminal background). You may also need to fill out a "mitigation for moral character" form.

10. Visit the Division of Alcoholic Beverages & Tobacco website and download the alcoholic beverage permit application.

11. Fill out the application form for a Florida liquor license with information about all the shareholders directly involved with the business.

12. Mail your application for a Florida liquor license to: ABT Licensing Central Office, 1940 North Monroe Street, Tallahassee, Florida 32399-1021 or your local licensing office.

13. Submit your completed application and appropriate fees to your local district office. Fees can range from $28 to $1,820-- the exact amount is determined by which county your business will reside in and the type of liquor license you are applying for. The application can be submitted by mail or hand-delivered.

14. The application must include a lease or deed to your business location and copies of any management contracts, franchise agreements, service agreements or profit-sharing agreements for your company. You also must include fingerprints for all company officers along with copies of arrest dispositions, if applicable, for any person with an ownership interest in the company.

15. The local FDABT office can typically answer questions you may have in completing the application.

16. Respond to any requests for additional information from the state. The FDABT will review your application within seven days of receipt.

17. Begin business operations once you receive your temporary or permanent license.

18. Don't buy any liquor from a distributor not licensed in Florida

Frequently Asked Questions About Florida Liquor Licenses

Resource: Florida Business Investments
http://floridaliquorlicenses.com/faq-fll.asp

How to Get a Liquor Store License in South Carolina

Retail Liquor Licenses (ABC Package Stores)

I. Requirement. In order to sell alcoholic beverages for off-premises consumption, one must have a retail dealer's license (§ 61-6-100 (3)). This license also allows you to sell wine containing 16% or more of alcohol by volume. It does not allow you to sell beer containing less than 14% alcohol by weight..

II. Application. Applications may be obtained by contacting the Alcoholic Beverage Licensing Section at (803) 898-5864, or by calling fax on demand at 1-800-768-3676 or (803) 898-5320. Application forms are also available on the Department's website at http://www.sctax.org. It is a crime to furnish false information on the application.

a. **Fees.** The initial application requires a nonrefundable filing fee of $200. Licenses cost $1,400 every two years.

b. **Good moral character.** All employees and all principals must be of good moral character (§ 61-2-100). When a license or permit has been suspended or revoked, no partner or person with a financial interest in the business may be issued a license or permit for the premises concerned (§ 61-2-140). No person within the second degree of kinship to a person whose license or permit has been suspended or revoked may be issued a license or permit for the premises concerned for a period of one year after the date of suspension or revocation (§ 61-2-140). All principals of a corporate entity must also submit a "Verification of Lawful Background for Applicants Principals" (ABL Form-920).

c. **Age and residence.** Principals must be at least 21 years of age. The Applicant, if an individual, must complete and submit a "Verification of Lawful Residence" (ABL Form -577) in accordance with the S.C. Illegal Immigration Reform Act.

d. **Location.** The location of the proposed place of business must be suitable.

e. **No more than three licenses**. An applicant cannot have any type of interest in more than three retail liquor stores. In addition, no license may be issued to more than one member of a household.

f. **Minimum distance from schools, churches, or playgrounds.** Locations established after November 7, 1962 must meet the following requirements:

A. If the church, school, or playground is located in a municipality, the establishment must be at least 300 feet away.

B. If the church, school, or playground is located outside of a municipality, the establishment must be at least 500 feet away.

C. The distance is measured using the shortest route of normal vehicular or pedestrian traffic.

D. The distance restrictions do not apply to renewals or to new locations licensed at the time the application is filed with the Department.

g. **Newspaper advertisement.** The applicant must advertise its intention to apply for the liquor license in a newspaper most likely to give notice to interested citizens (§ 61-6-1820). The advertisement must be published once a week for three consecutive weeks. Your application packet will list approved newspapers. It is the applicant's responsibility to advertise in the correct newspaper. Contact the Alcoholic Beverage Licensing Section at the number shown above if you are unsure which newspaper will give this required notice.

h. **Notice to the public.** A sign must be displayed at the proposed place of business for at least fifteen days. An agent of the South Carolina State Law Enforcement Division must place and remove this sign (§ 61-6-1820). If the sign is removed by any person other than the agent, the location will have to be re-posted.

i. **SLED investigation.** All liquor license applications are investigated by the South Carolina Law Enforcement Division. This investigation usually requires thirty to fortyfive days, and will be delayed if the application is incomplete, incorrect information has been furnished on the application, or if the applicant does not promptly return the investigating agent's telephone calls.

j. **Protests.** Any person residing in the county where a liquor license is being sought, or a person residing within five miles of the location, may protest the issuance of the permit (§ 61- 6-185). Such a protest will significantly delay a liquor application, as a contested case hearing must be held before the Administrative Law Court. Due to notice and scheduling requirements, it usually takes two to four months for a hearing to held from the time the file is transmitted to the Administrative Law Court by the South Carolina Department of Revenue. Files cannot be transmitted until the application is complete, the investigation is complete, all notice periods have run, and the applicant has requested a hearing. Therefore, it is extremely important that the applicant follow the instructions in the application packet, fully answer all questions, and furnish all required information with the application. Once the Department has transmitted an application to the Administrative Law Court, the Court will schedule the matter for a hearing. Once a file has been transmitted to the Court, all requests for information and all motions must be filed with the Administrative Law Court, 1205 Pendleton Street, Suite 224 Edgar A. Brown Building, Columbia, SC 29201. The telephone number of the Administrative Law Court is (803) 734-0550.

k. **Temporary licenses not to exceed 120 days.** A person who purchases or acquires by lease, inheritance, divorce decree, eviction, or otherwise a retail business which sells liquor from a holder of a retail license to sell liquor at the business, upon initiating the application process may be issued a temporary liquor license (§ 61-6-505). This license is valid until the biennial license is approved or denied, but in no case can the temporary license be valid for more than 120 days from the date of issuance. The fee for this license is $25.00. The location for which the temporary license is sought must have had a valid Alcohol Beverage License and not be considered by the Department to be a public nuisance. All principals must be of good moral character, and cannot owe the State government any back taxes, penalties, or interest. The principals must attach a criminal records check, not more than 90 days old, on all principals. If any principals are nonresidents of SC or have not resided in SC for at least two years, you must attach a current criminal history background check obtained from the state of residency or former residency for each nonresident. These background checks must accompany your application. See page 3, for a definition of a "principal". For SC residents you can obtain these checks online at **www.sled.state.sc.us** or at SLED Headquarters, 4400 Broad River Rd, PO Box 21398, Columbia, SC 29221(between the hours of 8:30 a.m. and 5:00 p.m. or by mail by forwarding your request to: SLED, PO Box 21398, Columbia, SC 29221-1398, ATTN: Criminal Records Department. You must enclose a self addressed envelope and furnish your full name, social security number and date of birth. Record checks from SLED require a $25.00 fee payable by money order or business check made out to SLED. No personal checks or cash are accepted by SLED.

l. **Local zoning.** Before filing your application for a liquor license, you are strongly encouraged to check with your local zoning authorities to insure that your business will comply with local zoning requirements.

m. **License saturation.** If other liquor stores in your area protest your application and are able to show that citizens in your area desiring to purchase alcoholic liquors are more than adequately served, the Administrative Law Court may deny your application (§ 61-6-170).

III. Expiration dates of licenses. Licenses expire according to the county where the licensed premises is located (§ 61-2-120). The expiration dates are the last day of:

a. February in years which end in an:

A. Odd number for Allendale, Bamberg, Barnwell, Beaufort, and Berkeley Counties;

B. Even number for Charleston, Clarendon, Colleton, Dorchester, Georgetown, Hampton, Jasper, and Williamsburg Counties;

b. May in years which end in an:

A. Odd number for Cherokee, Chester, Chesterfield, Darlington, Dillon, Fairfield, Florence, and Horry Counties;

B. Even numbers for Lancaster, Marion, Marlboro, Union, and York Counties;

c. August in years that end in:

A. Odd number for Calhoun, Kershaw, Lee, Orangeburg, and Sumter Counties;

B. Even number for Richland County;

d. November in years which end in an:

A. Odd number for Abbeville, Aiken, Anderson, Edgefield, Greenville, and Greenwood Counties;

B. Even number for Laurens, Lexington, McCormick, Newberry, Oconee, Pickens, Saluda, and Spartanburg Counties.

IV. License renewal. File your renewal application at least thirty days before your license expires. A timely renewal by mail will prevent you from having to wait in a lengthy line. If you allow your license to expire, you cannot sell liquor or wine, and you will have to pay a filing fee to obtain your license. You may be required to re-advertise, and a new SLED investigation may be required. If you owe delinquent taxes, interest, or penalties, or have been convicted of a crime, your license will not be renewed (§ 61-2-160).

V. Sales tax license required. In addition to your retail liquor license, before you sell any item, you must first obtain a retail business license (sales tax license) from the South Carolina Department of Revenue (§ 12-36-510). There is a one-time fee of fifty dollars for this license.

VI. Sign required to be posted.

a. "The possession of beer, wine, or alcoholic liquors by a person under twenty-one years of age is a criminal offense under the laws of this State, and it is also unlawful for a person to knowingly give false information concerning his age for the purpose of purchasing beer, wine or liquor.

b. A person may transport alcoholic liquors to and from a place where alcoholic liquors may be lawfully possessed or consumed; but if the cap or seal on the container has been opened or broken, it is unlawful to transport alcoholic liquors in a motor vehicle, except in the luggage compartment or cargo area.

VII. Sale of wine at locations with a liquor license. Your retail liquor license authorizes the sale of wine containing 16% or more alcohol content (by volume).

VIII. Hours. You may sell liquor from 9:00 AM until 7:00 PM, Monday through Saturday (61-6-1500(3)(a)).

IX. Cessation of operations. If your store ceases to operate or sells its assets, you must surrender your liquor license to the Department immediately. Liquor licenses cannot be transferred to the new operator. If you allow the new operator to use your liquor license, you will be held financially responsible for any violation committed by the new operator (§ 61-2-140).

X. Minimum age of employees. All employees must be at least twenty-one years of age.

XI. Retail price displays. You must display retail prices on the shelf under each brand and bottle size.

XII. Premiums, coupons, or stamps. You may offer discounts through the use or premiums, coupons, or stamps redeemable by mail.

XIII. Minibottles. In order to sell minibottles, you must obtain the necessary federal wholesale license, and you must procure a permit from the S.C. Department of Revenue. Regulation 7-200.1.

XIV. Lottery tickets. Lottery tickets may be sold in retail liquor stores. § 61-6-1540.

XV. Check cashing services. If properly licensed, check cashing services may be conducted on the premises of a retail liquor store. § 61-6-1505.

XVI. Transfer of liquor between stores. Liquor may be transferred between stores owned by the same person as long as the following requirements are met:

a. The transfer is made by common carrier, licensed wholesaler's truck, or truck or station wagon owned by the licensee and the driver has in his or her possession an invoice showing the license numbers of the stores involved, the brand, size and quantity to be transferred, and the date of the transfer.

b. Prior to the transfer, a copy of the invoice must be mailed to the S.C. Department of Revenue, ATTN: ABL Section, Columbia, SC 29214.

c. If the transfer is to be made by vehicle owned by the licensee, the vehicle must be registered with the S.C. Department of Revenue, ABL Section.

XVII. Sampling. Wines and alcoholic liquors may be sampled in retail liquor stores as long as they are conducted as follows:

a. No sample may be offered from more than four products at any time.

b. No more than one bottle of each of the four products may be opened.

c. The sampling must be held in a designated tasting area and all open bottles must be visible at all times. All open bottles must be removed at the end of the tasting.

d. Samples must be less than one-half ounce for each product sampled.

e. No person may be served more than one sample of each product.

f. No sampling may be longer than four hours.

g. At least ten days before the sampling, a letter detailing the specific date and hours of the sampling must be mailed first class to the South Carolina Law Enforcement Division.

h. No sample may be offered to, or allowed to be consumed by, an intoxicated person or a person under the age of twenty one years. This person must not be allowed to loiter on the store premises.

i. The tasting must be conducted by the manufacturer or an agent of the manufacturer, and must not be conducted by a wholesaler, retailer, or employee of a wholesaler or retailer.

j. No retail liquor store may offer more than one sampling per day.

XVIII. Prohibited acts.

a. Sell or possess liquor in containers of less than two hundred milliliters. § 61-6-1500(1).

b. Sell liquor between the hours of 7:00 PM and 9:00 AM. § 61-6-1500(2).

c. Sell liquor for consumption on the premises. § 61-6- 1500(3).

d. Sell liquor to a person under 21 years of age. § 61-6- 1500(3).

e. Permit the drinking of liquor on the premises. § 61-6- 1500(A)(1)(b).

f. Sell liquor to an intoxicated person. § 61-6-1500(A)(1)(d).

g. Sell liquor to a mentally incompetent person. § 61-6-1500(A)(1)(e).

h. Sell liquor on credit; however, this does not prohibit payment by credit card. § 61-6-1500 (3).

i. Redeem proof-of-purchase certificates for any promotional item. § 61-6-1500(4)

j. Possess wine or liquor with a broken seal. Regulation 7-501.

k. Interference with an officer. § 61-2-240.

l. Permit a person under twenty-one years of age to possess or consume liquor. Regulation 7-200.48.

m. Sell or keep non-alcoholic merchandise except items in sealed packages with liquor or drinking glassware packaged with liquor. § 61-6-1540.

n. Purchase of liquors from a person other than a licensed retail dealer. § 61-6-1630.

o. Purchase of liquors from a retail dealer with a check that fails to clear the bank. Regulation 7-402.

p. Refilling liquors. § 61-6-1500(B)(1).

q. Refusal to permit inspection upon demand of an officer or agent. § 61-2-240.

r. Sale of liquors on which the tax has not been paid. § 61--2600.

s. Purchase liquor or wine from a wholesaler with a check that fails to clear the bank. Regulation 7-300.3.

t. Purchase liquor or wine from anyone other than a licensed wholesaler. Regulation 7-300.2.

XIX. Penalties. The Department may revoke the license of any person failing to comply with requirements (§ 61-6-4270). However, in lieu of revocation, the Department may suspend the license or assess a monetary penalty. The penalty for a violation is dependent upon the severity of the offense. In addition, the Department may consider the number and severity of previous violations. However, for serious offenses, the Department may revoke the liquor license for the first violation. Some offenses are also criminal offenses, and violators may be arrested.

XX. Training. Employee and manager training emphasizing methods for selling beer and wine legally are available from a variety of 3rdparty vendors. For a list of approved vendors, see S.C. Revenue Procedure 04-4, available online under the Alcohol Beverage Licensing and Regulations Advisory Opinions.

XXI. This handout is for general guidance only. It does not include every law or regulation dealing with liquors, or every crime that can be committed on a licensed premise. You may contact the South Carolina Department of Revenue at 803-898-5864 or www.sctax.org, in order to find or be instructed on how to find a complete copy of the laws and regulations on liquors. Please be aware that the law regulating liquors can be amended at any time.

[1] Retailers may accept draft beer or wine equipment replacement parts of nominal value, party wagons for temporary use, and point of sale advertising specialties. A retailer may also accept the cleaning of draft or wine lines, setting boxes, rotating stock, affixing price tags to beer or wine products, and building beer or wine displays.
[2] The five percent may be collected from each attendee. The price of admission must be on the ticket, and you must retain the ticket stub for three years.
[3] "The courts will refuse to countenance any trick or subterfuge intended to evade the law..." See Pirates Cove v. ABC Commission, 258 S.C. 397, 189 S.E.2d 7 (1972).
[4] Selling items, selling tickets or charging admission are examples of business or commercial activity.
[5] Advertising the event on television, on radio, in the newspaper, with flyers, with billboards or with signs is evidence that the function is open to the general public. Admitting persons that have not been personally invited by the person giving the function is evidence that the function is open to the general public.

Source: www.sctax.org/NR/rdonlyres/5F5D735B-DCCC-42A3-A193-00FC915D6AC1/0/retailLiquor_Licenses.pdf

How to Get a Liquor Store License in Maryland

Alcohol laws of Maryland are unique in that they vary considerably by county, due to the wide latitude of home rule granted to Maryland counties.

Resources:
http://en.wikipedia.org/wiki/Alcohol_laws_of_Maryland
http://en.wikipedia.org/wiki/Montgomery_County_Department_of_Liquor_Control

www.baltimorecountymd.gov/Agencies/liquorboard/rules_regulations.html
www.baltimorecity.gov/Government/BoardsandCommissions/LiquorBoard.aspx
http://www.montgomerycountymd.gov/dlc/
http://www.aacounty.org/liquorBoard/index.cfm#.Ulaxa5LD_IU
http://frederickcountymd.gov/index.aspx?nid=1291
http://ccgovernment.carr.org/ccg/license/

www.city-data.com/forum/maryland/1851011-i-need-help-understanding-states-liquor.html

Alcohol Laws in Maryland   http://www.alcohollaws.org/marylandalcohollaws.html

Process

1. Obtain and complete an application. You can obtain an application either on the state of Maryland website or by contacting the Liquor License Board. The various counties have different application procedures, so check with your county to get the most accurate information.

2. Post a notice in your establishment in a place that is clearly visible to the public. This notice must be posted for 10 consecutive days. This is to inform the public that you are applying for a license. The state of Maryland will likely send out an inspector to make sure you have completed this task.

3. Submit to an inquiry by the Liquor Licensing Board. These people are required to determine if you are fit to have the license. This could mean a background check and an inquiry into your finances and your business reputation. You will not be granted a license if the board feels you may abuse the privilege.

4. Prepare to defend your application against any locals who may protest your application. Certain communities are very sensitive to the types of businesses that function in their area. Be prepared in case you are called in for a protest hearing. Chances are you will not be called upon, but your presence may be required.

5. Fulfill all requirements to maintain your license. A lapsed license could cost you your livelihood, as well as additional fines. You will be informed of the requirements when you begin the application process. Make this your priority.

How to Get a Liquor License in West Virginia

The WVABCA Licensing Division is responsible for ensuring applicants comply with West Virginia law pertaining to the issuance and maintenance of licenses, encompassing all aspects of the handling, serving, and sale of alcoholic beverages.

There are two types of retail outlet licenses:

Class A retail license, which means a retail license permitting the retail sale of liquor at a freestanding liquor retail outlet. Class A retail licensees are also referred to as a "Freestanding liquor retail outlet" which means a retail outlet that sells only liquor, beer, nonintoxicating beer and other alcohol-related products, including tobacco-related products.

Class B retail license, which means a retail license permitting the sale of liquor at a mixed retail liquor outlet. Class B retail licensees are also referred to as a "Mixed retail liquor outlet" which means a retail outlet that sells liquor, beer, nonintoxicating beer and other alcohol-related products, including tobacco-related products, in addition to convenience and other retail products.

Source: http://www.abca.wv.gov/liquor/Pages/LiquorRetailer.aspx

Application:
abca.wv.gov/licensing/Documents/Retail%20Liquor%20Application%20Packet.pdf

Annual Fees: http://www.abca.wv.gov/licensing/Pages/default.aspx

Frequently Asked Questions: http://www.abca.wv.gov/Pages/faq.aspx

WV Alcohol Laws: http://en.wikipedia.org/wiki/Alcohol_laws_of_West_Virginia

Opening a Liquor Store in Puerto Rico

Alcohol Regulations
Puerto Rico has no restrictions on the sale of alcohol other than a legal drinking age of 18; the law bans the sale of liquor to minors. If you own a retail business such as a grocery store, you can sell beer, wine and liquor freely, without obtaining a separate license. Liquor sales are conducted in bars, restaurants and stores, in hotels, and by small vendors in tourist areas such as beaches. The police will enforce public-drinking bans in the capital of San Juan and other cities, but the laws are not enforced during public festivals, street parades and the like.

Beer, wine and spirits is available for sale in supermarkets, convenience stores and drug stores as well as liquor stores.

Puerto Rico
http://www.hacienda.gobierno.pr/conocenos/ri_negociados/impuesto.html
Negociado de Impuesto al Consumo
P.O. Box 9024140
San Juan, P.R. 00902-4140
Tel: (787) 277-3900, (787) 277-3934, (787) 277,3936, (787) 277-3939, (787) 774-1201
Fax: (787) 277-3929

Required Forms:

www.hacienda.gobierno.pr/downloads/pdf/formularios/as%202914.1.pdf

Starting a Business in Puerto Rico
www.doingbusiness.org/data/exploreeconomies/puerto-rico/starting-a-business
www.ehow.com/how_6327386_open-business-puerto-rico.html

Liquor Stores for Sale in Puerto Rico
www.bizbuysell.com/texas/puerto-rico/liquor-stores-for-sale/?q=/wEFA249YQ==

How to Open a Liquor Store in Rhode Island

Class A (Package Store) License – Retail

Liquor Stores for Sale in RI
http://www.bizbuysell.com/rhode-island/liquor-stores-for-sale/
http://www.businessbroker.net/state/rhode-island-businesses-for-sale.aspx

The Division of Commercial Licensing and Regulation is responsible for regulating and monitoring the manufacturing, importing, exporting, storing, selling and transporting of alcoholic beverages.
Resources:
www.dbr.ri.gov/divisions/commlicensing/liquor.php
www.dbr.ri.gov/documents/divisions/commlicensing/liquor/Commercial_Licensing_
    Regulation_8.pdf

In addition to the state laws regarding the issuance of liquor licenses, Rhode Island also offers considerable discretion to its cities in allowing them to approve and
reject applications. In addition to state laws, applicants must meet all local laws before they can be issued a liquor license. For example, the city of Providence has its own five-member Board of Licenses that applicants must appear before and receive the approval of.

As of July 2013, Rhode Island liquor stores can open at 10 a.m. on Sundays. The law allowing package store to open two hours earlier on Sundays was passed by the General Assembly on July 3 and was signed into law by Gov. Lincoln D. Chafee on July 12. Closing time is still 6 p.m.
Source:
www.thebeveragejournal.com/rhode-island-liquor-stores-can-open-10-a-m-sundays/

All alcohol may be sold only in liquor stores.
Bars may stay open until 2 a.m. in Providence only on Friday and Saturday nights and nights before a state-recognized holiday.
Source: http://en.wikipedia.org/wiki/Alcohol_laws_of_the_United_States

RI Liquor License Fees
http://www.providenceri.com/license/liquor

RI Liquor License Applications
http://www.providenceri.com/license/applications

How to Open a Liquor Store in Wyoming

Wyoming (State-contracted stores)
Out of the 18 states that regulate alcohol wholesaling, only 10 (Alabama, Idaho, New Hampshire, Oregon, North Carolina, Pennsylvania, Virginia, Washington, and Utah) run liquor establishments. The others either permit ABC licensed private stores to sell liquor or contract the management and operations of the store to private firms, usually for a commission.

Wyoming does not operate retail outlets. Maintains monopoly on wholesale importation. Although licenses are issued by local licensing authorities, all liquor licenses must be approved by the state, and licenses are limited by population density. Wyoming has the least restrictive liquor retail outlet density with one store per 765 inhabitants.

Alcoholic beverage control states, generally called **control states**, are eighteen states in the United States that have state monopoly over the wholesaling or retailing of some or all categories of alcoholic beverages, such as beer, wine, and distilled spirits.
Resource: http://en.wikipedia.org/wiki/Alcohol_laws_of_the_United_States_by_state

Wyoming Liquor Division Information
                                   http://eliquor.wyoming.gov/information.htm
Address: 6601 Campstool Rd. Cheyenne, WY. 82002

Wyoming State Liquor Association   **http://wyoliquor.org/**
The WSLA has been at the forefront of the industry, protecting Wyoming businesses from destructive legislation and regulations while working to keep our state business-friendly to allow our economy, and our businesses, to grow and prosper.

Wyoming Alcohol Laws   www.alcohollaws.org/wyomingalcohollaws.html
State-owned, or package, stores sell wine and hard liquor in Wyoming. Beer is usually available in most grocery stores and convenience marts. Local ordinances regulate the hours that alcohol may be sold.

Jackson Hole Liquor Stores
http://jacksonholechamber.chambermaster.com/list/category/liquor-stores-418

How to Open a Liquor Store in Kentucky

The Kentucky Department of Alcoholic Beverage Control (ABC) is in charge of administering and enforcing Kentucky's alcoholic beverage laws. The state ABC also processes applications for and issues liquor licenses. In addition, there are city, county, and urban county ABC administrators throughout Kentucky. These local administrators must approve all license applications before they will be reviewed by the state ABC. KRS 243.370.

There are 84 different license types. Most licenses pertain to distilled spirits (liquor) and wine or to malt beverages (beer). Licenses are not available statewide. Alcoholic beverage licenses may only be issued in larger cities and counties in Kentucky or where the locality has voted in favor of allowing alcoholic beverage sales. See KRS Chapter 242 and KRS 243.230.

An ABC license may be issued for up to 1 year. KRS 243.090(1). License periods are staggered according to county and zip code (for larger counties) so that all licenses do not expire at the same time.

A temporary license may be issued for an organized charitable, civic, or community sponsored event such as a picnic, carnival, fair, festival, exposition, racing association, political campaign function, or other party. 804 KAR 4:250(3). It is not available for an event solely based upon a holiday or a private commercial venture. A temporary license allows the holder to exercise the same privileges as an ABC license holder at a fraction of the cost. If issued, the temporary license is valid throughout the length of the event, up to 30 days. KRS 243.260(1).

A person or business interested in selling, producing, transporting, or storing alcoholic beverages in Kentucky must first obtain one or more ABC licenses. According to KRS 243.020(1), "A person shall not do any act authorized by any kind of license with respect to the manufacture, storage, sale, purchase, transporting, or other traffic in alcoholic beverages unless he holds the kind of license that authorizes the act." There are various penalties for operating without the proper license(s). Usually, the violation of a liquor law is a Class B misdemeanor for the first offense, with elevated penalties for subsequent violations. KRS 243.990.

http://www.lexingtonkylawfirm.com/business-services/company-startup/abc-alcoholic-beverage-license/#sthash.yRoLKAgH.dpuf

Kentucky Department of Alcoholic Beverage Control
https://dppweb.ky.gov/abcstar/portal/abconline/page/license_lookup/portal.aspx

Resource:
http://en.wikipedia.org/wiki/alcohol_laws_of_kentucky

Kentucky has several dozen dry counties where the sale of alcohol is prohibited or where liquor sales are permitted only at certain approved sites. The full list of wet, dry, and limited counties can be found on the Kentucky Department of Alcohol Beverage Control website.

How to Open a Liquor Store In Washington D.C.

Resources:
Types of ABC Licenses, Endorsements and Permits

http://abra.dc.gov/page/types-abc-licenses-endorsements-and-permits
http://abra.dc.gov/page/abc-license-fees

Alcoholic Beverage Regulation Administration
http://abra.dc.gov/

An overview of DC's Liquor Laws

Liquor can be served by a licensed business from 8 a.m. to 2 a.m. on Monday - Thursday, from 8 a.m. to 3 a.m. on Friday and Saturday and 10 a.m. – 2 a.m. on Sundays. The day before a federal holiday, alcohol may be served from 8 a.m. – 3 a.m. On January 1 (New Year's Eve), liquor may be served from 8 a.m. – 4 a.m.

Off-premises retailers, such as grocery and other stores, may sell liquor from 9 am – 10 pm daily.

A person must be at least 18 years old to serve or sell alcoholic beverages and at least 21 years old to be a bartender.

A customer must produce valid I.D. if asked by the establishment to show it in order to be served alcohol.

It is illegal to use a fake I.D. to purchase liquor. An underage person who tries to buy liquor with a fake I.D. could be subject to a fine and have driving privileges suspended.

It is illegal to possess an open container of an alcoholic beverage in public space that is not part of an ABC-licensed establishment. An individual who breaks this law can be prosecuted and punished by a fine of up to $500 and/or up to 90 days in jail.